PC Computing for Absolute Beginners

Barbara Edwards

SIGMA PRESS
Wilmslow, England

Typeset and Designed by Sigma Press, Wilmslow

Cover Design by Design House, Marple Bridge.

First published in 1993
Sigma Press, 1 South Oak Lane, Wilmslow, Cheshire SK9 6AR, UK

First printed 1993

ISBN: 1-85058-286-6

British Library Cataloguing in Publication Data
A CIP catalogue record for this book is available from the British Library

Printed in Malta by
Interprint Ltd.

Acknowledgement of copyright names and trademarks

Many product names used in this book are protected by copyright or are trademarks owned by the companies publishing these products. Use of the name of any product without mention of its trademark or copyright status should not be construed as a challenge to such status. Full acknowledgment is hereby made of all such protection by the authors and publisher.

General disclaimer

The programs described in this book have been included for their instructional value. They are not guaranteed for any particular purpose and the publisher does not offer any warranties or representations, nor does it accept any liabilities with respect to the user of the programs.

Contents

1

Buying Your Computer and Other Equipment

1.1 A Brief History of the IBM PC and its Clones

PC is short for personal computer. This means a computer that is small enough to sit on your desk. About 15 years ago, most computers were mainframes, great big boxes of electronics that filled large air conditioned rooms. There were also minicomputers, but these involved a box or two and weren't exactly designed for the sitting room. Home computers were just emerging, but they were crude things with very small memories and in the earliest stages they often came as a kit that you had to assemble yourself. In Britain it might have been a Sinclair or BBC, in America, a Commodore PET, then Commodore 64 or an Apple. Their memories were usually too small to be of much business use. You had to be an enthusiast and tended to write your own programs, usually in the BASIC programming language.

Computers advance like world population. The current desktop computer is as powerful as the room-filling mainframe of only 15 years ago. At its best it is nearly as powerful as a minicomputer and the distinction between them is breaking down. Networking can provide added power as you draw on a string of other programs and information contained in a whole series of linked computers.

The whole computer world changes so rapidly that names and definitions soon cease to make sense.

In 1981, the large computer company, IBM, launched what it called the PC. It was not the most technically advanced machine around, but IBM knew how to market its product and presented the PC as the first real small business machine. This strategy took off. IBM used the word PC in a more specific sense to mean a particular kind of computer, not just anything that would fit onto a desk. It had a particular kind of chip (the brain or centre of the computer), the Intel 8086 or 8088.

Every computer needs some program to manage its housekeeping, a program that tells the computer what keys you are pressing on the keyboard, that loads up your software from disk or tape, that saves things and makes a note of where they are. This is what is called an operating system and in the case of the IBM PC, this was called PC-DOS.

Naturally things didn't stand still during the next 10 years. More sophisticated chips were developed, the Intel 80286, the Intel 80386 and finally the Intel 80486. Machines using the 80286 chip were first introduced in 1984, those using the 80386 in 1987 and the 80486 first appeared in 1990. Each new chip was more powerful than the previous one, but they were all part of the same family, in that they could do everything their predecessors could do plus a little bit more, and faster.

The 386 and 486 were major improvements on the earlier chips, the 286 rather less so. Being a family they continued to use the same operating system, PC-DOS, or MS-DOS the Microsoft version, which is essentially the same. Rather ironically, MS-DOS could only deal with a limited amount of memory, less than the full capacity of the 80286, 80386 and 80486. This left whole areas of the memory chips unused. To use the full memory capacity of the later chips you needed a new and more advanced operating system like Unix or OS/2 or a program like Windows 3.1. However these chips will always run MS-DOS as well so the family operating system has been maintained.

IBM had marketed a winner and other manufacturers soon latched on. They used the same chips (Intel is the only company licensed to make the 386, and the other chips were limited under various agreements to a small range of other companies) but built machines that were cheaper and often offered their own extra advantages – Figure 1.1. One of the largest rival companies was Compaq in the USA, Amstrad in Britain and Olivetti in Europe. They could run the same software as the IBM PC and they used the same operating system, MS-DOS.

From now on, I shall use PC in this more specific sense to mean a certain kind of computer, produced by IBM or another manufacturer. The PC means a computer:

❏ that runs on an Intel 8086, 8088, 80286, 80386 or 80486 chip

❏ than runs the operating system, MS-DOS (or PC-DOS).

1.2 What do the Different Chips Mean?

The only thing the computer's brain, called a Central Processing Unit or CPU, can actually understand is a 0 or a 1, an on or an off. Everything it deals with, the instructions it is given and the words and numbers it works on, has to be translated into 0s and 1s. Each single 0 or 1 is called a bit. One major difference between the chips is the number of bits that can be processed at one time and that can pass between the various components in the computer's brain, along what is called a bus. Another important difference is the amount of available memory.

Figure 1.1: A typical IBM clone – the Dell System 325P. It's a 386 PC with a 50 Mb hard drive, 5.25'' and 3.5'' floppy drives, and VGA colour monitor

The 8086 was the first PC chip to appear. It could process and pass 16 bits at one time. It could access up to 1 Megabyte memory (1 Megabyte is written as 1 Mb and is actually 1,048,576 bytes, each byte being eight bits long, in other words approximately 1 million bytes). However it was difficult to manufacture and was soon replaced by the 8088 chip. Although this could process 16 bits at one time it could only pass 8 bits along its bus. Another name for the 8086/8088 chip machines was the PC/XT. By the mid 1980s, the 8086 chip had become easier to manufacture and was used more often than the 8088. PCs with these chips are now bottom of the range and can be obtained quite cheaply, often for as little as £300 at the time of writing.

The next chip up was the 80286, and when it was announced in 1984, its machines were called the PC/AT. It processes 16 bits at one time like the 8086 and has a 16 bit bus. Its main advance is that it can address or point to a much larger memory, about 16 Mb in all. However at this stage, the PC Operating System, MS-DOS could only access 1 Mb of this, so the increased memory was not of much practical use. Its only real advantage was that it could run much faster, not what you would call a great technical breakthrough. In the autumn of 1991, a 286 cost about £800 to £1,000 which was a lot to pay for a machine not that much better than the 8086/8088. I have seen some really cheap 286s in the Tottenham Court Road at about £300 to £400 and these could be worth considering. Make sure, though, that the so called bargain really is a compatible PC and will run the software that you want.

The 80386 was a major development. It processes 32 bits at one time and has a 32 bit bus. In its full version it is known as a 386 DX. The 386 SX is a cutdown version of the 386 DX. It has a 32 bit processor but only a 16 bit bus, a bit like the difference between the 8088 and the 8086. It can address or point to 4000 Mb memory which is a vast increase on the old 8086/8. However most conventional programs running on all but the very latest version of DOS can only address 1 Mb of this directly, so the vast memory is not that useful and again increased speed could be your main benefit. However a growing amount of software is beginning to make better use of this memory and you have the option of adding on another operating system which will allow you to access it – operating systems like UNIX or OS/2 or other software with the same ability. It has good potential for expansion and add-ons.

If you are running a growing business or want to do computer aided design, scientific processing or professional desktop publishing, this is the minimum standard of machine you should aim at. If you have a smaller business, which needs little more than simple accounts and word processing, it could be an unnecessary luxury. If you are a hobbyist or recently retired, there is still an enormous amount you can do on one of the simplest machines, like the 8086/8. They will cost a fraction of the price of the 386 and you can always upgrade at a later date if your business is expanding or you find that you have become a real computer enthusiast.

The latest chip is the 80486, which began to appear in mid to late 1991. It still has a 32 bit bus and processor, but it has made a considerable technical advance in being able to use memory much more effectively so that it can use as little as one quarter of the 386 equivalent memory.

1.2.1 Different Speeds

Another important difference between the chips is the speed at which they work. This is called clock speed. The computer times its activities down to the split second and this is the only way it can hold its complicated life together. It sets up a pulse beat and on each pulse beat, in regular order, something happens. It is a bit like being run by a ticking metronome. The more beats, or the faster the clock, the more the computer can fit into a given slice of time. So a very important measure of your computer's performance is its clock speed, given in MHz, or millions of cycles per second.

IBM clones or copies, try to offer more than an IBM, for example a faster clock speed, at a lower price.

The 8086 ran at a clock speed of 5 MHz; the 80286 jumped to 12.5 MHz; although its later versions managed to achieve about 16 MHz.

The 386 started where the 286 left off, at a clock speed of about 16 MHz. A year later, by the end of 1988, it had reached 20 MHz. By mid 1989, it was 33 MHz, probably the chip's limit.

The 486 does things slightly differently. It allows faster processing for a given clock speed i.e. 25 MHz on a 486 will be faster than 33 MHz on a 386.

1.3 Computer Memory

The computer has an internal memory and the larger this is, the more program instructions it can store at any one time. This memory is divided into two main types: ROM or read only memory and RAM or random access memory.

Instructions are put into ROM by the manufacturer. They stay there throughout the computer's life, whether the computer is switched on or off. These are usually just the bare essentials, like the program instructions needed to look for the rest of the operating system when you boot up at the beginning of a work session or the instructions that show up or echo whatever keys you press on the keyboard. Older type computers used to store rather more in their ROM, like the BASIC programming language, but manufacturers realised that what was in ROM couldn't be changed or adapted and that most things in computing change, very rapidly.

RAM, on the other hand, goes blank every time you switch the machine off and is free and empty every time you switch on. When you load up a word processor or a game, it goes into RAM. The rest of the operating system, MS-DOS, goes in there as well when you switch on or boot up and the other programs sit on top of it. These are the internal DOS commands like COPY and you can use them at any time. Programs that load into RAM and stay there, whatever else you run, are called TSRs, Terminate and Stay Resident programs.

Your word processor and other applications will be designed so that the main part of each program stays in RAM throughout use – the more unusual features will be called in and swapped for other bits, as and when needed. The computer copies bits from the disk where the program is permanently stored, but doesn't interfere in any other way, so the program is left intact.

When you start a computer session, the bare essentials stored in ROM will cause the computer to check out that all its bits and pieces are there, and will look for the rest of the operating system. When it has found this, it will load it into the bottom of RAM, and leave it sitting there throughout your session. One part of the operating system, a file called COMMAND.COM, gives you the A or C prompt, which allows you to load in another program.

Supposing you then decide to run a word processor. You either put a floppy disk in the drive or the computer will look for the part of the hard disk where it is stored. The computer then copies the main part of the word processing program into RAM, above the operating system. You produce a letter. The computer may need to copy other parts of the word processor to do this, perhaps replacing some parts it already has in RAM. At this stage, there are two copies of the word processing program, one on the disk, the other, the parts it has copied into RAM. The letter you are writing will be stored in RAM while you are working on it. When you instruct the computer to save your work, a copy is made on the disk. At this stage, there will be the original letter in RAM, and a copy on disk. Switch off, RAM is flushed out, and all you are left with is the disk copy.

If you go on to use a spreadsheet program, this writes over the bit of RAM where the word processor was stored. If you then go on to play a game, the game writes over the bit of RAM where the spreadsheet was stored. When you finally switch off, RAM is empty again. Because the computer copies the programs from a disk, the original will still be there. Anything you save during a work session, like a word processed letter, a spreadsheet worksheet or a game score, will be on the disk as well, at the end of the session. But in RAM itself, nothing will remain.

Different types of programs use more or less RAM. Spreadsheets tend to do everything in RAM. Databases tend to go back to the disk more often, both to store the information you are interested in and to copy more bits of the whole database program. Game play tends to go on in RAM, but graphics (pictures) are very heavy on memory and will probably need to be loaded from disk every time there is a major change of scenery. RAM is immediately available to the computer's main brain, so any program that can be stored mainly in RAM will tend to be much faster than one that has to keep on copying things from disks.

Some programs are small enough to fit into RAM so that the computer can copy in the whole program when it is first loaded up and never needs to go back to the disk again. This means that you can take the disk out of the drive, if it is a floppy, and carry on without it. Other programs will want to go back, and copy some more from the disk, so you must leave it there.

Since some, or all of the program, is copied into RAM at one time, it does matter how much RAM you have, and this is something that you must consider when you are buying a computer. Since programs running under the main PC operating system, MS-DOS, can only use a certain amount of memory, the vast memory of the 386 is not of that much concern for most ordinary programs. RAM is more of a problem if you are running an 8088 or 8086. Very old PCs may have as little as 256K (the K stands for Kilobyte, which is 1024 bytes, or roughly speaking characters and is the way computers measure memory). This will be quite limiting in terms of what you can run. The more likely choice is between 512K or 640K. If you have 512K be careful when you buy software and make sure it will run on your machine. At the moment a lot still will, but there will be less of it as time goes on.

Many of the big packages, like the major spreadsheet Lotus 1-2-3, are now being developed to go into the memory areas of the 386 and 486 above what most DOS applications can reach, what we call expanded or extended memory (there is a difference). This means that the newest versions will only run if you have a 386 or above. If you are going to run big package software, make sure the computer is up to it. Older versions do have their uses, they are tried, tested and very much cheaper. But make sure you have plenty of back up copies of your software, in case it becomes obsolete.

1.4 Disks and Disk Drives

Application programs and work or data are all stored on disks, ready to be copied and worked on next time you boot up your machine. Disks are read/write like video and cassette tapes. They can be written to again and again, which makes them quite economical. There are new alternative storage devices appearing, like CD-ROM. This works like a compact disc and can be used to store computer programs, data, pictures and sound. Like a compact audio disc, it cannot yet be written to, although researchers may eventually come up with ones that can. At the moment, this is used for storing large amounts of quite permanent data like educational material, ranging from unpleasant looking tropical diseases for trainee doctors through to early school animal facts. There is about to be an explosion in CD-ROM for home entertainment.

As far as conventional computer disks go, they are round like records and compact discs. They are made of plastic or aluminium in the case of a hard disk, and are coated with a magnetic material. The disk drive has an electronic head which can use electrical signals to magnetise or demagnetise small points on a disk. These correspond to the on or off, or 1 or 0, which is the only language the computer understands. When the disk drive head *reads* from a disk, it has the ability to sense the magnetic state of a small spot on the disk and turn it back into an electrical signal.

Now, like everything else for the PC, disks come in different sizes and shapes and you will need to make a decision over which to go for. There are floppy disks and hard disks. Floppy disks are disks which you keep away from the computer. When you want to use the programs or data they contain, you put the disk into a floppy disk drive, usually into a slot on the front or side of the computer.

A hard disk, on the other hand, is a closed box that you can't get into. If you could, it would lose one of its advantages: it is a dust free, untouched, sterile environment. This means that you can store programs and data more densely and since the surroundings are so clean, you can sit the disk drive head on a miniscule cushion of air just above the disk surface and it can still read and write. Because it doesn't come into physical contact with the surface, it can move around the disk faster than the head of a floppy unit, about 12 times as fast, in fact.

A hard disk drive will have several circular disks stored one above the other and each will have a head resting just above and below. All the heads move in line and the part of each disk platter that they cover at one time is called a cylinder. The hard disk drive only really became financially viable during the late 1980s.

1.4.1 Floppy Disk Drives

New software comes on floppy disks, so you will want a floppy disk drive as well as a hard disk drive. It is still possible to purchase computers that don't have hard disk drives. You will find that this does restrict the software that you can run, particularly if you want to use databases which tend to be very heavy on disk use. However if you are on a budget, there are still plenty of programs that you can run on a floppy disk-only machine and it may be possible to add a hard disk drive at a later date. If you are in this situation, try and go for a second floppy disk drive.

There is some software, like Wordstar, used in writing this book, that can manage without a hard disk but does require two floppies. Having just one floppy disk drive without a hard disk, means an annoying amount of disk swapping as you run your programs. Again, if you are on a real budget it may be possible to add a second floppy disk drive at a later date. If you do have a hard disk drive, one floppy will generally be quite enough, although the next paragraph gives you a reason why you might want two different ones.

There are different sizes of floppy disks. There are the larger, 5.25'' ones that really do look floppy. In fact, all floppy disks are floppy, and all come protected by a plasticised sleeve. The 5.25'' disks have a bendy sleeve, the other smaller disks, have a rigid plastic sleeve. The 5.25'' floppy disks have a large rectangular hole through which you can see the brown magnetised part of the disk itself. Do not touch this, because finger marks or scratches can damage the magnetised surface and mess up the data and programs stored there. To make matters even more confusing, these disks themselves come in two sizes – they can either store 360K bytes or twice this, 720K.

The other type of floppy disk, with the rigid sleeve, measures 3.5''. The magnetic surface is completely hidden. There is a large metal shutter at the end which gets pushed back when you put it in the disk drive, so that the head can actually reach the magnetised surface. You can pull the shutter back yourself to see this, but having done it once, just to have a look, don't do it again. You will soon have a worn out, damaged disk, that you can dissect for the fun of it. Being tougher, these type of disks are a better bet for children.

To make matters even worse, this kind of floppy disk also comes in two sizes, the double density double sided ones that store 720K and the high density ones that store 1.44 Mb (1 Mb is 1000 Kbytes). Computers that have high density drives can read the 720K 3.5" floppies, but there seems to be some doubt as to whether they can write to them as well. The very newest high density disk drives should be able to write as well as read the 720K drives, so it may all depend on the age of your computer.

If you have such a high density drive, make sure that you have the high density 1.44 Mb disks for storing data and work, and taking backups of programs. The disks look very much the same and the most useful indicator is the label on the side of the box. If you look carefully, though, you will see that the 1.44 Mb disk has an extra little rectangular hole on the opposite side from the rectangle with an open/close shutter.This tells the drive what type of disk it is.

Suppose you get software on the wrong sized disk. Some people get round this by buying a computer with both a 3.5" and a 5.25" disk drive. They can then copy from one type of disk to another. The only problem occurs when you go from the 3.5" to the 5.25". Since the latter only takes half as much data, you can't fit everything onto one disk, and if you have a large program with lots of files, you will have to split them between two or more disks and you may not get the combinations of files you need to make the program run properly. If you don't have two different disk drives, you can connect two computers with different types of drive, using the cables and software supplied by a program like Laplink. You can also get outside companies to do this for you, but they tend to be expensive.

Until a year or two ago, most properly boxed software and magazine freebies, came on the 5.25" disks, and it could be a real problem if you only had the 3.5" disk drive. However, more and more software (including magazine freebies) is now appearing on the 3.5" and this will probably become the norm, so if you are going to have one floppy disk, opt for the 3.5". If you have a more powerful PC that will take it, it is generally best to opt for the high density 3.5" drive. It can read both high density and double density, whereas a double density disk drive, can only read its own disks.

Your decision could be affected by what your friends and workplace have, bearing in mind that some people and institutions change their computers as often as their cars. It may be worth not being able to do much work at home this year because you are the one with the more recent disk drive. Instead you may have many more compatible years ahead when your workplace and colleagues catch up with you.

So choosing a floppy disk drive is not an easy decision. However there is one crumb of comfort in the fact that you can often add extra disk drives at a later date. When you buy a computer ask whether this will be possible, and whether you will be able to use standard ones, or will need to get them from a particular clone manufacturer.

Amstrad and Olivetti, in particular, tend to do things their own way, so ask some careful questions. Unfortunately, you sometimes get some less than careful replies, so be persistent.

1.4.2 How to Choose a Hard Disk Drive

What about hard disk drives? Technically, there are differences, but as it sits in the machine and doesn't have transferable disks, the technicalities are not usually part of the purchasing decision. What you do need to decide is how big it is going to be. To a large extent, this depends on the size of your pocket. Try and go as big as you can, without going bankrupt. At the time of writing, 40 Mb bytes is a reasonable size for the family or small business. It is large enough for most of the major software. 20 Mb could be enough, if you are a very small business or just a family. The trouble is, that in as little as two years' time, these figures will probably look very feeble. Newer versions of the latest software tend to occupy more disk space than ever and even 40 Mb can soon get filled up.

Again, ask your dealer if you will be able to upgrade at a later date, to a larger hard disk drive.

There are some other aspects of hard disk performance, which you might want to ask your dealer about so that he realises that you have some knowledge and can't be completely fooled. The read/write heads have to move in and out, and the disk has to rotate, all mechanical actions that take time, however short. There are several statistical measures of how long all this takes, the most common of which is the access time, the statistically average time for the disk drive heads to move from one random point on the disk to another. This is measured in milliseconds, abbreviated to ms, and such times vary between 18 ms and 100 ms. The lower this is, the faster and better the disk drive. Try to get one which is under 65 ms. If you use large database packages, which tend to use a lot of disk read/writes, this could be a measure to think about quite seriously.

If you are going to move the computer around a lot, you may be interested in its ability to cope with physical knocks. Some hard disk drive manufacturers test their drives under *shock therapy* to determine how many Gs (force of earth's gravity) their machines can withstand without data loss. Common ratings are 10 or 20 Gs – the higher the rating, the more knockable the computer. This though, is a minor consideration, compared with size, price and speed.

1.5 Monitors

More bad news. Monitors don't come in one variety either, so there are even more decisions to make. This is going to be a fairly brief account because monitor technology is quite complicated and you may want to look at more technical literature.

In fact, there are two things that are needed for producing a display on a monitor screen. You need some electronics inside the computer itself. This usually comes on what is called an expansion card and is called an adaptor. However, a few manufacturers like Amstrad in its 1512 PC put the electronics on the motherboard, where the main brain chip of the computer is stored. This has the unfortunate effect that you are stuck with what was there originally.

You also need the actual monitor itself, the bit that looks like a TV screen. This must be able to work with the electronics inside the computer. Fortunately when you buy a new PC, the internal electronics and the actual monitor will match. If you decide to upgrade though, you will need both a new expansion card and a new monitor. For the rest of this section, it is assumed that you will get the whole package, adaptor card and matching monitor screen.

1.5.1 Different Types of Monitor

A major distinction is between monochrome – or text only, and graphics. The former can only produce text or chunky pictures, made out of bits of letters, like you get on Ceefax. It will not produce business graphs or pie charts and you cannot play games that use pictures, which most of them do. This was one of the earliest kinds of screen display but the quality is still excellent, and if nearly all your work will be word processing, it may be something to consider. Children, though, like games and making pictures, so it is not a good family option. It does not have colours, although the writing on it may be green or amber. The word monochrome means literally *one colour* but it is in fact a very particular kind of monitor, one that does not do graphics.

All the others do graphics, which means that they can draw proper lines or circles, and you can run games and make business charts and diagrams. One of the earliest monitors that could do graphics, was the Hercules monitor, and although rather old, it is still good quality. The problem is that it won't produce colours, just black and white.

The next type of graphics adaptor to appear on the market was the CGA, short for Colour Graphics Adaptor. It provided for four colours which was an improvement, but the screen was rather fuzzy, worse than the older Hercules. If you are buying a cut price bargain, you may get a CGA monitor, and if the price is really low it could be worth it. However it is not considered a good piece of technology, and it is better to look for the next rung up. Funnily enough, until recently, most of the software was stuck at CGA, and the people who did go up the ladder, found that there was only a limited number of things they could run. Now, two years later, the tables have completely turned. Today, the latest games will not run on CGA, so bear this in mind if you are an avid games player.

The next development was the EGA, or Enhanced Graphics Adaptor, which provided clearer pictures and 16 colours. This hadn't been around very long before the next upgrade appeared, the VGA, or Video Graphics Adaptor. This is analogue rather than digital which means that it can produce much more variation in colour. It also provides an even sharper picture. This is the state of the art at the moment and if you are an ordinary family or business, unless you can get a real bargain of a CGA, this is what you should look at. The only problem, yet again, is that there is not one version of VGA, there are now three: the VGA, Super VGA and Extra Super VGA – the ESVGA. The Super VGA is better, the ESVGA better still. However, quite a lot of software only supports the ordinary VGA, so you won't always get use from the superior display. VGA needs quite a different monitor from CGA and EGA, an analogue rather than a digital monitor.

The latest adaptor is XGA. This may become the standard of the future, but at the moment, it is too soon to tell.

You may also come across what is called a multisync monitor. This has the *smart* ability to sense what adaptor card you have inside the computer and to adjust itself accordingly. This has the advantage that you can change the adaptor card without having to purchase a new monitor screen.

If you are engaged in a graphics hungry profession, there are even better graphics screens, at a price, of course. This might be necessary if you are publishing magazines, with professional desktop publishing, or doing computer aided design.

1.5.2 Definition or Sharpness

Computer graphics pictures are made out of little squares of coloured light or black/white. These are called pixels and the more you can get on the screen, the more detail you will produce. Graphics resolution is the number of little squares or pixels that fit across the screen multiplied by the number that run down it. For example, the old CGA monitor has a resolution of 320 x 200, which means 320 pixels across and 200 down. The new VGA has a resolution of 640 x 480. The table below shows the resolution and number of colours available for each adaptor.

The VGA series are usually able to switch between different resolutions, being what we call multisync. Very high resolution uses a lot of memory, and it can be useful to run at a lower resolution and to have more memory free for gameplay or sophisticated spreadsheet facilities. It also means you can run software which has only been written for lower resolution monitors.

Just to confuse matters, the CGA, EGA and VGAs come in mono or black and white versions. They will do all the graphics you could think of but these will be in black and white or in various shades of grey (up to 16 for a VGA) depending on exactly what monitor it is.

Graphics adaptor	Resolution	Colours
Monochrome	Text only 720 x 350	None
Hercules mono	Graphics	None
CGA	Graphics 320 x 200	4
EGA	Graphics 640 x 350	16
VGA	Graphics 640 x 480	256 Not same time
Super VGA	Graphics 800 x 600	256 Not same time
Extended SVGA	Graphics 1,024 x 768	256 Not same time

1.5.3 Portables

Portable screen technology is a bit different, because, at the present state of the art, the cathode ray tube television type monitor is too bulky. Most of them use LED technology, but another option is gas plasma. They come in the same standards as those given above, mainly CGA and VGA. The first colour LED-based screen has just appeared on the market, but you have to be very rich indeed to be able to afford it, so for most portable users, colour is not yet a realistic option.

1.5.4 Flicker

The other thing you may want to consider when you purchase a monitor is how much flicker it produces. Computer displays are produced by constantly writing on the screen, line by line, just like television. You may appear to have the same picture on the screen, but, in fact, it is being repeatedly redrawn. If this happens too slowly, the image can look fuzzy; if it happens too quickly, you get an unpleasant flickering. It can be difficult to get the right balance. It is a good idea to see the monitor in action before you actually purchase it.

1.6 Windows and Graphical User Interfaces

Windows is what is called a Graphical User Interface (GUI). These are not bits of hardware or computer equipment. They are, in fact, types of software but I have included them here because they run on certain types of hardware and may affect your choice of computer.

The first graphical user interface was created for the Apple range of computers. It was designed to provide a natural way for a human being to relate to the computer, by putting little pictures on the screen, and creating something like an ordinary non computerised working desk. You pick up folders, work on them and put them back in the filing cabinet.

If something isn't working out you throw it into the wastebin or trashcan. If you decide it wasn't such a mistake after all, you can scrabble through the rubbish and take it out again. On the desktop you have to hand a diary, calculator and a quick notepad. You can move quickly from one type of task to another, write a bit of a letter, do some spreadsheet calculations, go back to the letter and start drawing a picture.

Although it is usually possible to operate a graphical user interface from the keyboard, a mouse is really essential. You glide the mouse around the real desk and the cursor moves around the computer screen. To pick up and open a file, you press the mouse button. To copy a file, simply pull it on to the blank file it is being copied into. To throw something away, just drag it across the screen with the mouse until it is on top of the picture of the trashcan, press the mouse button and in it goes.

It was called an intuitive system because it could be used as naturally as your own work desk (it is assumed that you don't drown under piles of unorganised paper).

The system was brought to perfection on the Apple Macintosh series of computers. Apple was careful to preserve its copyright and prevented other companies from producing anything quite as effective. However as time has gone on, others have been developed like Workbench for the Commodore Amiga.

The PC had started off with the command-driven, text-oriented MS-DOS and most early users were familiar with this rather unfriendly way of relating to their computers. What you start off with and get used to, will, for some time, be what you are happiest with. Children who start on Amigas, zip around their computer with a mouse in a way that make most adults feel quite envious. An adult who has started with MS-DOS, will find it much more difficult to adjust to the Windows/mouse environment. However PC GUIs seem set to be the growth area of the future.

Funnily enough it was Amstrad who started GUIs for the PC. They supplied GEM with their PC1512 series, and if you have acquired one of these at a bargain price, you will have it. It has a menu at the top and a lot of files squashed on to the screen. GEM was really quite good but it didn't take off anywhere else in the PC world, partly because the PC1512 series was too slow to make good use of it. You do need a sophisticated chip to make GUIs worthwhile, and at that stage only the Motorola 68000 series used by the Apple Mac, the Amiga and Atari was up to it. The irony is that it is the Atari that has kept GEM going, although it is, of course, its own and not a PC version.

At the moment, the main GUI for the PC is called Windows. The latest version is Windows 3.1 and you need a 386 to run it. There is a version for the 286 but it is inferior and there is not much in the way of software to run on it, so Windows at that level is really a non-starter. Compared with the Apple Mac's GUI, Windows is certainly a much less natural way of communicating with the computer. In fact, if you don't know MS-DOS, you might find it a bit strange. However it does have one great big advantage: the ability to multitask or to run more than one kind of application at one time, so you can get the desktop effect of moving from one thing to another. It also allows you to use the extra memory beyond the usual power of MS-DOS, which can only handle 1 Mbyte at a time. This, in itself, makes it a very valuable tool.

There is other PC software that lets you multitask, in particular Desqview, but this doesn't have the graphical appearance.

Now if you are planning to buy a PC, you could say that it all sounds very nice but it is really an optional extra. A year a two ago, I would probably have agreed, but it now looks as though GUIs will become an essential feature in PC computing. Windows has been pushed very hard by its company Microsoft and a vast amount of major software, both commercial package and shareware, is being written to run under Windows. There is probably enough investment now, to mean that there is no turning back. Being able to tap into the reservoirs of unused memory is very attractive and as large packages tend to develop more features and use more memory as time goes on, I am sure it will continue.

At the time of writing in late autumn 1991, the giant company IBM has allied with Apple, which will provide a further push in the direction of GUIs. IBM's new operating system for the PC, called OS/2, has a friendly pictorial interface called Presentation Manager. If they release this to clones, there may be a serious rival to Windows, but two rivals rather than one market leader, will only strengthen the case for GUIs.

So what has all this to do with hardware? If you are in the budget market, don't bother, there is still plenty you can do. But if you are buying something more expensive, do try and get something that will run Windows properly. This means buying a 386, even if it stretches you, rather than a 286.

If you do have Windows, you can work without it if that makes you happier. In fact, you have both options so you are covered either way.

1.7 Buying a Printer

Unless you are buying a PC solely for the purpose of playing games (Amstrad have just started marketing a new PC package on this basis) a printer will be an absolute must. Even if you are planning to mainly play games, it is likely that you have some other applications in mind as well and most of these will need a printer. If you are a small business, there is no point in having a computer without one. If you are going to do any word processing, you obviously need a printer unless you have the type of electronic typewriter that can work through, or be what is called interfaced to, the PC.

Just like the computer itself, choosing a printer will depend very heavily on the applications you are going to run. If you plan to use a top range desktop publishing program or a computer aided design (CAD) package you will need a powerful printer to match your software expenditure. If you want to make full use of an expensive word processor with several different fonts or typefaces, you will need a printer that can match that capability. You will need one with the ability to do graphics if you want to produce business charts and diagrams, or print out the children's pictures. In this situation you may be keen to have colour. If your children are very artistic, remember that four colours is usually the maximum that a printer will provide.

So the prime consideration is what software you are going to run and what you are going to do with it.

Printers all use what are called consumables, small parts that need to be replaced regularly like cartridges or inked ribbons or, in the case of laser printers, toner. Sometimes, particularly for colour printers, these can be quite expensive, so consider their approximate cost when you are planning a purchase.

There is the problem of what is called compatibility. Printers can often be one of the devils of computing. The larger software packages often provide support for a range of popular makes, but the smaller ones may not bother. Make sure that the software you want to run, will work with your printer. Look carefully at lists of printers in the software manual and the printer manual itself and ask the dealer some very direct questions, in writing, if possible. For example: Will the Natsui 254 or whatever it is, run the latest version of Wordperfect or Lotus 1-2-3?

There are no absolute standards for printers but fortunately there are some. Many printers claim to be compatible with three leading machines, the IBM Proprinter, the Epson FX and Epson LQ, and for Laser printers, the Laserjet+. Laserjet II and Laserjet III series. A printer may allow you to switch between these standards, thus widening the choice of workable software.

Stick to the usual beginners' advice of going for a well established manufacturer and a well established model. Look at the reviews in the magazines. Apart from the fact that well known manufacturers' printers are more likely to run with your chosen software, it will be easier to go on finding their consumables in the years ahead. Also stick to up-to-date technology. I have a Panasonic Daisywheel printer. There is nothing wrong with it and Panasonic is one of the biggest names. The trouble is that the daisywheel has now been superseded and I once spent a whole afternoon ringing round to find where I could get a replacement ribbon.

Although you will need some kind of printer almost as soon as you start running your computer, any future purchases of new computers or printers can occur at different times, which spreads out the cash flow. If you opt for a budget printer now, it can always be used by the children or for draft quality when you move on to something more sophisticated. A small bubble jet might not be as good or as versatile as a laser, but the quality is still very acceptable and you can leave greater sophistication to a later date. You will then have an excellent portable printer to take on your travels.

You will also want to consider the printer speed. Unfortunately, some types of printer measure this in *characters per second* (cps), whereas others use *pages per minute* (ppm). It is possible, though, to provide a rough conversion between the two.

Another thing to consider is noise. Some printers are rather unpleasant in this respect and might prove the last straw for your beleaguered ear drums.

You also need to consider:

❑ Whether you need a specially wide carriage (you pay for this), for say DTP or CAD or just very big spreadsheets

❑ Whether your chosen printer can output in landscape mode to allow you to produce large spreadsheets sideways

❑ Whether you want to use continuous feed stationery or individual sheets

❑ Whether you want to use multi-sheet carbonised stationery, where you feed in several sheets at one go, and the print is carbonised on to lower layers. You will need an impact, dot matrix printer for this purpose

❑ Whether the printer will be situated less than three metres from your computer or kept at a greater distance, possibly connected or networked to other computers. In this case you must have what is called a serial rather than a parallel connection. Parallel connections allow eight bits (an on or an off) to travel at the same time, whereas serial connections just pass one at a time. This is necessary if your data is to pass more than three metres from the computer. Most printers are supplied automatically with a parallel connection, so if you want to network or distance the printer make sure it is possible to have a serial connection.

The last but not the least consideration is price and this may well be a determining factor. If you are running a professional design office or publishing house, you will need to go to some expense. If not, the good news is that printer technology has improved to such an extent that you can now get really very good quality for a relatively modest outlay, say about £250.

So what are the options? There are now three major types of printer: the dot matrix, the laser and the ink jet. Unlike earlier types, they can all produce graphics, although whether they do this with the particular software that you want to run, may be another matter.

1.7.1 The Dot Matrix Printer

The dot matrix printer head has a grid made out of little pins. When printing, selected pins are pushed forward against an inked ribbon, to hit the paper. The selected pins form letter and other character shapes. In fact they can produce any kind of shape, which makes them versatile and good at producing graphics.

They are called impact printers because the pin ends actually touch the paper through the ribbon. This means that they are the only type of printer that can use carbonised paper. They tend to be fast but on the whole, rather noisy. Some of the more modern and expensive ones claim to be much quieter.

They use an inked cloth ribbon which can be used again and again like an old fashioned typewriter ribbon. This means that they are very economical in terms of consumables which can be useful in a family situation. It is hard not to grit your teeth at the five year old's half finished frequent print outs, when you are paying 5p a sheet.

Output quality varies with the number of pins – the more they have the clearer and more detailed the print out. Early models had only 9 pins and were very crude by modern standards – 18 or 24 is now more or less standard and there are even higher numbers. Dot matrix printers often provide two quality levels. One way of doing this is to go over the same line again, but slightly phased out – this takes longer than printing it just once. The other way is to use a variable number of pins, in which case the better quality will not take much longer than the draft.

The more popular makes provide IBM Proprinter or Epson compatibility. Many have a tractor feed for old fashioned continuous stationery with holes at each side, but usually allow individual sheets to be fed in as well. Typical dot matrix printers are shown in Figures 1.2 and 1.3.

Figure 1.2: The Epson 850 with optional sheet feeder. Photo courtesy of Epson UK

Figure 1.3: The Panasonic KX-P1123 24-pin dot matrix printer.

Prices vary with quality of course. You can get a budget dot matrix printer for just over £100 if you shop around. This will satisfy most family needs but the word processed output may not be as good as you would like, particularly if you get used to the better quality of other people's ink jet and laser printers.

1.7.2 The Laser Printer

At present, this is the best type. It is fast and silent but is also very much more expensive. The relatively large difference in price between the laser and other types of printers, may not justify the improvement in quality. Figure 1.4 shows a typical laser printer.

They work rather like photocopying machines, and this means that they should be kept well ventilated to avoid ozone build up. They contain a light sensitive drum which is activated by a laser beam. This picks up toner – a fine black powder. The paper winds round the drum and is given a static charge which allows it to pick up the toner. It is then heated up to bond the ink to the paper. There are also LED and LCD printers which work in much the same way, but without using lasers.

Laser printers print one page at a time. Since the output from your computer is continuous, they have their own special memory or buffer, where the computer output builds up until they are storing a full page. They need to have the electronics to manage this and usually build on this to provide a sophisticated set of controls. You can get additional software to make even fuller use of the laser printer. The trouble is that this extra sophistication comes at a price, like learning how to use the special printer programming language, which means that a busy, unsupported business person may never reap the full benefit of an expensive printer.

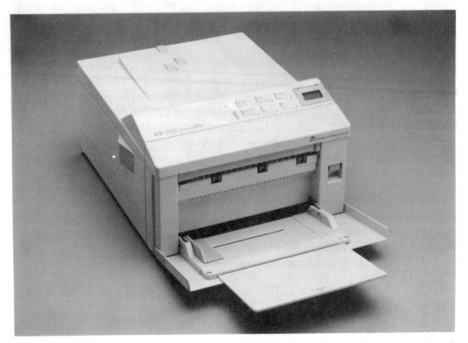

Figure 1.4: The Hewlett-Packard Laserjet III. Photo courtesy of Hewlett-Packard

There are different standards of compatibility, the latest being Laserwriter III. Try to get this, if you can. Make sure that your particular software will be able to make as much use as possible of the attractive features offered in the advertising brochure.

The consumables tend to be expensive. However, the quality of printout is very good and although the others are doing very well at catching up, the laser printer is still the queen of the industry. At a price though!

1.7.3 The Bubble Jet Printer

This technology has gone through some recent improvements. It works by having a set of nozzles which selectively shoot ink on to the paper. It is non impact because the nozzles do not touch the paper.

You need to be slightly careful with the type of paper you use but this is true for laser printers as well. If it is too absorbent you get a smudged effect. The printout emerges quite wet and you must be careful not to put anything else on top of it until it has had a few seconds to dry. A friend informs me that her swimming pool notice got too wet to read, so if you use documents in an atmosphere that is not dry, another printer might be more appropriate.

The quality is excellent, not quite as good as a laser printer, but good enough to provide your personal and small business correspondence with a professional look.

The prices are low in comparison with laser printers and pound for pound they are a very good bet. They are nice and quiet, and reasonable but not brilliant in terms of speed.

Unfortunately, they are expensive in terms of consumables. The print cost can be as much as 5 or 6p per sheet compared with about 2p for the laser printer and much less for the dot matrix. They maintain their print quality until the ink runs out and the cartridge needs changing. Dot matrix printers, on the other hand, tend to get weaker and weaker until you decide you really must change the ribbon.

The technology means that you can have a much lighter, more compact printer and this can be useful in a home situation where you may want to put things away or carry them round from room to room.

They do not usually provide for continuous stationery. You may need to feed the paper in sheet by sheet which can be very tedious. Sheet feeders are usually available but can cost another £50 or so.

1.8 Extras

There are several other bits and pieces of hardware that you can add on, either when you first buy a computer or as time goes by. You can add extra disk drives, either hard or floppy.

Additional hard or floppy disk drives can often be stored inside the computer itself, although you can have external ones too. If you have a portable PC with a hard disk drive, it makes a lot of sense to have a detachable floppy. You will only use it for copying in the original program disks, or copying your data or work to backup or to send to friends or business contacts. You will probably be able to manage without it on your travels, which gives you less to cart around and lose.

The other add-ons will be used outside the computer, because they are often input or output devices. They need to be connected to some kind of slot on the back or side of the computer. This can be done in two ways. Either you use what are called ports, which are already built in at the back of the computer. These come in two varieties, serial or parallel and have already been mentioned in the section on printers.

The other method is to put an expansion card in the computer itself. This will have the appropriate connector on it. Your computer will have spare expansion slots somewhere inside and the big problem is how many. An expansion card is a narrow board containing electronic circuitry like the main motherboard on the computer, where its main brain, the central processing unit or CPU, is stored. Some devices must use an expansion card. Others can use either a port or a card.

To make matters more confusing, some manufacturers build devices on the motherboard itself or on a direct link to the main bus or channel that connects one part of the CPU to another. This has the advantage that you either need fewer expansion slots, or you can use them for other things but it does make the built-in devices difficult to upgrade.

The easiest way round all this, is to work out what devices or add-ons you have got already and what others you want to add later. To cover yourself, try and get as much expandability as possible. This will be extremely important if you want to have a mixture of the latest developments in business and games playing.

Add-on devices develop so rapidly that all I can do in this section is give you a very general idea of what exists. If you are planning to buy one, read the reviews in the computer magazines.

1.8.1 The Mouse

The mouse is a small plastic device which you move around on the desk. As you do this, the cursor moves around on the computer screen. It has two or three buttons on top, and you press these to pull down a menu from the top of the screen, to make a menu choice or to carry out some action, like dragging a picture of a file on to another, to copy it over. It means you can move around the screen very quickly which is almost essential if you are going to use a paint or design package. It is also a necessary part of using Windows which expects you to carry out actions by moving from one little picture or icon to another. If you buy a top range computer with Windows, you would expect the dealer to throw in a mouse.

Otherwise you may find you don't need one. Some of the newer machines, like Amigas, Ataris and Apple Macs are mouse driven, and the machine is fairly useless without one. The PC, however, started without the mouse and relatively little software was written that used it. So if you do get a mouse, unless you run Windows versions of software, you can expect that only a small amount of your software will allow you to use it.

A mouse generally operate by having a little tracker ball on its undersides. As this rolls around the desk, it sends signals to the computer, which works out how far the mouse has travelled and links this up to the cursor. There are two direct ways in which a mouse can be connected to the PC. One is on to the PC bus, which is the pathway along which data travels around inside the central processing unit. The other is via a serial port. The problem with the latter is that you may have only one or two of these, and if you use one for your mouse, that leaves one less for something else.

Standard mice varieties are the Microsoft, Genius and Logitech. It is better to stick either to a big name or to make sure that your mouse is fully compatible with one of the main ones. You cannot generally swap mice between computers with different operating systems, like the Apple Mac and Amiga. However there are some on the market, like the Naksha mouse, which can be switched between different types of computer. They come with different connections and internal software.

1.8.2 Joysticks

These come from the joystick found on aeroplanes, and are used in games, where you want rapid movement around the screen and also the ability to press a fire button to shoot at missiles and other monsters. It is easier to use than a mouse.

The PC has come to joysticks rather late in life, unlike many of its popular rivals. Make sure that you purchase a joystick that can be run on your PC, and you will likely need some conversion software and an expansion card. Again, it ties up an expansion card from other potential uses.

1.8.3 Modems

This translates signals sent from your computer into a form which can then be sent down the telephone line. They are translated back at the other end and fed into another computer. You can link yourself up to geographically distant parts of your business, even to the other side of the world. You can access what are called bulletin boards and download very cheap software. You can also get into whole databases or libraries of information, things like literature abstracts of journal or newspaper articles, company information and legal reports. You pay a price for all these things, of course, and on top of that, there is the telephone bill.

You need to do this kind of translation because the computer uses digital signals, using just two voltage levels for on or off, the only things that it can understand. The telephone system uses an analogue system to cope with the ups and downs of human speech, covering many different levels of sound.

The most popular way of classifying modems is by their speed, which is measured in bits per second (bps), each bit being one on or one off. This is called the baud rate. The figure gets higher as technology improves. An old model might be 300 baud, a not quite so old one would be 1200 baud. The most common is now the 2400 baud and there is a movement towards the 4800 and 9600. Figure 1.5 shows an example of a fast speed model.

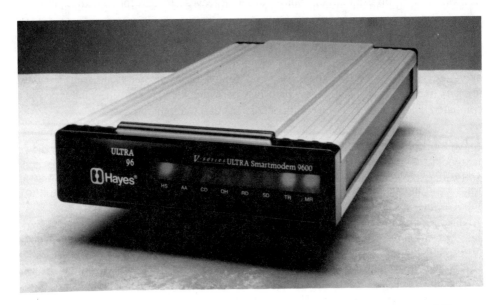

Figure 1.5: The Hayes V-series Ultra Smartmodem 9600. Photo courtesy of Hayes Microcomputer Products

1.8.4 Fax

You can put a special Fax card in your computer. This will allow you to fax documents produced with your word processor, spreadsheet or graphical software.

1.8.5 Sound Enhancers

On its own account, the PC has rather primitive sound, unlike the speech and vastly superior sound capability of, say, the Amiga. Even the old BBC computers were more sophisticated. The PC has only one sound channel, so you can only produce one note at a time, no chords or harmonics. Many games now come with a wonderland of modern musical sound. To get round this you can buy a sound system to give your PC extra channels, and also to provide a set of speakers to send it out. These also sometimes provide a speech facility. They come as part of the new Amstrad PC games package or can be purchased separately, retailing at about £100 to £150. However, they do have the advantage, like many add-ons, that you don't have to buy them straightaway. You can wait till a later date when you are feeling more affluent.

1.8.6 CD-ROM

This will probably be one of the major storage devices of the future. Rather like the old story of VHS, Phillips and Betamax, there have been some problems in deciding exactly what the main system will be. CD-ROM stores computer material, text, pictures and moving film on what is more or less a compact disc. You can't rub it out, so it is more suitable for more permanent material. It has the advantage that you can store vast quantities of information on one small disc, and you can easily combine writing, photos and films and put bits of all three on the screen at one time. You can zoom in for a closer look and select more material on any area, written, film or photo that might happen to interest you.

This is what is meant by hypermedia, and it is seen as the educational achievement of the future, although to my sceptical mind a nation that finds it hard to buy new textbooks, is unlikely to find the money to get into such a huge hardware and software explosion. Although the material is fixed, you can be very selective in which bits of its vast quantity, you dip into.

Kodak are working on a system, where you can feed in your family photographs, and they will all appear on a CD-ROM. This should be available in the middle of 1992.

If it is very important to you to be in the forefront of modern technology, then maybe buy it now, but with caution. It is probably better to wait for the manufacturers to settle down to some kind of standard and for the price to fall, which I am sure it will.

1.8.7 Scanners

A scanner passes over writing, drawings and photographs, and produces a copy which can be turned into a computer file and stored on a disk. It can then be loaded into a desktop publishing or paint package. It can be edited or changed, made smaller or larger, bits cut out and other bits drawn in. Scanners can be very useful for producing teaching or training material or for magazines or other published material that uses illustrations.

1.9 Rivals

1.9.1 The Amstrad PCW Range

Look very carefully at the label. One that needs watching is the Amstrad PCW range, the latest version being the PCW9512. It is easy just to see the PC in the label and immediately think that you have got a PC, a not unreasonable assumption in the circumstances. In fact these machines are NOT PCs, they do not use the same operating system (they use the older CP/M not MS-DOS) and they are definitely not compatible. Unless you are looking at the very latest model, appearing in late 1991, you will find it even uses a different sized disk, a 3.25'' rather than a 3.5''. The PCW was designed as a word processor, that happened to have computing facilities as well. It came as an all-in-one package with a printer and the word processing software, LocoScript. About four or five years ago, they were a very good buy, being rather cheaper than the corresponding PC equivalent. Now the 8086 chip based PC is cheaper. PCWs were also well supported by cheap, easy-to-run, small business software, but again the PC can now do better and has the advantage of being much more widely supported in all business worlds.

LocoScript will run on a PC as well. In fact, it will work in much the same way, as regards menus and what it does, whether it is on the PC or PCW. However you cannot run exactly the same program from exactly the same disk, even if they are the same size. You need either LocoScript for the PC or Locoscript for the PCW. The reason is that they run different operating systems: the PC, as we have seen, runs MS-DOS, the PCW runs the older CP/M.

1.9.2 Apple Mac, Amiga and Atari

There are rather more serious rivals. The Apple Macintosh uses yet another, quite different family of chips and a totally different operating system, called in its latest version, System 7. They are very nice machines, particularly if you are interested in graphics and art. Quite a few secondary schools and some businesses have adopted them. In business, they are not as widespread as the PC and they have tended to be rather expensive, until 1990, when the Classic was marketed at about £500. If you use one yourself at work, it might be a good buy. If you are a non computer user, and your children use them at school, they could be worthwhile. On the other hand, in Britain at least, the PC is used more widely in business, so if you don't have an Apple at work or at school, go for the PC.

Other possible rivals are the Commodore Amiga and Atari ST 500 series. They both use the same family of chips, the Motorola 6800 series, but they are not compatible, because they use different operating systems, Amiga Dos and STOS respectively. They are strong on art and music, and the higher (2000 series) of Amiga is used in the professional art and graphics world. There are word processors, databases and spreadsheets for both, but the choice is limited compared with the PC, so they are not ideal for business.

If you are buying a computer for the children only, the Amiga or Atari could be ideal. For the same price as an 8086 PC, you will get a full 32 bit machine, which is vastly superior. The 386 PC has some technical strengths, but it costs more, about four times as much. However, this usually includes a monitor, a hard disk drive, and if you added these to your Amiga the price differential would not be so great. Although you would at least have the option of a lower initial expenditure, leaving the add-ons until you have the spare cash.

If your children are teenagers moving on to their second computer, the Amiga or Atari could be ideal. If they are younger, it has a lot to offer: a good, full LOGO, speech, wonderful graphics and sound but there is very little in the way of books for beginners, and it is too easy for young children to get stuck on games.

If the adults want to compute, the decision could be different. If they use a PC at work, and just want to do a very small amount of computing at home, the Amiga or Atari could still be the answer, as it will give the children a lot to do, and it is possible to get what is called a PC emulator, which will let you run PC software on what is an incompatible machine. It works a bit more slowly than the PC, but for occasional use that might not matter.

If the adults are heavy users of the computer, and they have the PC at work, go for the PC. It makes an excellent family computer and provides plenty for both children and adults. There is a huge amount of shareware available. Although the PC is seen mainly as a business machine, nearly all the major commercial games come in a PC version, so there is plenty of leisure as well. If you are a games freak, make sure you have plenty of expansion slots though. To get the best quality out of games, you will probably want to add a joystick, and mouse if you haven't got one already. You may also want extra music and sound facilities, as the PC's own inbuilt sound and speaker system is fairly crude. Also the most up to date games are better on at least a 286 chip and will often not run on CGA monitors, so make sure you have VGA.

Many parents in Britain will ask about the BBC Micro, which is used at my child's school. This is certainly better provided for in terms of educational software. However, its rather chunky, bite sized graphics look old fashioned in comparison with the Apple Macintosh, PC, Amiga or Atari. They have what are now considered very small memories and are quite limited when it comes to word processing, spreadsheets and databases. Most secondary schools have already moved on to more powerful computers and the primary schools are going that way as well. Most of these new machines will be PC compatible (that is able to run PC software) if they are not actual PCs themselves. The Acorn 3000 and Archimedes are modern, technically excellent machines, and they have some very avid devotees. However they are relatively expensive and not that widely used or supported.

With children, it is well worth considering what their friends have. They will want to swap disks, to compare notes and discuss how programs run and maybe even to make joint purchases of extra hardware.

However, just in case you are wondering why you bought this book, let me praise the PC. It is an ideal family computer, the machine most likely to be used by adults at work, but also provides plenty for the younger members to do. Shareware means that there is lots to do on a limited budget. Children adapt easily to different types of computer between home and school, probably more so than adults. This adaptability is a useful preparation for adult life. Children and adults can learn together and this will probably benefit both parties (provided there is a certain amount of tolerance on either side!).

So if you are buying for the family, go for the PC. If it is just for the children, in value for money terms, the other options may be a better bet and the choice may hang on what their friends have.

1.10 Which Manufacturer do you Choose?

So you have decided to buy a PC. What kind of PC do you purchase and which manufacturer do you choose?

As far as the type of PC goes, to a large extent you get what you pay for. If your upper limit is definitely £500, you have no real choice, you will have to get an XT with the 8086 chip. You will also need some sort of printer to make use of your PC, and this should be included in your estimated price. Financial limits can, though, be a false economy. Another £300 and you could get something vastly superior. If you stick to the lower band, you may find you grow out of your computer very quickly and want a new one before your finances are ready for it. It may be worth stretching yourself a little bit more to get into the next band.

You will also need software. If you want the big packages, these do not come cheap. £350 for a big label word processor and £450 for a major database package, can cost you as much again as the hardware. However software can come later – you can survive for quite a long time on shareware and wait for the big packages until your purse is a little fuller.

You will also need spare blank disks for data and back up copies, print ribbons, ink and so on for your printer – what we call consumables. This can add another £40 to £50 to your original hardware costs.

However, if you are on a budget, the software can wait so stretch yourself on the hardware. Consider what you are going to use the computer for. Are you going to use it in your business? Is this likely to expand? Look carefully at your future forecasts. The business user will probably grow out of an 8086 but if your cash flow is crucial at the moment, an 8086 might be best for now, with a view to upgrading in say two years' time. Because the PC is the member of a family, you can transfer your data and programs on to the new compatible machines without too much trouble.

If you use a PC at work, what kind do you have? If you have a fast 386 with a mouse and icon driven Windows, you could be quite irritated by the 8086 and also find that it can't run the much more powerful software you are used to. On the other hand, you might take the view that you are so well equipped at work, that you won't be doing that much computing at home, and an 8086 could handle the odd weekend report or document.

Consider how each member of the family will use the computer.

If you are running a business, cost out what you will save by using the computer. I used to type wills at home and it nearly drove me mad. On average, I would retype each one 2.5 times before I got it correct and it would take over three hours. I would go into the office the next day, and beg them to buy me a word processor. Now it would have made me a lot happier, but at the rate of 15 wills a year, it just wasn't worth it. So do some hard sums. You also need to allow for the fact that you have to set the computer up and train yourself and your staff. You then need practice and mistake time before you become fully productive. If you want to set up a database, you will need to plan it, collect your data and spend several hours inputting it before you reap any benefit at all.

If you are retired or a non business family, the simplest PC may be quite as much as you need. Your main use will probably be word processing and with the help of shareware and other budget packages, there will be plenty to do and discover.

This may seem controversial advice, but either go for the budget priced 8086 or try and go much higher up, to the 386. At the moment there is still a buoyant market for the 286, but the price tends to be much higher than the 8086 and apart from speed, it does not provide that much of a technical advantage. Of course, if you can find a 286 that is £100 or £200 more than the 8086, it might be worth considering, but make sure that it is a fully compatible PC.

The reason for going for a 386 rather than a 286 is paradoxical. You will probably only ever use a fraction of the capability of the 386, but it does allow you to run Windows 3.1 and this looks set to become an industry standard. This is a mouse driven, pictorial menu system which manages to use more of the PC memory and can run more than one application at the same time, what we call multitasking. Increasingly, commercial software is making use of it.

Having decided what chip to buy, how do you select the manufacturer? I think everyone wants an easy answer, like the Damvig (fictional name) 999x but unfortunately in computing, fashion comes and goes faster than the High Street. This month's flavour could be next month's bankruptcy. Our local computer club is a bunch of quite senior industry professionals. A couple of years ago, they all went for a single manufacturer and you got the impression that nothing could be better. A year later, the story was quite different, various faults had set in and they wouldn't have made the same decision again. Now if the experts can't get it right, what are the rest of us going to do? All I can do is to offer some tips.

Don't buy anything too old. In about the mid 1980s, PC type machines were manufactured, which were not really compatible, machines like the Sharp and the Apricot. They can be expensive bargains, as there is relatively little software that will run on them.

❏ Sort out your specifications before you go shopping. What chip do you want? What kind of monitor? What software do you want – will the prospective machine run it? What kind of disk drives and what size? Make sure you get what you want.

❏ Read the computer magazines and look at reviews. These also come and go and change their names from week to week. Some current titles are given in the Appendix. The reviews are not foolproof but they give you some kind of idea.

❏ Ask about the possibility of upgrading and adding on at a later date. Can you do this and how easy will it be to get the extras? Some of the clones do things very much their own way, like Amstrad and Olivetti, and may need their own special add-ons. However, being established firms, that might not be the end of the world.

❏ Stick to the larger companies. You have probably heard that there is lots of money in computing and there probably was before the 1991 recession, but there is also an enormous turnover of companies and personnel. The individuals turn up somewhere else but there is no company left to sue or to provide spare parts. The little man round the corner probably does have some real bargains but leave them to the initiated. This is also true of second hand computers unless you know you are buying from reliable people with a good reason for selling, and that the machine they are offering is not obsolete. Usually there will be no manufacturer's guarantee.

❏ Local dealers may offer support like setting up the hard disk for you and loading the software. They may provide advice when you get stuck. This could make all the difference between your becoming a successful computer user or putting your new box of hardware back in the cupboard. It could well be worth paying a little more for this kind of assistance. However, you need to be careful as there are some sharks around.

❏ Local technical and adult education colleges offer excellent introductory courses for small business users and they might be worth looking at. If you get a good tutor, he or she will help you with specific problems. Small business clubs can be useful and there are the government funded Training and Enterprise Councils. They can be a valuable source of local knowledge. Another good source of information is a PC user group. The meetings can be very daunting if you are a beginner, as they tend to be full of over knowledgeable enthusiasts, but they are often willing to offer you free advice on what is worth buying. Be a bit careful, because being so keen, they may go for much more powerful equipment than you actually need.

Finally, you need to consider exactly where you are going to buy your PC. The choices are:

❏ **Your local dealer or shop.** These vary a lot, both in terms of prices and support. The chain stores, like Dixons, often offer very good prices for the most popular budget type computers, but they tend to run a few lines at one particular time, and six months later they have moved on and offer no more support for what you have bought. If you are buying a budget computer, you may find them quite reasonable. They tend to stock established lines from larger, more reliable companies.

❏ **Mail Order.** It is best to use a credit card for this, as you have more legal redress if the goods are not of merchantable quality. You can save a lot of money this way. Buy the magazines and look carefully at all the advertisements. There are some companies, like Dell, which deal exclusively by mail order, and provide very good value for money. Computers often fail during burn out time – the first 72 hours of use – and if this happens to you, you need to be happy with wrapping up parcels and dealing with carrier companies. *Note:* when you receive a computer by post, sign for it as "UNINSPECTED", otherwise the carrier may try to wriggle out of his responsibility in case of damage.

❏ **Visiting Tottenham Court Road.** There are many dealers in this part of London, who give the kind of discounts you get through mail order, and they may, in fact, offer the latter as well. You do need to know what you are buying, and be prepared for an unpleasant journey home through the centre of London. If something goes wrong while your computer is under guarantee, you may be able to send it back to the manufacturer rather than staggering back to the Tottenham Court Road.

❏ **Computer shows.** There are some very good offers at shows, but they are hot and crowded and your journey home will probably be a bit of a nightmare. It can be well worth the cost saving if you are feeling strong.

2

Buying Software

2.1 What is Software?

The first chapter in this book dealt with hardware, the actual machinery that makes up the computer, the printer and the things you might want to add on. This is not much use on its own, because it won't do anything at all until you put some instructions in. This is what software is, the instructions that tell the computer what to do.

A bit like the horse and carriage or the CD player and compact discs, one is of little use without the other. This book started with hardware but software is just as important. Don't buy your computer until you have looked at software and made some careful plans about the sort of things you are going to do with your new machine. What sort of things does software do?

Housekeeping

Your program files and work are stored on disks, either hard or floppy. It is necessary to keep a record of what is kept where. When you ask for one of these files, it has got to be copied into the computer's main memory. When you have finished your work, it needs to be copied on to a disk in some spare space. You will send work to the printer, this needs to be organised and the computer needs to interpret the messages you give it when you type on the keyboard. All this takes a great deal of organisation, and this is what the Operating System does.

In the last chapter, I said that the PC was defined by having the operating system, MS-DOS, but that it could run other operating systems as well, like Unix and OS/2. You can get different versions of DOS. To make matters more confusing, your dealer may give you something different, called DR.DOS. This is an alternative to MS-DOS, and is produced by a different company, called Digital Research. It has some rather attractive features but it is built on MS-DOS and is not really a separate operating system, so my definition still stands.

Applications software

These are the programs that actually do something: let you write letters, memos and reports (word processing), produce financial and statistical material (spreadsheets) or store and retrieve information (databases). The background housekeeping is vital to the running of your machine, but you won't have to worry much about it. Most of your dealings with the computer will be in using applications software. It is ready made, designed with the mass market in mind. This means that most of it provides more functions than you will need or want. It also includes desktop publishing, computer aided design, accounts packages and a huge games market.

Bespoke or custom built software

There are so many good application packages around that can be adapted to your particular use, that you will probably never come across this. It is a suite of programs written for one specific user by a team of professional systems analysts and programmers. As such people like to be well paid and programming is very time consuming, it is extremely expensive.

Utilities

These are little programs that often do the kinds of things that the main operating system has not got round to. They may provide better ways of showing what files you have got on your disks, or sort them into a different order. They may display a title in large, moving letters or make special sounds. If you have a portable computer, you can get a utility that will display a better cursor. You can use them to produce a menu system of all the files and programs you store on your disks. Once you have gained a little experience, they can be quite fun to mess around with.

The sort of software you buy will depend on your individual needs and interests. If you are running a dog kennel or a hairdressers, you may find an applications package that suits your particular business. If you are a teacher, you may find some educational software that helps in your job and programs for storing marks and providing quiz outlines. Whoever you are, though, you will almost certainly need a word processor and possibly a spreadsheet and database as well and last but not least, some games. The rest of this chapter discusses this kind of main core applications software in more detail. I have left databases out because they tend to be a bit more specialised. However they are covered in Chapter 6 along with how to plan and set one up using a famous shareware package PC-FILE.

2.2 Choosing a Word Processor

Almost everyone will require a word processor at some stage. This produces written material, letters, reports, even books. Word processors vary from the very simple to something extremely complex. Desktop publishing (DTP) is the next stage up and produces magazines and books like this one, many complete with illustrations brought in from drawing packages and scanners. The most sophisticated word processors, like WordPerfect (Figure 2.1), are beginning to develop many of the features of DTP so that the distinction becomes a bit blurred. However the most advanced DTP packages can be used to typeset, which cuts down one of the stages in publishing. As one stage in computing moves on, so does the next.

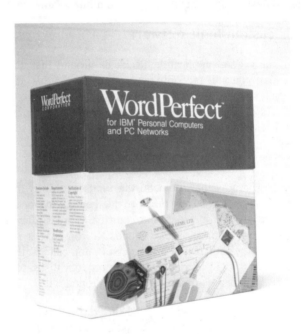

Figure 2.1: WordPerfect's features now include DTP facilities

You need to consider what you are going to use your word processor for and who in your family is going to use it. If you have a secretary or a family member employed as one, outside the home, it is worth buying a large package because they will be used to something of this quality and will want to keep up their skills. The really big packages are WordPerfect, Wordstar, Microsoft's Word for Windows and Display-write 5. During 1991, WordPerfect was the market leader.

If you are newly retired or a family without secretarial contacts, and want something that isn't much bother and is easy to learn, there are some excellent simple integrated packages, like Logotron's Eight in One, First Choice, Works or C-A Office (Figure 2.2). Integrated software puts several different types of application into one package: a spreadsheet, database and word processor. This has the advantage that they will all have the same kind of menu system, so once you have learnt one it is easy to turn to the others. On the other hand, by doing everything, they probably do less well on each individual application.

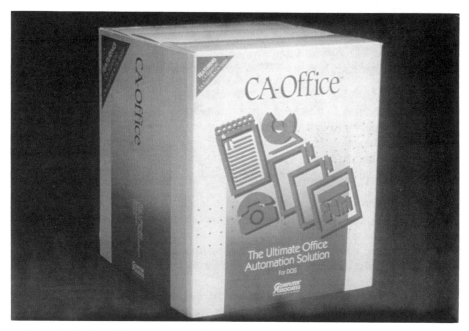

Figure 2.2: C-A Office – an excellent integrated package. Photo courtesy of C-A Associates

Another possibility is shareware. The main ones are Galaxy and Galaxy Lite or Word Fugue (these are Wordstar clones) or PC-Write or Write Lite. Galaxy Lite and Word Fugue comes as inspection copies. This means that you are just meant to try them out and see whether you like them, and if you do you should register and pay a working price. You then get a proper manual, some more working facilities and upgrades. This will cost you approximately £30.

Galaxy Lite forces you into registering because after you have used it 10 times it keeps on putting messages all over the screen and you can hardly see what you are doing. It is attractive and quite easy to use and although I don't have the full registered version, the manual you get on the shareware disk is very well written and clear. If you buy a shareware Wordstar clone, you have the option of buying Wordstar proper when you have acquired more money and you can then import your files. Being a clone, the match is not perfect but with some minor adjustments, your files will be quite viable.

A professional writer would probably need a large package. The publisher can then feed his files straight into a DTP. It is worth getting enough training to make use of some of its advanced features as they will be very helpful in your work.

Children may seem to be a problem, as schools often have their own special word processors which are not always compatible with the PC. However, children are very adaptable and even if you are a reluctant computer user, you will probably learn enough about word processing to be able to teach them the basic first steps of your particular word processor. If it is an advanced package, there will be plenty for them to grow into, and they will get a good start early in life. Very young children like big print and there is a very simple shareware Kid's Wordprocessor which provides this facility.

When you are planning to buy a word processor look carefully at printers at the same time. There is no point in having an advanced package if you don't have a printer that can use it. Ask the dealer if your chosen printer will take full advantage of the word processing package and is also compatible with the computer that you are going to buy. It is safer to stick to big names and popular brands.

A single word processor will provide a very wide spread of different features and the average user will only need a fraction of these. Book writers want to handle long documents and to use indexes. Companies will want to indent paragraphs, use minuting columns, and perhaps put in figures from spreadsheets. Advertisers want beautifully presented letters with special typefaces.

Below are some of the features you can find in word processors so that you can see what is available. Make a list of the things you require and look for a word processor that will meet those needs.

❏ **WYSIWYG** stands for What You See is What You Get. This means that what shows up on the screen looks just like what your printer would produce. In the very early days of word processing this was impossible. Your written work looked like a long string of text with some strange characters in the middle. Instead of seeing a paragraph break you would just get a symbol like [lf] wrapped in with all the words.

> That was a long time ago, and word processors are now getting so complicated that it is getting more difficult to achieve once again. Text may be written in columns, may even be spread around pictures, may have many different typefaces, and headers and footnotes (chapter and book titles at the top of a page or the bottom, just as in this book). It is almost impossible for all this detail to appear on a screen, particularly if you do not possess a very high resolution professional monitor.

❏ **Different typefaces or fonts.** Most computers offer bold or heavier type, italics and underlining may also be on offer. Can you change the print and use fancy fonts, switching in the middle of a document? Will this show up on the screen? This is where the Windows versions of word processors, in particular Word, at the present time win over. They treat letters and characters as though they were pictures or graphics and that makes it much easier to show all the different typestyles.

❏ **Is it comfortable to use?** This is a difficult one. When you are a beginner, a menu system is ideal. When you have got used to a word processor, this can be an irritation particularly if you have to select your way through a whole series of menus before you can get anywhere. You then want quick short cut ways of doing things like using function keys or funny combinations (Wordstar is keen on <Alt> plus letters like S, T, V or KR).

❏ WordPerfect uses the function keys on their own, or with Shift, Alt or Control at the same time. This means that each function key can be used in four ways. Fortunately, it provides a special plastic template you can set over your function keys to act as a reminder. If you are a beginner though, this can all be very confusing as many of the key combinations don't make much sense in themselves. If a word processor offers too many new features, even the seasoned user will find his or her memory overstretched.

❏ **Spell checking.** This is now quite a standard feature. How quickly does it work? What does it do if it comes across proper names or technical jargon? Can you add your own words to the computer's dictionary? Many packages are American and keep on highlighting completely legitimate British spellings.

❏ **Thesaurus.** This provides alternative words so that you can avoid repeating yourself. Again it is becoming a quite common feature. Another variant is the grammar or style checker. This has its limitations as the computer has not yet acquired the ability of a Shakespeare but you could find one entertaining.

❏ **Special effects.** A scientist or academic writer may want to use superscripts or subscripts, as in H_2SO_4 or $a^2 + b^2$. Does your word processor provide these facilities?

❏ **Headers and footers.** Someone who writes long reports or books may want the heading constantly repeated at the top, possibly in very small print, and maybe differently on odd and even pages. They may want page numbers automatically put in.

❏ **Mathematics.** Some advanced packages will do simple arithmetic like adding up columns of figures. Displaywrite 4 offers this feature but I found it very cumbersome to use.

❏ **Portability.** Can you bring in material from your database or spreadsheet? Can you send written material from your word processor into your friend's different package? This is where Windows really comes into its own. It provides what is called Direct Data Exchange or DDE so that any material can be easily imported from one application to another and because you have multitasking, you can have them both on the screen at the same time.

If you are writing material for publication, can your text be exported to a professional DTP package? This will probably mean you have to go for WordPerfect, WordStar or Word.

❏ **Importing pictures.** Can you import graphics material or drawings from some recognised paint package. If you can, a whole library of clip art may be at your disposal. WordPerfect can do this and Word for Windows, being part of a graphical system, is excellent in this respect.

❏ **Indexes.** Some packages provide an indexing facility which searches for words and builds up a book index. This would be ideal for an author.

❏ **Search and Replace.** Most word processors offer a search and replace facility. This can be surprisingly useful. Suppose you have written a long report, and have consistently spelt a word wrong. The computer will correct it for you.

❏ **Macros.** Does the package allow you to use macros? If you find yourself doing the same series of key presses over and over again, you can write a macro and one or two prearranged keypresses will do it all for you.

❏ **Size.** If you write long documents, will your word processor handle them?

❏ **Drawing.** Can you do simple line drawings to produce boxes and rectangles? This can be useful for surrounding special text or drawing say family trees. Don't expect a full artistic facility though.

❏ **Outliners.** Some word processors provide outliners. These allow you to set out headings and explanatory text for chapters and their subsections. You can then fill them in with your writing. They can be very useful for presenting plans for what you are going to write. The writing becomes easier afterwards too.

❏ **Literature.** Are there good manuals or books on your chosen package? Are there cheap classes and user groups in your area? Will it be reasonably easy to learn and to get support and help?

2.3 Choosing a Spreadsheet

A spreadsheet is an electronic grid. It can do all kinds of calculations, both for accounting and also for mathematics and statistics. If you are a number cruncher, you will almost certainly require a spreadsheet. Even if you are not, a spreadsheet provides a convenient grid structure which can easily be used for lining up columns of text. It can also act as a database for storing rows of information, which can then be sorted. It is a very versatile package which can be put to many different uses.

It is not necessary to buy a large spreadsheet package, to get the full flavour of how to use one. Shareware offers a marvellous option, called As-easy-as. This is a clone of the current leading package and unless you are a very advanced user, you will find that the books and teaching guides work in the same way, with only minor differences. As-easy-as is used in all our local educational institutions both as an educational tool and for financial management. If you are not sure whether you want a spreadsheet or not, start here. Chapter 5 gives some introductory uses for As-easy-as. There is a cut down version called Alite, also available as shareware. It works a bit differently, because the major manufacturer started to sue companies that made clone copies, which means that future packages will need to change.

If you are a seasoned calculator and want a big package, the main options are:

Lotus 1-2-3

This has been the market leader for years, to such an extent that other major commercial spreadsheets will often provide two modes of operation, one just like Lotus. They will also tend to make sure that their saved material is compatible with and can be put into Lotus, what is called in computer jargon, imported.

Lotus has gone through several versions. You may not need the latest, which is, of course, the most expensive – Figure 2.3. Version 2.2 needs a minimum of two floppy disk drives, and the latest versions need at least a 286 or 386 processor. Lotus 1-2-3/G provides its own graphical user interface (which just means that you do everything by opening and closing windows on your screen with the mouse) and there is now a version just appearing for Windows.

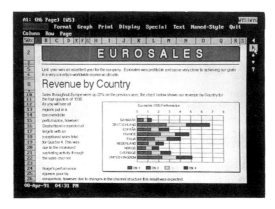

Figure 2.3: Lotus 1-2-3 – the market leader for years

Supercalc

This is now going into Version 6. In 1990, its producer, Computer Associates decided to offload the previous version, Supercalc 5, at a budget price of £79. I am not sure what it did to their profits, but as a marketing ploy it was very successful. For the first time in spreadsheet history, in terms of new sales, Lotus was no longer the market leader. If you want to use a large commercial spreadsheet, this could be an excellent buy. It also has powerful mathematical functions.

Quattro

This package by Borland is another possibility. Borland have recently taken over Ashton Tate, the large database supplier, and look set to become a world leader. This package will fit in with their other products, has a new version that can be run under Windows, the graphical standard of the future, and is strong on graphical presentation, in the form of charts, graphs and slides.

Excel

Microsoft, the makers of MS-DOS and Windows, and the major world company in competition with IBM, offer Excel which runs under Windows. This was a spreadsheet originally found on the Apple Macintosh series of computers.

What kinds of things can you look for in major commercial spreadsheets?

❑ **Multiple pages.** You can treat your spreadsheet as a huge book full of analysis paper, with various kinds of linkages provided between the pages. Sometimes this will be on a single cell only, sometimes on more than that. If you change the relevant cell, the other pages should automatically be re-calculated.

❑ **More sophisticated functions or calculations.** If you are a heavy scientific user or use advanced financial calculations, check that your chosen spreadsheet can meet your needs.

❑ **More sophisticated graphing and charting facilities.** Like the facility to produce 3-D graphics. Quattro even allows you to shift the angle of view of the 3-D perspective.

❑ **Spreadsheet publishing.** You can have all kinds of different typefaces and fonts and you will spend as much time sorting out the presentation side of your spreadsheet as you do setting it up.

❑ **Macros.** Most spreadsheets allow you to write macros – little programs or collections of commands. The more sophisticated the package the nearer the macros get to a full programming language.

❏ **Compatibility and portability.** This is a very important consideration if you regularly want to put bits of your spreadsheets into your word processed correspondence or reports. You may want to be able to view your word processor and spreadsheet on the screen at the same time. This is one of the main functions of Windows.

Another way to achieve this effect is to buy an integrated package like Smart. The trouble is that the Smart spreadsheet has an unusual way of referencing cells and generally such packages tend to be a jack of all trades and master of none. If compatibility is of great importance to you, a loss of quality from individual packages may well be worth it.

On the other hand, it might be another argument in favour of going for Windows, because one of the main aims of Windows is to provide a common look to all the major applications that run under it, so that you have little difficulty in moving from one to another. You can have at least two open on the screen at one time and one of the major features of Windows is what is known as DDE, Direct Data Exchange, which means that you can easily move material across from one application to another.

❏ **Formatting.** If you have used a conventional spreadsheet before, you will know that there are one or two things that are a bit tedious. The chapter on As-easy-as will give you an introduction if you are a newcomer, and there are some bits of that which are a bit awkward. One is formatting, having to decide what kind of numbers you are going to feed in, whether they are percentages, have decimal places or are currency. Another is the problem of deciding how wide your column is going to be and having to make a small sequence of moves to change them. Some of the latest spreadsheets have the *intelligence* to notice the size of your entries and to adjust the column width accordingly. Another annoyance is when you have put in a long column full of figures, have moved on to another screen, and want to add them all up. Quattro's Autosum can do this for you at the press of a button and you don't have to worry about where you started from.

❏ **Mouse use.** Some of the big packages like Lotus and Quattro already allow you to use a mouse. This will become a standard under Windows. You can use the mouse for pull down menus and also for rapidly and easily moving around.

❏ **Audit trails.** Another advanced feature is the ability to provide an audit trail of past entries and a Solveit facility which allows you to analyse and assess the effect of individual changes.

❏ **Presentation.** There is usually a growing emphasis on presentation, with, for example, the ability to produce 35 mm slides.

2.4 How to Buy Good Software for Children

If you ask children for their top choice of software, the answer will almost certainly be a game of some variety. Parents may have a completely different view of the matter and some even ban games altogether.

2.4.1 Should Children Play Games?

The answer is a definite yes, although the what, where and when may be something else. Some of the more recent educational research shows that playing games is one of the best ways of learning how to use computers. They help you to get used to the keyboard and to develop manipulative skills. You have only got to watch children using a computer mouse to appreciate that they quickly develop an ease which fewer adults possess. Games usually involve menus with different choices and they also often allow you to save a game in the middle and load it up another time. This gives children skills in handling menus and disks.

The move towards the mouse, pull down menus and icons in the PC, with Windows, means that it is worth getting your children practised in this kind of environment.

Text adventure games, with or without graphics, involve reading and writing text and this can be an excellent way of getting a child to practice reading and spelling without being aware of it. The earlier series of Kings Quest is ideal in this respect.

A particular brand of graphics adventure, called a **Role** Playing Game, has a character or group of characters under your control in a fantasy or scenario. You must build up their various characteristics such as strength, speed, wisdom and so on, which will vary depending on certain actions that you take. Success in these games revolves round making the right decision at the right time. A typical example is the Bard's Tale series – Figure 2.4. Some involve warfare, economics, logic and strategy in often quite complex situations. Classics here are Star Trek (Figure 2.5), Sim City, Populous and Sim Earth. You can colonise planets, build cities or redesign whole civilisations in quite life-like simulations.

Games can feed the imagination. A mediaeval setting develops historical awareness. Games can provide inspiration for drawings and stories. My younger boy likes me to join in his bedtime computer adventure game. Together we people our cellar with spiders, swords, oversize flies and strange bits of chewed meat. I add a few dusty wine bottles for my own pleasure. The story becomes a social exercise between the two of us. Flying and driving simulations can develop your child's road skills, without having to risk being involved in traffic accidents.

Computer games can be useful for your child's social life. It gives you something to entertain the visitor, something for them all to discuss at school. When your children have visitors, you will notice that they often play together and discuss what they think is good or bad about their games.

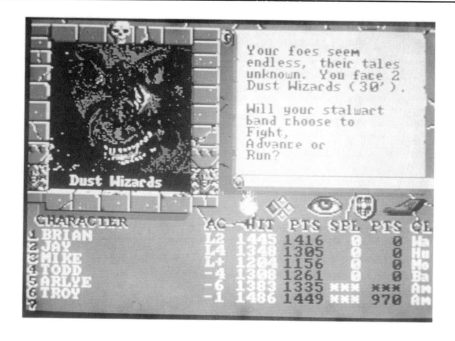

Figure 2.4: Success in Role Playing games depends on making the right decision at the right time

Figure 2.5: Star Trek – based on the TV series

Children enjoy playing games and enjoyment is the most important goal in children's computing. If they see computers as fun and something that they like to use, this will be the very best foundation you can give them for their future lives. Whether we like it or not, computers will be an ever increasing part of everyday life and children need to be as natural about them as most of us are with pen and paper. Many children, particularly girls, are getting a negative view of computers at school and it is vital that there is a counterbalance to this at home or they may grow up being outsiders to a tool that will be essential for their economic survival.

Playing games and enjoying them may make a child interested in programming. My younger child is now asking questions like: "How do they make the ship blow up when the tornado reaches it?" and: "How do you send the tornado there?". There are some complicated programming ideas behind all this.

Games allow children to feel in charge, in a world where they are open to commercial manipulation and control at ever younger ages.

When I was a child, we were free to roam around fields and streams. Nowadays, if your children are gone for more than 10 minutes, you wonder who has kidnapped them and most younger children have a personal world severely circumscribed by dangerous roads of fast traffic. They have to be taken everywhere, from one structured activity to another. The computer actually allows them to be in charge for a change.

2.4.2 The Flip Side of Games

Games do have their negative side as well.

They become the commercially hyped up end of the computer software market. They are now very expensive at about £25 and one arcade game may be little different from another. The type of play is often much the same, the hyped up monster being just a little different or the background slightly altered in terms of scenario. The trouble is your child will want the latest or he will see himself as socially unacceptable. Your pocket will tend to suffer quite heavily. However, I think this is more a problem of consumerism than of computers and your solution will depend on your own personal lifestyle. If your child always has the latest designer clothes, the latest commercial game will probably be regarded as a necessity.

If your style is more moderate, you can resist the commercial pressures just as you would anything else. Look at the price lists six months later and you'll probably notice that last year's hyped up *must be the best game ever* is now being sold at bargain basement price. So it is financially well worth waiting.

Your children may over-react in the other direction if you put a total ban on the latest games. However you don't have to play straight into the advertiser's hands. You can keep the very latest to special treats, like just one game at Christmas or birthday time.

You can also encourage your children to become careful consumers themselves. They'll soon begin to realise that one game is much like another. Encourage them to buy magazines and read reviews. They usually get a demo disk which may be quite enough for the younger child of 7 or 8. They are less likely to get to the higher levels that the full game provides and a glimpse of the background scenario and resident monsters will give them as good an artistic glimpse as the full program. Encourage them to be critical about their games, to ask questions about whether they get boring or give them new ideas or something to think about.

Most reviews give percentage points for the features of games, which may give your children a good early understanding of the mathematical idea of a percentage. Even the games magazines have articles about computer hardware which may lead to a real interest in computing.

The other flip side of the coin is computer addiction. Horrifying articles and television programs appear to upset parents. It would be naive to say that there is no such problem. Computer games can be great fun and children can spend many hours playing them, when they could be doing something more fruitful. It can be very hard to drag a child away from the computer when it is really engrossed. As a parent though, you can exercise some control. Playing computer games can be a reward for other activities like doing homework or clearing up. It helps if you have a family computer that has to be shared with other people and it is quite likely if you have a PC, that this will be the case. It is probably not a good idea to leave the computer in a younger child's bedroom as it can be more difficult to control.

The worst addicts are probably teenagers. If younger children are taught to be discriminating computer users, they may have got over the games-only stage. Any child new to computing will play games obsessively for two or three or even four weeks. You will usually find after that time, the computer is sometimes left idle and the bike is on the road again. The early initial excitement does tend to wear off. Addicted teenagers might well be addicts to other things like early sex or drugs. With Aids around, computer addiction is probably preferable. Some addicts are probably technically minded males who have replaced their train sets and motorbikes with computers. They may be uncommunicative and withdrawn but they are probably the type of characters who would have been like this anyway.

Most of the games are rather masculine. There is a lot of shooting and fighting. There is relatively little that appeals to girls which is worrying when economic life is pitted against them enough already. If you have girls, it is probably even more important to make sure that they have a nice computer to hand and that they are happy with it. Because the games are generally so unfeminine, pick out the few that do appeal like Kings Quest, and look to other areas of software that they will enjoy more. Girls are more likely to enjoy creative writing than boys, so look at a good word processor and desktop publishing. A good paint package and animator is another possibility. They enjoy making cards and using clip art. If your daughter enjoys programming, foster it.

Let the boys get on with it, but really nurture the girls. Most women who get on in the computer industry have had a mentor behind them.

2.4.3 Non-Game Software for Children

Build up a software library for children, which has some good things in it apart from games.

Word processors

There are word processors written especially for children. If they are very young, these can be attractive. Children of 4 or 5 like to see their writing in big print. The commands and menu choices are usually very simple and obvious and may be driven almost entirely by pictures or icons, which is good for children who are not yet that familiar with reading.

Beyond this kind of age, children usually adapt quite easily to adult word processors, particularly if they have a little adult help, and they just use them for the simple and obvious operations, like saving, editing and printing a file, or providing simple enhancements, like some bold here or there. A spell checker may be attractive and a good way of learning spelling without adult pressure, not that there seems to be much pressure on spelling these days.

It is not really necessary to buy a separate word processor for the children. If you have a large package like WordPerfect, you can still teach quite young children how to do the basic things. Older children will be very lucky, because they will get a head start in a commercial leader, and have plenty of scope to do wonderful text work and to learn about computer packages in general.

Don't worry about using what they have at school. Children are usually very adaptable and one of the problems with schools is, that having chosen years ago to go down the BBC path, they cut themselves off from what the business world was doing. Using a large PC package at home will redress this balance.

If you don't have a large package, don't buy one specially. Let them use what you have.

Spreadsheets and databases

If you know something about spreadsheets, pass this on to your children. Encourage them to use the spreadsheet as a first resort for solving mathematical problems. All *too* few mathematics teachers are doing this, but the business world certainly is. This is a situation, where you may well have more resources than the teachers!

You do not need to spend much money on children's spreadsheets. If you have a big package let them use that. If not, As-easy-as, the main shareware package, is ideal.

With databases, big packages are probably a bit much, although the odds are that, if you possess one, you can help them with it. The shareware PC-FILE is excellent and can be used for almost anything. There is no need to buy dedicated educational databases.

Art packages

One of these should be near the top of your shopping list. Most children, be they artistic or not, get a lot out of them. Learning to draw with a mouse is probably as important for the new citizen as learning to draw with a pencil. Personally I find this rather regrettable, as I love the texture that you get from crayons and charcoal, but that is modern life.

The child who doesn't like traditional art very much may feel quite differently about a computer. Even if not tempted to become a mouse artist, he or she may enjoy altering ready-made clip art pictures.

Choose a good, standard package like PC Paintbrush or De Luxe Paint. Drawings or graphics get saved in different ways, called file formats. If you choose a big package with a popular format, it will be easy to put your drawings into other packages. A large word processor like Wordperfect will accept some graphics pictures. You might want to buy a scanner, scan ordinary art drawings or photographs, and then alter them on your paint package. This kind of swapping round from one package to another, is one of the ways in which modern computing is going.

If you buy Windows, it provides a small paint package, which is compatible with other Windows programs.

Some of the latest versions of the big paint packages allow you to animate or create moving cartoon pictures. If you have a standard paint package which produces standard graphic files, you can transfer your drawings into a special animation package.

Some children may want to use a simple computer aided design (CAD) package to design cars or other objects.

Easy-to-use budget desktop publishing packages, like Timeworks, are well worth thinking about. Children also enjoy making banners, cards and calendars with programs like Printmaster or Printshop.

Educational software

This is a disappointing area although it is getting better than it was a year or so ago. Remember that most children do use this kind of software at school and it is important that home provides different experiences. Some of it is not really that exciting and probably needs the coercion that a school environment provides. Some of the better educational programs like history or archeology simulations are written for group activities and are accompanied by extensive non computer resource material, so are not really suitable for the home.

The kind of program that you will find commercially available is the drill type for practising spellings and maths. If your children enjoy these, they will provide extra practice in these skills. If they are not converts to these activities, the software will not perform miracles and may put them off computers for life!

In fact your children will receive more real education from carefully chosen spreadsheets, word processors, paint packages and games than they will from most formal educational software.

Having said that, there is some educational software around and some names and addresses are given in the Appendix.

Programming languages

There is no need for children to program unless they really want to. We are already at a stage where programs almost write programs. If your children are inclined that way, encourage it, but if not certainly don't force them into that kind of existence.

Having said that, programming can be a wonderful hobby for the more mathematically inclined child, who is bored by what is on offer at school. In Britain, children are not considered capable of doing algebra until they are at least 12 and yet a bright 9 year old may have little difficulty in dealing with computer variables. Programming can be very creative and satisfying and can give an understanding of how computers work.

Never force programming on any of your children, but if they do enjoy it, buy them books and manuals and encourage them. Start LOGO when they are 7 or 8, probably with your help. Let them go on to BASIC. When they have exhausted that, invest in C or PASCAL. At this stage, buy a proper compiler, books and manuals and leave them to it.

2.5 How and Where to buy Software

2.5.1 Where do you buy Software?

There are three main sources for buying software:

❏ Your local dealer or software supplier

❏ Mail Order

❑ Computer Shows

Local dealer, shop or software supplier

You will often get free software thrown in when buying your first computer. This can be very useful particularly if it is something like Windows or a good integrated package, like Works. Even if it's good, it is probably not worth the claim in the advertising literature, as you could often get something that performs the same function for less money. It also tends to tie you to whatever software is the dealer's flavour of the month, and although this saves you doing your own research, there may be other packages more suited to your particular needs. You are very likely to stick to what you are first given, particularly if you are a beginner. If you get a pack of games, it will be a fairly general one and probably only half of what you are given will really appeal.

Your local dealer may be a chain like Dixons which mainly sells hardware but keeps a little software as well. Sometimes you will have a shop that concentrates more on software, particularly if you are buying games. You tend to pay the full retail price for software bought this way, although there may be the occasional offer.

There is so much software available that anything other than an emporium can only keep a small proportion on shelf. This may be well chosen but it will obviously limit your selection. There is a tendency to stock the most recently reviewed and advertised software. Well established and only slightly older alternatives may well be omitted. Totally new software may sometimes have bugs that people have not yet noticed, so you may not be getting the best choice.

However on the plus side, you do often have a friendly person who can give you advice or help. If you are buying the more expensive software, they may give you a demonstration. If they have used it themselves, they may offer some useful tips and advice and may continue to give you help and support.

In America, they have giant software (and hardware) supermarkets where you can go and browse and often watch some of the programs actually running. The first of this kind has just opened in Britain at Croydon, but no one yet knows whether this idea will work as well as it does in the States.

Mail order

Mail order has the advantage of being very much cheaper, often by as much as 30%, which is quite significant. You can phone up, use your credit card and quite possibly receive your software by return of post. Some firms use a courier service. They vary a great deal in terms of efficiency. Most are quite good, but the odd one can take literally weeks to supply the software. Once you have found a good one, stick to it. I have found with games that they sometimes advertise software before its release date and then the wait may be quite long.

Although the price saving is very good, you get next to nothing in the way of support and no chance to review the software before you buy it. This means that you need to know what software you really do want before you place an order. One of the best ways is to have a good look at what your friends are using and to ask their advice. Local user groups may be very helpful in this respect. The other method is to read the reviews in the PC magazines. These are not wonderful, but they are certainly better than nothing and they give you some idea.

Even though they now make annual charges, it is useful keeping up a credit card specifically for mail order. This gives you more rights legally if the goods are unsatisfactory, than you would get if you paid direct. It is also very convenient. When you start, just make one or two purchases from any particular firm until you have established which is the most satisfactory in terms of service. Keep a careful record of the date and cost of orders made and any registration number which the firm gives you. If the software is incorrect or late in coming, chase it up.

Computer shows

These take place in major cities. Sometimes they are quite general, like the Computer Shopper Show (Computer Shopper is a magazine) or they may relate to a particular type of software or machine, like business, databases, the PC or the Amiga. Many magazines let you buy tickets in advance, with £1 or £2 off. It is worth doing this, because shows are popular and the queues are appalling.

You really do get some very good bargains. You can save 20 to 30% on the cost of hardware and software and it may be worth using shows to make large purchases, like the computer itself, particularly if you have strong arms for the journey home! You also get quite a good chance to look at demonstrations and to learn about new products.

The drawback is the crowds, particularly if you are taking a young family. You will get hot, uncomfortable, cross and will spend a lot of money on soft drinks. If you work for a medium or large company and go to the business shows, you may find things a bit more comfortable. Perhaps you will get a reasonable lunch at your company's expense!

2.5.2 Different Types of Software

Buying commercial software

This can be bought at all the outlets given above. You will get a box with some kind of logo or picture on the front, frequently covered in cling film, hence the term shrink wrapped. This shows you that no one else has opened it and copied it or tampered with it in some unhealthy way. Inside the box you will find a set of disks containing the program files. These should be copied on to your hard disk or, if you have a floppy only system, on to spare floppy disks (see Chapter 3 – DOS in a Nutshell to see how to do this). The copies become your day to day program disks, and you keep the originals as backups in case something goes wrong with your hard drive or your daily floppy disks.

The box will also contain a manual. These are better than they used to be, but tend to have a list of commands in alphabetical order. A few may have a tutorial section to teach you the rudiments of the package. You will probably find a book more helpful when you are first learning a package. The manual provides a useful reference when you get to an advanced stage.

The other thing you will often find is a registration card. Do send this card off. Being registered means that the manufacturer will give you the opportunity to buy upgrades at a reasonable price. If anything goes wrong with the original software, you may well be given a corrected copy. Registration sometimes allows you to telephone the manufacturer for free advice, but usually you have to pay a registration fee for this kind of service. If you are a newcomer, using a big package, it is probably worth paying the fee.

Buying shareware

Shareware and public domain programs are distributed for next to nothing, and cost little more than the disk they are stored on. They came from the pioneer days of computing, when people distributed their proudly written programs just for the love of it. A similar thing happened with educational programs in Britain. Sometimes the authors hadn't got enough money to pay for the heavy advertising and promotional costs that are needed to launch a commercial program. Sometimes, they were just not very good programs. This means that the quality can be quite variable.

Although shareware programs are subject to copyright, you can give copies to other people but only licensed libraries are allowed to sell them. Because the concept of shareware is try before you buy you are often asked to register or to send a subscription to the author. As he is often in America and has changed his address, this can be difficult. Public domain, on the other hand, really is public and you can do what you want with it

Shareware has its own outlets. The shareware companies copy and distribute programs that come down through bulletin boards and appear from a whole collection of sources. The reputable ones claim to check these programs for viruses (it is certainly not worth their while being known to have one).

You will sometimes find ready made packs of the most popular shareware programs in your local software dealer or even a book shop. Otherwise, you really do have to buy it mail order. The major suppliers may have a stand at shows, but they will do little more than supply disks and catalogues.

This means that the only way of assessing shareware is to ask around among your friends and to read reviews. There has been a real growth recently in magazines dedicated to shareware alone so there is no difficulty in finding these. More general magazines also often have a page or two devoted to shareware. The suppliers will be found in the advertising material. The Appendix contains the names of some of the currently published magazines (there has recently been quite a shake up in this area) and of the suppliers of shareware.

With shareware you get the disks and nothing more. However after registering you will normally get a full version of the program and supporting manual. Most shareware has a document manual stored on the disk. It may be included in a zipped file, which is a special way of saving programs in a smaller amount of disk space. Chapter 3 tells you how to unzip the file and extract the manual.

_3_

MS-DOS in a Nutshell

3.1 General Introduction to MS-DOS

So you have made up your mind, purchased a PC, dragged it home and you are itching to go, straight into the free game the dealer gave you. Now for the bad news. You must attend to some housekeeping before you do anything else. If you were lucky enough to have a dealer who set up the hard disk and installed the software, you can play straight away but you may still need some of this chapter to find where the game is and how to load it up.

Housekeeping is done with something called MS-DOS (or possibly PC-DOS if you have a proper IBM). DOS stands for Disk Operating System, MS stands for Microsoft, the famous software company that wrote it. Disk Operating System sounds rather unexciting, so why all the interest?

Nearly all the software your computer runs is stored on a disk, either hard or floppy. The computer needs to know exactly what you have got and where it is stored. As bits of programs can be scattered all over the disk, this takes some organisation. MS-DOS does all this in quite a friendly way so that you don't have to worry about the physical side of the disk drive at all.

If you have a very powerful PC, like the 386, it will be able to run more than one operating system, like Unix or OS/2, but MS-DOS will still be there.

MS-DOS is a whole series of little programs stored on a disk. Each separate clone manufacturer will supply a slightly different set but all the most important parts will be there. It provides a direct way of communicating with the computer without having to know anything about what is going on behind the scenes. It relates to you through a program called COMMAND.COM (more of this later) and indicates that it is willing to talk to you when it shows:

```
A:\
```

followed by a flashing cursor if you have a floppy disk drive, or:

```
C:\
```

followed by a flashing cursor if you have a hard disk.

These are called the A: prompt and the C: prompt, respectively.

This does not look very thrilling, but, believe it or not, it is the entry to all kinds of worlds, a step or two away from your dealer's free game.

MS-DOS has programs that allow you to copy the whole of one disk on to another, to load software to and from the hard disk, to take backups or copies of single programs and work, and to set the time and date. It gives a record of everything you keep on disk and lets you use a mouse or printer without having to give the least thought to the complicated organisation involved. It allows you to write menus for your favourite programs and to take a closer look at what is going on inside the computer, if you are so inclined.

MS-DOS divides its collection of programs into two categories: internal and external. When you first get the computer going at the beginning of a working session, the internal commands are loaded into the computer's memory and they stay there, tucked neatly beneath any other running programs, until you switch off. This means that you can use them at any time without needing to worry about where they are stored. The external commands, on the other hand, are not loaded automatically into memory and to use them you will need to know where they are stored and to call them up from there.

Like all major software programs, there have been several different versions of MS-DOS. It first appeared in 1981 and went through four major versions in the next 10 years. Another version, version 5, appeared in the summer of 1991. You are most likely to have version 3.2 or 3.3 on your home PC although it is possible you have version 4 or more. Later versions offer more facilities, although some of these, like networking or linking to other computers, will not bother you much at home. Generally versions 4 and 5 are more user friendly which means that they are easier to use. They also allow you to use a little bit more of the computer's memory if you have a higher grade PC, like a 386.

You use MS-DOS by typing in commands at the A: or C: prompt. So far, I have tried to make MS-DOS seem quite friendly, but it does have its flip side. You need to get the commands absolutely correct, down to the very last space or the spelling of programs or data files, although it doesn't mind whether you use upper or lower case. It can do some very powerful things, and wrong spelling or punctuation can lead to quite nasty results, without any warnings at all. It is all too easy to wipe out all the contents of a valuable work disk in just a few seconds. I once lost two days' writing this way - all with one incorrect MS-DOS command.

So it needs to be used carefully. You should think about what you want to do and check commands before you press the Return key to register them. In family situations, with children clamouring for supper, the doorbell ringing and the radio on full blast, it is all too easy to make horrible mistakes. For this reason, I have, where possible, included a few procedures you can use to make MS-DOS safer.

If you have youngish children, you will probably want to keep MS-DOS to adults only. It is possible to do many of the things that MS-DOS does in other safer ways. For example, you can delete work or copy it to another disk from within your word processor and this will quite probably provide you with more warning messages.

The rest of this section describes what to do if you are using MS-DOS 3.2 or 3.3. If you are lucky enough to have the latest version, MS-DOS 5, you have an attractive graphical shell and mouse and can do everything through pictures. There are books that will tell you what to do with this version. In any case, you can still use the direct commands given in this book and the kinds of operations you use the DOS Shell for are the same as those described in this chapter.

3.2 Copying Software using DISKCOPY

When you get a new computer, MS-DOS and any other software supplied with it, like a word processor or spreadsheet, will be stored on a set of floppy disks, usually contained in a fancy box with a manual. Now disks can easily get damaged if they get very hot or have something spilt on them or find themselves near electromagnets. They also get worn out. If you use a disk every day, you can expect it to last for an average of two months. You can also make horrible mistakes and write computer files on to a disk that is full of your favourite programs.

For this reason, the first thing you should do is to copy the main program disks - called making backups. If you have a hard disk you will copy the floppies on to that and may decide not to make floppy copies of the originals. However, do copy your MS-DOS disks because these are the ones that get you going and if something goes wrong with your hard disk, you will need MS-DOS to set it up again.

If you have only floppy disk drives, you should take copies of all your major software. Large package software often comes on 5 to 10 disks. Some of these will cover optional extras like setting up an unusual printer or adapting the package to different types of hardware. As a beginner with an ordinary printer, you will probably never use these, so just copy the main program disk for a start - you can always go back and copy the others later. Once you have taken copies, put the originals back in their box and store them somewhere safe.

Whenever you buy new software, go through the same procedure. You will often find, however, that you cannot do this with games. This is because schoolkids with empty purses and lots of social contacts are all too likely to copy each other's software. To avoid this manufacturers put copy protection on their disks. If the original disk gets corrupted, provided it has a proper label on it, you may be able to send it back and the manufacturer will give you a replacement. Sometimes you are expected to fill in a registration card. The adventure game Kings Quest allows you to copy disks, but forces you to start the game with the original floppy in the drive. Other manufacturers have clever ploys like making you put in special codes which differ each time the game is played and can only be found in the official handbook. In some cases, you may have to be prepared to lose the cost of the game which, at £24.99, is not amusing.

To copy or backup a disk, you need the original and a blank one. You want the computer to read the contents of the original disk (what we call the *source* disk) but to otherwise leave it unchanged. To be on the safe side you should write protect it, to prevent anything being written on to it. This will act as a safeguard against doing anything horrid, like copying the blank disk (the *destination* disk) on to the beautiful new original.

To write protect a 3.5'' floppy, you slide over the write protect shutter so that it leaves an open hole. This is a little rectangle at the bottom of the disk, with a little plastic shutter, which can be pushed over so that you have an open hole, or pushed over again so that it is covered up - Figure 3.1. If you have a high density disk, there will be another little rectangular hole on the other side of the disk. This will always be open because it doesn't have a shutter and it is this hole which tells the computer that it is using a high density disk. To write protect a 5.25'' floppy disk, you need to cover the notch on the side, by sticking a little tab over it.

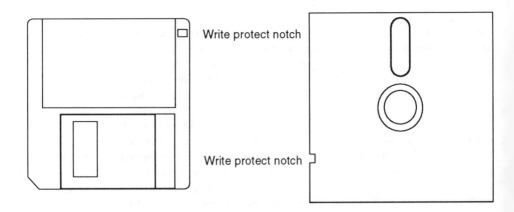

Write protect notch

Write protect notch

Figure 3.1: Floppy disks and their write protect systems

The destination disk, however, must not be write protected if the copy is to be successful. If you are using the 5.25'' disk make sure the notch on the side is not covered with a little tab. For the 3.5'' disk, make sure the shutter is moved over so that the hole is covered.

If you have two floppy disk drives, get in the habit of putting the source or *copy from* disk in drive A:, and the destination or *copy to* disk in drive B:. It is possible to copy in the other direction, but swapping direction is a wonderful way to make mistakes.

To copy a whole disk on to a new clean disk, you can use the MS-DOS command, DISKCOPY. If the destination disk isn't new, all the old contents will be removed, so be careful. If you don't have a hard disk, you may want to use another type of command, called FORMAT together with COPY, so that you can boot up straightaway from your program disk. You are told how to do this later in this chapter. If you are in this situation, just use DISKCOPY to backup the main MS-DOS disk and use the COPY and FORMAT procedure on your other main program disks.

DISKCOPY is an external MS-DOS command and needs to be loaded up before use. If your MS-DOS programs are all on one disk, insert that disk in drive A:. If MS-DOS uses more than one disk, insert the disk that contains DISKCOPY (you may need to see the section on DIR to find out how to locate this).

If you have one floppy disk drive only, with or without a hard disk drive, type:

```
DISKCOPY A: B:<Rn>
```

The computer will instruct you to put the source disk in the drive, then to put the destination disk in and so on. You will be kept quite busy constantly swapping disks.

If you have two floppy disk drives, put the source disk in drive A:, the destination disk in drive B: and type:

```
DISKCOPY A: B:<Rn>
```

The computer will do the copying for you.

In the above commands <Rn> means press the Return key. You must always do this to enter the information into the computer's memory. I will continue to remind you of this for the rest of this chapter, but thereafter, I will assume you will remember to do so without being prompted.

If you have two floppy disk drives, but they take different sized disks, things will be a bit more difficult. If your software comes on 5.25'' disks, there is no problem. This will be the source disk and you will copy from whatever drive, A: or B:, happens to be the 5.25'' floppy disk drive. If this means that you are copying from B: to A:, just type:

```
DISKCOPY B: A:<Rn>
```

If, on the other hand, you have got your new software on a 3.5'' disk only, you will need to split it up in some way or copy it into the hard disk and out again. This means that you will need to use the COPY command described later in this chapter.

3.3 Formatting Floppy Disks

A disk is made out of thin plastic covered in a magnetic coating. Computers think in machine code, which is nothing other than 0s and 1s. These can be represented by a magnetised or a non-magnetised spot on the disk. These spots are arranged in concentric circles which are then split up into sectors rather like the segments of an orange. The disk has a hole in the centre which sits on a spindle. The disk drive head which reads from and writes to the disk, stays in a fixed position and the disk rotates around it. The head can deal with one sector at a time and can move forwards and backwards over it. This is different from a gramophone record which has a spiral track so that the player head moves along a fixed path towards the centre of the record. The computer disk drive head, on the other hand, can move freely from one part of the disk to another with a mixture of turning and in and out movements. It does not have to follow a set path.

When you buy a new box of disks or start off with a new hard disk, the concentric rings are already set out but the sectors aren't. This makes new disks very flexible - they can be used on different types of computer, the Amiga, Atari and Macintosh as well as the PC. However, you do need to set the sectors out before your particular computer can use them. This is what is called formatting a disk. Once you have formatted it for your PC, the other computers like the Amiga and Atari will not be able to use it until it is formatted to their own particular pattern.

When you use DISKCOPY, it formats the disk as well as copying files on to it. You will need to format the disks you are going to use to store your work or data. If you have a hard disk drive, that also needs to be formatted before use.

3.3.1 Computers Without a Hard Disk

The first thing you should do is to format some data disks. You may want to create one for each family member and one for each of your major work areas, like word processing, spreadsheets or databases. If you have a paint package you will need a data disk to store the children's drawings, and one or two to store half finished games. It is always worth having a few formatted disks spare, because you can easily find yourself in the middle of a game and want to save your current position. It may insist on having a data disk inserted and if you haven't got one, that is it.

FORMAT is an external MS-DOS command so you will need to find it on your MS-DOS disk, or preferably the copy you have just made. If you have more than one disk, use DIR to see which it is on. FORMAT is a very dangerous command because it wipes out whatever is on the disk you format and if you don't use it correctly, you could wipe out your MS-DOS disk. To avoid nasty mistakes, write protect it. Always be careful when you use this command and use DIR to check that what appears to be a blank destination disk really is blank. You would expect to see a message to the effect that the computer can't read that disk, which is another way of saying the disk has never been formatted and really is blank.

If you have a single disk drive, put the MS-DOS disk containing FORMAT.COM in the drive and type:

```
FORMAT B:<Rn>
```

You will be instructed to put a blank disk in the same drive. Take the MS-DOS disk out, and insert the blank one.

If you have a double disk drive put the MS-DOS disk in drive A:, the blank disk in drive B: and type:

```
FORMAT B:<Rn>
```

The red disk drive lights will come on and off and messages and numbers will appear on the screen, like:

```
0 79
1 79
```

0 and 1 are the cylinder head numbers which roughly speaking means the top or bottom side of the disk. The second figure is the number of tracks or concentric rings, and shows exactly which one is being formatted at that moment.

When the computer has finished formatting the disk, it will ask:

Format another (y/n)?

If you have finished formatting for the day, type N or n and press <Rn>. To do more, type Y or y <Rn>.

It is worth formatting several disks in one go - while you have a tea break (providing you don't spill it on the disks or keyboard) so that you have plenty of formatted disks to hand when you run applications and suddenly want to save things.

If you don't have a hard disk drive, you will need to use MS-DOS to boot up every time you turn your computer on. This gives you the A: prompt and you then have to swap disks when you want to run one of your application programs. You can save yourself this hassle by using FORMAT to make the backups of your main application disks self bootable. You can then start your computing sessions with one application disk. This is very useful for young children who get muddled having to use MS-DOS first.

To make an application disk bootable, follow the procedure above but end the FORMAT instruction with:

/S

This is known as a switch and is really just means selecting an option. Many MS-DOS commands provide additional choices or features. S stands for system and it puts the MS-DOS system files on the disk that you are formatting. The main file is called COMMAND.COM and it is this which gives you the A: prompt.

Now go forward to the section on COPY to copy the main application program files to your bootable disk.

3.4 Setting up and Formatting a Hard Disk

I often think it rather unfortunate that computers have to be set up or installed before you can use them. The beginner has to start computing by carrying out a once off procedure that is never used again. If you buy your computer from a local dealer, he may have the same view as me and carry out the installation for you. If so, bypass the next section on partitioning and formatting a hard disk.

3.4.1 Partitioning a Hard Disk

If your hard disk is more than 32 Mbytes you come up against a strange problem. MS-DOS 3.3 and earlier versions are only able to access 32 Mbytes so your hard disk is beyond the capability of MS-DOS! To get round this, you can split the hard disk into two sections or partitions, not exceeding 32 Mbytes in size. You call the first partition drive C: and this is what you will boot up to when you switch on. The second you can call drive D: and you can treat it as though you had another separate disk drive. This is what is called, in computer terms, making a *logical drive*. In real life, it is physically part of the one hard disk drive but in your logical mind you pretend it is a separate one.

It strikes me that it is worth making a virtue out of necessity and putting the children's programs and saved activities on to drive D:. You will need to work out roughly how may programs and how much work the adults are likely to store and do the same again for the children. Programs that you don't use regularly or swap over frequently can always be run from floppy disks. You can delete programs stored on the hard disk and change them for fresh ones. If children use paint packages, their stored pictures will occupy quite a lot of memory as graphics are very hungry in this respect.

Before you partition the disk, it has to be physically formatted at a very low level. I have assumed that this has been done by the dealer and if you are a complete beginner, it is worth making sure that this has happened, as it is not the ideal first computing task for the novice. If he hasn't, you will need to struggle with the manual as it tends to be different for the different clones or types of PC.

To partition a hard disk:

Put the write protected copy MS-DOS disk containing FDISK in drive A: (you may need to use DIR to find where this is). Key in:

```
FDISK<Rn>
```

The computer will answer with something like:

```
ZEDBASE Personal Computer
Fixed Disk Setup Program Version 3.3
(C) Copyright ZEDBASE

FDISK options

Current Fixed Disk Drive:1
Choose one of the following

1. Create DOS Partition
2. Change Active Partition
3. Delete DOS partition
4. Display Partition Data
5. Select Next Fixed Disk Drive (if more than 64Mb)

Enter choice: [1]
```

Press <Rn> to register this option.

If your hard disk has already been partitioned, you will get a message like:

```
DOS partition already exists
```

You can then skip the rest of the procedure as it has already been done, by pressing <Esc>. The A: prompt will reappear. If the disk has been partitioned it will probably have been formatted as well so you can go on to load your software.

Otherwise, you get the message:

```
Create DOS partition

Current Fixed Disk Drive: 1

1. Create Primary DOS partition
2. Create Extended DOS partition
```

Choose option 2 and press <Rn>.

You will get a message like:

```
Create Extended DOS partition

Current Fixed Disk Drive: 1

Partition      Status    Type      Start     End    Size
C: 1           A         PRI DOS   0         419    420
Total disk space is 807 cylinders.
Maximum space available for partition is 387 cylinders

Enter partition size...............: [387]

Press ESC to return to FDISK Options
```

Press <Rn> to accept the partition size.

You will get a screen like:

```
Create Extended DOS Partition

Current Fixed Disk Drive: 1

Partition      Status    Type      Start     End    Size
C: 1           A         PRI DOS   0         419    420
   2                     EXT DOS   420       806    387

Extended DOS partition created

Press ESC to return to FDISK options
```

Press <Esc> and the next screen asks you to give the Extended DOS partition a drive designation - use D:. The screen looks like this:

```
Create Logical DOS drive(s)

No logical drives defined

Total partition size is 387 cylinders

Maximum space available for logical drive is 387 cylinders.

Enter logical drive size..........: [387]

Press ESC to return to FDISK Options
```

Press <Rn> and the screen then shows:

```
Create Logical DOS drive(s)
```

```
Drv          Start       End         Size
D:           420         806         387
```

All available space in the Extended DOS partition is
assigned to logical drives.

Logical DOS drive created, drive letters changed or

added

Press ESC to return to FDISK Options

Press <Esc> twice. If your hard disk is more than 64 Mb you will need to choose
Option 5 from the main FDISK menu and go through the procedure all over again. If
not you are back at square one and you can boot up again by putting your write
protected copy DOS disk in drive A: and pressing <Ctrl><Alt><Del> all at the same
time to do a warm reboot or switch off and on again. You are now ready to go on to
the next stage, of formatting each partition of the hard disk in turn.

3.4.2 Formatting your Hard Disk

Once you have set up the partitions, the next thing to do before you can use the hard
disk, is to format drives C: and D: (or just C: if your hard disk is 32 Megabytes or
less and you haven't had to partition it). Notice that formatting wipes away any
existing programs and work so make sure the hard disk is blank before you do this. If
you want to set up the hard disk again after you have used it, you must copy off
anything that matters, before you use this procedure.

Put the MS-DOS system files on to drive C:, so that when you switch on to boot up,
the computer automatically goes to the C: drive. To do this, type:

FORMAT C: /S<Rn>

As mentioned earlier, the /S is a switch symbol. This really just means you can select
an option. Many MS-DOS commands provide additional choices or features. S stands
for system, the basic MS-DOS files that cause the computer to go through the boot up
process. The main file is COMMAND.COM which will give you the C: prompt.

Because FORMAT is rather a dangerous command, it gives you a warning.

Think and then key in y or Y to proceed with the format.

When it has finished it will give you a message and return you to the A: prompt. It
tells you how many bytes the system files occupy and how much free disk space you
have left. There will be some bad bytes, no hard disk is ever perfect.

Go on to format drive D. Key in:

```
FORMAT :D<Rn>
```

This time, leave out the switch /S, because you will get in a mess if you try to make two hard disks bootable.

It is now possible to copy the rest of MS-DOS and your other software on to the hard disk, using the COPY command. But before you do this you need to look at the DIR command.

3.5 The DIR command

You will often want to see what you have got on a disk, be it floppy or hard. Your labels are never as clear as they might be and six months later you have little memory of what you have written. A disk may contain hundreds of files: programs, letters and spreadsheets.

Start with a floppy disk. Any disk will do. Put the disk in drive A:. If you have no hard disk and have booted up to the A prompt, type:

```
DIR<Rn>
```

If you have a hard disk and have booted up to the C: prompt, type:
```
DIR A:<Rn>
```

```
READLITE ME        1024 13/02/90   16:31
LITEDISK BAT       6569 26/01/90   16:20
GETYN    COM        875 10/01/90   16:19
LITE     EXE     151040 14/02/90   15:44
LITE     HLP      72171 13/02/90   13:46
WORDS    MAS     110428 19/09/89   18:41
ED       DEF         90 03/01/90   17:40
ED       TRS        993 24/01/90   15:01
ED       SPC        886 25/01/90   20:27
ED       MDS       1008 07/04/89   17:55
LITE     PIF        369 26/01/90   11:16
NEWL100  &DO        241 24/01/90   15:53
PROLITE  DIR       1008 14/02/90   15:45
GEMINI   BAT         72 15/03/90    1:10
WELCOME  MSG       1300 15/03/90    0:24
STORY1   DOC       1009 01/01/80    1:03
LIST     COM       3072 10/02/85   15:44
NEWL100  DOC        815 01/01/80    1:53
WORDS    USE         11 01/01/80    1:06
PRAC1               226 22/11/91   20:57
LETTEMP               2 22/11/91   21:33
        21 file(s)      353209 bytes
                        367616 bytes free
```

Figure 3.2: The result of the DIR command

DIR which is short for directory, gives you a list of all the files on the disk - an example is shown in Figure 3.2. Just DIR on its own will give you the files on the current drive. If you want a listing of the files on some other drive, make a space, followed by the drive letter and a colon. You can do a listing of what is in a subdirectory with for example:

```
DIR \GAMES<Rn>
```

You get four bits of information about all the files on your disk. The first, which is up to eight letters long, is the actual file name. It can be the name of a program file, or some written text, your own or someone else's, it can be a spreadsheet or some graphics (pictures, or bar or pie charts).

You then get another three letters. This is called an extension. You can make up your own, like BKE, WLH - these are initials of various members of my family. They could be used to show who they belong to. However some applications use their own extensions and save files with their own particular three character ending. This can be very useful in telling you what kind of file you have.

For example, FRENCH1.BAS, has a BAS extension which shows me that it is a program written in the BASIC programming language.

SPIDER.BUG is a file containing a program written in the Ladybug Logo programming language because this is how it saves all its programs.

Lotus 1-2-3 puts .WKS on the end of its files, while dBase IV uses .DBF.

In SIMUL.COM, the COM stands for compiled. This means that, whatever programming language SIMUL was written in, it has been compiled - translated into the mixture of 0s and 1s which is the only language that the computer can understand. This means it is a program that the computer can run straight away and provided it is stored in the current directory (the one you are in at the moment) all you have do to run it is type:

```
SIMUL<Rn>
```

The extension .EXE stands for *executable* and for practical purposes, this means much the same thing.

.BAT stands for Batch file. This is something you can also run by just typing the filename. It works a bit differently from .COM and .EXE because it is just a list of commands to be carried out. One of these may be to run another program. A fuller description of Batch files is given later in this section.

.DOC or .TXT means a document or text file. This is a file of written words which could be loaded up on your word processor.

What do the other two bits of information about each file mean? First you see a number opposite the filename. This tells you how long each file is in bytes.

You then get a date and a time. This indicates when the file was first saved, or an amendment was made. For something like MS-DOS, it could be three years or so ago, which is probably not very interesting. However, when it comes to your own work or programming, it can be very useful, particularly if you have used a rather meaningless file name and can't remember what it was about.

Right at the end, underneath the listing of all the files, you are told how much space in bytes you have left on your disk. The last figure can be very useful when you are running out of disk space. One byte is worth one character of the alphabet, a single digit, other symbol or a space.

How do you deal with everything whizzing past you on the screen? You can use another switch command /P. Type:

```
DIR /P<Rn>
```

for your floppy disk drive computer or:

```
DIR A:/P<Rn>
```

if you have a hard disk drive and want to see what is on the disk in floppy drive A:.

You get one page at a time and an instruction to *Press any key to continue......* Press any key and you get another page and so on until you get to the end of the directory listing.

Another method is to type in:

```
DIR /W<Rn>
```

or:

```
DIR A:/W<Rn>.
```

This fits more filenames across the screen because it leaves out the length and the date and time when they were saved. You can see the result in Figure 3.3.

If you want to print out your directory listing, first make sure your printer is switched on, or your computer will snarl up and you will have to switch off and reboot. Type:

```
DIR A: > PRN<Rn>
```

or just:

```
DIR > PRN<Rn>
```

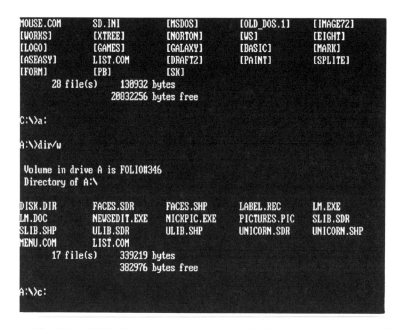

```
MOUSE.COM      SD.INI         [MSDOS]        [OLD_DOS.1]    [IMAGE72]
[WORKS]        [XTREE]        [NORTON]       [WS]           [EIGHT]
[LOGO]         [GAMES]        [GALAXY]       [BASIC]        [MARK]
[ASEASY]       LIST.COM       [DRAFT2]       [PAINT]        [SPLITE]
[FORM]         [PB]           [SK]
       28 file(s)    130932 bytes
                   20832256 bytes free

C:\>a:

A:\>dir/w

 Volume in drive A is FOLIO#346
 Directory of A:\

DISK.DIR       FACES.SDR      FACES.SHP      LABEL.REC      LM.EXE
LM.DOC         NEWSEDIT.EXE   NICKPIC.EXE    PICTURES.PIC   SLIB.SDR
SLIB.SHP       ULIB.SDR       ULIB.SHP       UNICORN.SDR    UNICORN.SHP
MENU.COM       LIST.COM
       17 file(s)    339219 bytes
                     382976 bytes free

A:\>c:
```

Figure 3.3: Using DIR /W reduces the amount of information about each file to fit more on screen

You can use DIR on your hard disk as well. You will, though, see things like this:

```
DOS <DIR> or [DOS]
```

and

```
WS <DIR> or [WS]
```

as well as the ordinary list of files you get with the floppy disk. <DIR> indicates that you have a sub-directory of that name. In this situation, there are two with the names DOS and WS. To get a directory listing of the files they contain, the easiest method for the beginner, is to use Change Directory to put yourself into the directory you are interested in. e.g.:

```
CD \DOS<Rn>
```

to put yourself into the directory called DOS and then:

```
DIR<Rn>
```

to display a listing of the files in this directory.

Move back to the root with CD\ and then repeat the process for another directory.

3.6 Organising your Files into Subdirectories

Before long, you will have more than a thousand files stored on your hard disk. This leaves a lot to go through, when you want to find just one. It also means that you can easily forget what goes with what.

MS-DOS gets around this by allowing you to put your files into collections, like the separate drawers of a filing cabinet. You could collect all your MS-DOS program files into a drawer or *subdirectory* called DOS, all your WordPerfect files into another subdirectory called WordPerfect, all your accounts into Sage (a business book-keeping package) and all the children's stuff into Child.

Make a list of the main programs that you are going to run frequently and will want to store on your hard disk. Give your subdirectories short, easy to type labels that you can easily remember. The name that you key in to call up the program, like WP for WordPerfect or WS for WordStar, might be a good idea. If you are going to run a lot of small programs, think of a name that would cover several of them, like Utilities. Children may well like to have their own drawers so you could label these with their names. Your list might look something like this:

    WP for WordPerfect
    DOS
    DBASE
    ASEASY
    SAGE
    SUSAN
    MARY
    JOSEPH
    GAMES (ones all the family like)

If the family all uses the word processor or database, just create one subdirectory at the moment for the word processor or database. You can always make subdirectories below other subdirectories for the different family members.

When you have made this list, set them up on your hard disk. To make a new directory, type in at the C: prompt:

```
MD WP<Rn>
```

MD is short for make directory.

Do the next one:

```
MD DOS<Rn>
```

and the next one:

```
MD SAGE<Rn>
```

and so on, down the list.

These categories might seem rather general. Games could cover arcade games, strategy games or adventure games. Susan may want to use her own paint package or fantasy game. Can you split the directories up a bit, put some dividers in? The answer is, yes you can. You must use DOS's own structure to do this, what is called a tree structure. What you do is to make directories within directories. Under each of the major directory headings in the list above, you make *subdirectories*.

Really it is what you might call an upside down tree. It starts at a single point at the top. This is called the root and is given the symbol \ (notice that this is found on the left hand side of the keyboard and goes the opposite way to the switch sign you have already met in your formatting). The root is where you are when you start at the C: prompt. Several *branches* slope down from this to the next level, the ones on your list. The root is a directory, the *big drawers* its subdirectories. Branches can come out of these subdirectories, into another lower level of subdirectories, in this example, from Games to Arcade, Strategy and Adventure and from Susan to Paint or Fantasy. These are also called subdirectories. A typical directory structure is shown in Figure 3.4.

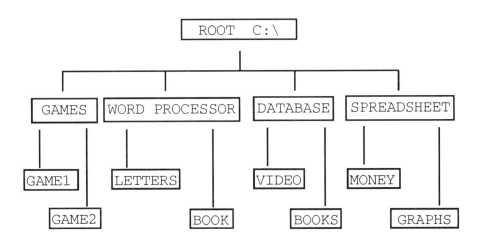

Figure 3.4: A typical directory structure

You will want to know where you are when you use subdirectories. It is well worth drawing a plan or a map of your own directory structure. So far you have only actually created subdirectories, you are still in the root directory. You will always be somewhere, and the directory you are in at any particular time is called the *current directory*. You are going to want to move into the various subdirectories, so that you can copy files into them, see what files you are keeping there and to run your applications. To do this, you use the MS-DOS command Change Directory or CD for short.

To make a subdirectory beneath another subdirectory, get into the subdirectory at the top, which is called the parent. So get into Susan with:

```
CD SUSAN<Rn>
```

You are now in the Susan subdirectory and you can see this from the prompt:

```
C:\SUSAN>[flashing cursor]
```

You can then make the subdirectories beneath it, in this example, Paint and Fantasy with:

```
MD PAINT<Rn>
```

and:

```
MD FANTASY<Rn>
```

Return to the root with:

```
CD\<Rn>
```

change into the subdirectory Games with:

```
CD GAMES<Rn>
```

and then create the subdirectories Arcade, Strategy and Venture with:

```
MD ARCADE<Rn>
MD STRATEGY<Rn>
MD VENTURE<Rn>
```

To go to another subdirectory branching out of Games you just type:

```
CD ARCADE<Rn>
```

You are now in the Arcade subdirectory which, in turn, is in the Games, subdirectory and the computer demonstrates this with the prompt:

```
C:\GAMES\ARCADE>[flashing cursor]
```

Suppose you then want to go to a subdirectory on another branch of the tree, like Sage. Please note that at this stage you cannot go directly to another subdirectory on another branch. You need to travel back up the branch you are on and then down the new branch.

You can do this by typing:

```
CD\<Rn>
```

This takes you right back up the Games\Arcade branch to the root. You can then type:

```
CD SAGE<Rn>
```

In fact, you could have got there in one move by typing CD \SAGE but when you are a beginner it is probably less muddling to do it in two stages. It also keeps you more aware of the need to definitely travel along branches.

To get from the Sage subdirectory to the Paint subdirectory of the Susan subdirectory, you type:

```
CD \<Rn>
```

to return to the root and then:

```
CD SUSAN\PAINT<Rn>
```

If you put a directory in the wrong place, you can always remove it. First you must make sure it doesn't contain any files (if it does, you must delete them first). You must also make sure that the subdirectory you are planning to remove doesn't itself have subdirectories. If it does, you must remove these as well. So suppose that you want to remove the subdirectory Arcade within Games and that at the moment, you are in the root directory. Move to the Games subdirectory with:

```
CD GAMES<Rn>
```

Then type:

```
RD ARCADE<Rn>
```

RD is short for Remove Directory

3.7 Making Bootable Floppies

Take the blank disks that you formatted with the /S switch in Section 3.4. If you have a double disk drive, place one of these disks in drive B: the drive you are going to use to *copy to*. Take the software disks you are going to copy over to your bootable disks, your main word processing disk (the one that has the main word processing program on it), BASIC or Ladybug Logo.

Write protect these disks by pushing the little flap until the hole is open on a 3.5"
disk or stick on the tab over the indent on the side of the 5.25" disk. Put the first of
these in drive A:

Then type:
```
COPY A:*.* B:<Rn>
```

Put the next program disk in drive A:, the next formatted /S switch disk in drive B:
and repeat the instruction. You don't need to type the whole instruction again - just
press function key F3 and the whole instruction appears again - F3 repeats the whole
of the last instruction. Press <Rn> to register it with the computer.

Continue until you have copied all the program disks. When you want to start your
computer to run one of these programs you don't need to bother with the usual boot
up disk, you can start straight away with the program disk - the system files you put
on it when you formatted with /S will do the booting up for you. These files, do
though, take up some room and if the original program disk almost fills up a disk you
will find the disk runs out of space and not all the files will be copied. MS-DOS will
give you a message to this effect but you could check beforehand by using DIR and
seeing how much space is left.

Use COPY *.* here rather than DISKCOPY because you want to keep the system
files that you put on the blank disk with FORMAT /S. DISKCOPY formats the disk
as well as doing a copy and wipes away anything that might have been there
including system files.

3.7.1 COPY can be Dangerous

A word of warning. If you are using files that you regularly change or update like
your spreadsheets, database entries, programs or bits of word processing and you
copy a new version of one of these on to a disk with an older version of the same
name, the new version will overwrite the old one, without any kind of warning
whatsoever. So make sure you are copying the new on to the old and not the other
way round.

It may be better to do your saving from the word processor itself. This is more likely
to give you a warning if a file has changed. The other thing you can do is to give
your files version numbers. For example call it CHAP1 when you write it on the
word processor. Save the first version as CHAP1a, the second as CHAP1b and so on.

3.8 Copying Several Files at Once

If you put a single ? in the name of a file to be copied, in a copy command, all the
files that have that name but with one different character where the ? is, will be
copied. So:

```
COPY DOSD?
```

copies the files DOSD1, DOSD2, DOSD3 and DOSD4.

If you put a * in the name it stands for any number of different characters. For example:

```
COPY ASEASY.*
```

will copy over ASEASY.DOC and ASEASY.EXE.

```
COPY B*.*
```

will copy over any file that begins with a B, whatever comes after that. The ? and * are called wildcards.

It is worth planning your file names carefully to take advantage of the ? and * wildcards. Group similar types of documents together with two or three meaningful common letters in a filename. For example LETBT051.DOC could be short for letter to British Telecom written in May 1991 (the 1 stands for the 1 in 1991, the 05 for month 5). You could then copy over all your letters with:

```
COPY A:LET*.DOC B:
```

all your 1991 documents with:

```
COPY A:*1.DOC B:
```

all your letters to BT, whatever the year and date with:

```
COPY A:LETBT*.DOC B:
```

or all your letters to anyone in May 1991 with:

```
COPY A:LET*051.DOC B:
```

So think about how you are going to group your work when you give it a filename. If you want to make collections of files belonging to individual members of a family or group, start all the files with an initial. For example:

BLETSL05.DOC

WSPIDER.BUG

MVENTURE.BAS

could be our family files belonging to B for Barbara, W for William and M for Matthew. I can copy all my files over with B*.*, all William's with W*.* and all Matthew's with M*.*.

3.9 Taking Backups

You will probably hear the advice that follows, time and time again, and from the largest organisation to the smallest computer freak in the land, it is advice that is regularly ignored.

Disks get corrupt and come up with a read/write error. Then you can't get anything off them, let alone write anything to them. Sometimes if you are very clever and have some special software like Norton's Utilities, you can recover some or all of the contents. But don't count on it. Disks get cooked on radiators or in the back of cars, they have wine trickled down them and get upset by electro-magnetism from modern machines. The contents of your careful work go with them. Disks have the wonderful property of storing vast amounts of information - but if one disk goes down, two whole books can go with them.

Hard disks go down too - in fact you can be quite sure that one day your hard disk will fail. One manufacturer quotes 20,000 to 80,000 hours as the average time they last, but recently I have come across three examples of a hard disk failing within the first six months of use.

You will have a backup of your actual program disks, in the originals you stored back in the manufacturer's box after taking the first backup copy. But your precious work will have no backup unless you take frequent copies. For word processing save your work every half an hour or so and at the end of your session copy your work file to another disk (or just swap to another work disk and save again from your word processor, if it allows it) and maybe copy to a third disk. Keep these in different places. I used to take three backups of all my work and carry them round in the same disk box. I realised one day that if I left this on the bus, all my work would be gone. So spread yourself round a bit! If you are doing something very important, leave a copy in another house or with a friend.

Copy out all the work you have stored on your hard disk at the end of the week or at the end of the day, if you are very productive. This is where a careful use of filenames will help you. You can do this with COPY *.* although MS-DOS does have a special BACKUP command and there are special programs that do this. This is beyond the scope of this book.

3.10 General Care of Disks

Disks are really quite delicate. They have an outside plastic cover but they can still be damaged quite easily.

❑ Don't let them get too hot i.e. don't sit them on a radiator or leave them on the back window of a car on a sunny day.

❑ Don't spill coffee, juice or wine over them.

❑ Don't let them get dusty - it's a good idea to keep your disks in a protective plastic box.

❑ Be careful to keep modern machinery containing electromagnets away from them. Particular examples are portable telephones, televisions and microwaves.

❑ Never insert or remove a disk from a drive which has its drive light on. If the light is stuck on, switch off the machine before removing the disk. This rule should be particularly impressed upon children who tend to want to do things in a hurry and are quite keen to wrench disks in and out of jammed machines. Don't allow them to pull disks apart to see what is inside. It won't be that long before you can let them have free play with a corrupted disk!

❑ The 3.5'' disks have a tougher plastic coating than the 5.25'' ones. If you have children, try and choose a PC that uses these. If there is a bargain, though, that uses the 5.25'' disks, it might be cheaper to buy more disks instead.

❑ Keep copies in different places.

3.11 Setting the Time and Date

The section on DIR showed that the disk directory stores the names of files and also the date and time when they were saved. This can be very useful a year or so later when your filenames do not look as meaningful as you meant them to be and you are wondering what you had been doing. It also allows you to sort your files into date order.

Many PCs come with a built-in battery clock. This will automatically record the correct date and time and will tell you when you last used the computer - a bit like big brother watching you. The recorded times of using a bank cash machine were used by the police to help catch a man who had murdered a couple and stolen their bank cards. Big brother will stop watching you when the clock batteries run out. At this point have a look at the manual. You will also need to reset the time when the clocks go forwards or backwards.

If you don't have an built-in clock you will need to put in the date and time every time you switch on the computer. You only really need to bother if you are going to save your work, so if you are only going to play games that won't be saved, just press <Rn> twice when you are asked for the date and time.

If you wish to set the time and date you do so using the form:

dd/mm/yy or

mm/dd/yy

depending on the prompt. You must use one or two figures, get month and date the right way round and use a / or -, nothing else.

For the time put a colon, :, between the hour and the minutes. You don't need to bother about seconds, just enter

```
hour:minutes<Rn>.
```

If you want to change the date or time any time after bootup use the MS-DOS commands, DATE and TIME. At the A: or C: prompt, type:

```
DATE<Rn>
```

to change the date and:

```
TIME<Rn>
```

to change the time, and then type in the new ones following the pattern given in the prompt.

3.12 Configuring the System

There are two MS-DOS files called AUTOEXEC.BAT and CONFIG.SYS, which contain information relevant to your particular system, such as what disk drives or other attachments you are running, or how many files or buffers (temporary stores of data) you can have open at any one time.

These two files will be on your MS-DOS boot up disk, if you only have floppy drives. If you have a hard disk drive, they will be stored in the root directory. When MS-DOS first boots up, it looks for these files, and loads them up into memory. AUTOEXEC.BAT is a list of MS-DOS commands, which it carries out straightaway. CONFIG.SYS contains country codes so that your keyboard puts in your own language characters and also sets up device drivers, which basically tells the computer what attachments you are running.

This is what my AUTOEXEC.BAT looks like:

```
@ECHO OFF
PROMPT $P$G
PATH C:\MSDOS;C:\
C:\MSDOS\KEYB UK 437 C:\MSDOS\KEYBOARD.SYS
MOUSE.COM
```

The PROMPT command tells the computer to give me the A: or C: prompt. PATH tells the computer where to go searching for files, if it can't find them straightaway in the root directory. KEYB 437 sets up the UK keyboard.

This is what my CONFIG.SYS file looks like:

```
DEVICE=C:\MSDOS\SETVER.EXE
COUNTRY=044,437, C:\MSDOS\COUNTRY.SYS
FILES=20
BUFFERS=20
BREAK=OFF
SHELL=C:\MSDOS\COMMAND.COM C:\MSDOS\ /p
```

These files can both be altered to suit your convenience, but this is a topic best left to more advanced books. However, as a beginner, you will occasionally use software that requires you to change one of these files, particularly CONFIG.SYS. For example, it may need FILES = 24, not 20. Fortunately, the very latest software sometimes does this kind of change itself, in its installation program, so only go on to read the rest of this section if you find you do have to do it yourself.

The first thing you will want to do is to have a look at CONFIG.SYS or AUTOEXEC.BAT to see whether or not they contain what you want. To do this, use the MS-DOS command, TYPE with:

```
TYPE AUTOEXEC.BAT<Rn>
```

and:

```
TYPE CONFIG.SYS<Rn>
```

In both cases, the contents of each file will be shown on the screen.

If you do need to make a change, you can do this with your word processor. Load it up in the usual way, and retrieve the files using the label:

```
C:\AUTOEXEC.BAT
```

and:

```
C:\CONFIG.SYS
```

if you have a hard disk drive.

If you have floppy disk drives only, treat your MS-DOS disk as your data disk.

Make the changes, and save the file back again, remembering first to remove the write protect tab from the MS-DOS floppy if you took the precaution of sticking one on it.

3.13 Very Simple Batch Files

You have already met AUTOEXEC.BAT. A batch file is just a set of MS-DOS commands like TIME or DATE or the name of an EXE or COM file, like LADYBUG or BASICA, which has the effect of running the program of that name. It ends in the extension .BAT.

You can do wonderful things with batch files, like writing whole programs of commands, making menus for your favourite applications and many other ingenious things better left to more advanced books.

However, I will give you one simple example: a batch file to make booting up easier for children. MS-DOS has its own simple little word processor, called EDLIN in its older versions, and the new and much improved EDIT in version 5. EDLIN is pretty horrid, and for that reason, as a beginner, use your own favourite word processor instead.

To make a quick start for Ladybug Logo, load up the word processor and create a file called BUG.BAT. Type in the following list of commands. You can press <Rn> at the end of each short line, to start a new line, but don't mess around with any other fancy controls, like going into bold or italics.

If you have floppy disks only, use your bootable Ladybug disk as your data disk and type:

```
ECHO OFF
CLS
GRAPHICS
LADYBUG
```

That is it. You must copy the GRAPHICS.COM file from your MS-DOS disk on to your bootable Ladybug disk, so that it is sitting there when your batch file wants to call it up.

If you have a hard disk drive, you can get the batch file, BUG.BAT to change directories for you. Type in:

```
ECHO OFF
CLS
CD MSDOS
GRAPHICS
CD..
CD LOGO
LADYBUG
```

It is assumed that GRAPHICS.COM is among the other MS-DOS files, saved in a subdirectory called MSDOS, and LADYBUG is in a subdirectory called LOGO. Save this list as a file named BUG.BAT at the root directory, that is, at the C:\ prompt, with the full label C:\BUG.BAT.

All the child has to do to load up Ladybug, is to type BUG at the C: or A: prompt (in this last case, the bootable Ladybug disk must be in the A: drive).

3.14 Dealing with Shareware

A lot of shareware consists of applications and little utilities that work in the same, slightly unfriendly way as MS-DOS.

Shareware just comes on a disk, no fancy box or manual. Many shareware programs do, in fact, have a manual, which is stored on the disk in a text or written file, ending with the extension .DOC or .TXT. You should have a look at this, and if you find it worthwhile, you may want to print it out. You can always do this with your word processor. You will need to use the full title of the document file, like:

```
WFUGUE.DOC
```

and to tell the word processor where it is stored. If you are using floppy disk drives only, you can put the shareware disk in as a data disk, and there is no problem.

If you have a hard disk drive, you could copy the document file into your normal subdirectory where you store your work or data files. However, it is probably preferable to load the .DOC file up from wherever it happens to be, with something like:

```
A:WFUGUE.DOC
```

if it is in the A: drive, or:

```
C:\WF\WFUGUE.DOC
```

if it is stored with the Word Fugue program files in the WF subdirectory of your hard disk.

Another method is to use a little utility called LIST which shareware companies often provide on any shareware disk that has a .DOC file on it. All you do is to type:

```
LIST WFUGUE.DOC
```

or whatever the filename happens to be and you get shown the .DOC file one page at a time, pressing Page Up and Page Down to move from one page to another. Use LIST to have a good look round the file, and if you think it is useful and want to print it out, load it up on your word processor.

Another utility you will come across with shareware is PKUNZIP. Shareware frequently comes archived or zipped up. This means that all the spaces in a file and other unnecessary characters are taken out so that the file is compressed and can be stored into a smaller space on the disk. The spaces and characters need to be put back before you can use the files.

Do a DIR to see what is on your shareware disk. If files end with the extension .ZIP, they have been compressed. You will usually see another file like PKUNZIP.COM which is the key that will uncompress them. Generally, you type:

```
PKUNZIP HUGO.ZIP
```

or whatever the filename happens to be, but follow the instructions given on the disk, like typing G for GO, because this will tell you what disks you need handy or how to sort out your subdirectories. One ZIP file can literally explode into a whole list of program files.

Word Processing

4.1 What Word Processing Does

One of the most valuable things your new computer will provide is word processing. This means producing written material or text. The finished result will look like a piece of typewriting, but getting there is completely different.

With old, ordinary typewriters, as you type each individual letter, it prints out on the paper. Type it wrong and you get a printed mistake. Get to the end of a line and you have to press the carriage return bar or the typing goes on beyond the edge of the paper. If you have a long word at the end of a line, you have to think where to put the hyphen. You have to work out when you are at the bottom of the page, which can be quite difficult when most of it is wrapped round a roller. Leave out a word, phrase or sentence and you've had it and must start again. There were some little mechanical aids like a bell ringing when you got near the end of a line or self correctable ribbons if you spotted a mistake.

The word processor operates differently. It shows up the typed characters on the screen, not on the printer. It has what is called word wrap which means that the computer notices when you get to the end of a line and automatically puts you on the next one. It may hyphenate words or it may keep them whole. You do not have to press Return, you just carry on typing quite obliviously. The computer sorts out where the page ending will be. What you are typing is on the screen and when you spot mistakes, even several rows later, you can go back and change them. To add something extra is no problem, the computer re-arranges all the writing to fit round it.

You only bother to print it all out when you are finally satisfied. This could be several days and revisions later. In between, you save it on a disk ready to call it up again and do some more work on it.

The very latest typewriters often have a memory and can do some of these things. But they tend to be quite expensive and can't do all the other things that computers can, like games or accounts, databases or spreadsheets. They might have a use in an office but at home the computer is more versatile.

The ease with which text can be changed and revised makes word processing a tremendous asset for the writer and teacher. Forgotten to put in a paragraph? No problem. Want to describe the geography of mountains before that of lakes, and you have done it the other way round? It's easy to move a whole block of text and put it in front of another.

Suppose you want to produce standard legal documents with the same wording but a slightly different collection of paragraphs on each occasion. Once you have got all the possible paragraphs, you can just call up the ones you want, in any order. You can get the computer to print out a whole series of such documents, putting in different names and addresses each time. It does have its flip side I suppose: you get so much junk mail as a result.

So to sum up, with a typewriter:

❏ You type and at the same time it prints out

❏ You read it, spot mistakes and think of different things to write

❏ You type the whole thing again with corrections

❏ You spot more mistakes

❏ You do a complete retype

❏ After a few retypes, you leave it like that. You know you could have worded some things better, but you have got to stop somewhere. Business letters have the odd handwritten correction. Time is money and the next retype may still produce mistakes.

But with the word processor:

❏ You type in the text and it appears on the screen

❏ You have a look back at what is on the screen. You can change or edit it (in computer jargon) until it is just the way you want it

❏ You print it out

Unless you are a perfect writer or typist, who never thinks of something better later (and who is like that?), word processing allows you to produce a much more polished product in much less time.

If you are producing standard, repetitive material it can save days or months of work.

Word processing has probably raised standards. We now expect perfect text. Some writers say it affects your style and not always in a positive way. Iris Murdoch, the famous novelist, will not use a word processor and still handwrites all her novels. If you type at secretarial speeds, your word processed writing will be more like speech, a bit chatty and looser. The carefully thought out literary phrase is less likely to appear and this could be a negative thing. On the other hand, you could argue that the fact that you can change word processing so easily, will make writing more refined as you read it over later and improve it. Future writing may take the form of a quick initial write, and then an editing or rechange. One day, somebody will probably write a Ph.D thesis on what word processing does to literature.

Word processors also give more choice as well as saving time. You can often choose different fonts or typestyles, changing them within the same document. This will depend on having the right printer. You can select page size and where margins will be. If you don't like the first choice, there is no problem in making a change – quite a contrast to the days of the old fashioned typewriter.

Notice the headings at the top of printed books and the page numbers at the bottom. Set them up for one or two pages and your word processor will automatically put them in on every page with numbers changed appropriately.

Some more advanced word processors allow you to write in columns like a newspaper. They can provide what is called a style sheet, a special layout that you can use for writing screen or radio plays. They may provide an outliner. You plan all the headings to use when writing a book or report and then fill it in with the actual writing.

Most word processors will check spelling, something that few people can fail to appreciate. If you use unfamiliar technical words you can add these to the computer's own dictionary. A Thesaurus will give alternative words and even style checkers to check grammar usage and sentence construction. Word processors can count the number of words, which is useful when producing books or scholarly reports.

Even on a budget, there are many interesting things you can do with text. Shareware has two or three very good word processors. The rest of this chapter gives an easy introduction to two of the best known ones: Galaxy Lite and Write Lite. Galaxy Lite snarls up the 10th time you use it, but the 11th seems to work without registration messages all over the screen. The authors of both ask you to register and buy the full version, but even at about £30 they are quite good value. Both have larger versions: Galaxy and PC-Write respectively.

There are other shareware packages like Formgen that allows you to print out and design all kinds of wonderful forms and Label Maker that will print out simple labels.

Although not shareware, Printmaster and Printshop are both quite cheap. They are visual, picture driven packages which means that, after some initial help, children can use them. They make cards, banners, calendars and certificates with ready drawn pictures, what is called clip art. You could get some coloured paper from your local art shop and produce really quite impressive products.

4.2 Starting Word Processing

4.2.1 Installing Galaxy Lite

With a hard disk, you will want to install Galaxy Lite. With floppies only, you will need to make a working copy on a blank formatted disk and you may need to unzip the shareware Galaxy Lite disk to do this.

If you have a hard disk

Create a directory in which to store the Galaxy program files. If you follow the Galaxy manual, call it GLITE. At the hard disk root C: directory, type:

```
MD GLITE
```

You can set Galaxy up so that it regularly saves files to some other subdirectory like say C:\GLITE\LETS. You can change it on any particular occasion so that it saves files to another subdirectory instead, like C:\GLITE\REPS. Make sure you first create these subdirectories (you can create new ones later) with commands like:

```
CD GLITE
```

to go into the Glite subdirectory, and then:

```
MD LETS
```

To carry out the installation

Put the Galaxy Lite shareware disk in drive A:. If you have floppies only, put a spare formatted disk in drive B:. Start the Install program by typing:

```
INSTALL
```

What this program does is to build a special file, called GLITE.INI, which creates a set of default values, things that will happen unless you specifically change them.

The install program is quite friendly and provides a lot of prompts and explanations. You work through a menu. First you are asked for the destination drive, which is the drive where the Galaxy program files will be stored, B: if you are using a second floppy disk drive, or C:\GLITE if you are using a hard disk.

It then builds the GLITE.INI file. Suggested values are given but they can be changed. Look at them carefully. They are things like whether you start with insert on. Most word processors do this, so stick with <Yes>. You won't get right justification unless you make a deliberate change. You can change the answer so that you can create files that will feed into Wordstar itself. Change this if you are going to purchase Wordstar in the very near future. Press N for No to the 43/50 line option on an EGA or VGA screen. It produces horribly small writing that nearly pulls your eyes out.

You are asked if you want to designate a default data directory. The suggested answer is <No>. If you accept this, your work files will be stored on the same drive as the program files. If you want to use a different subdirectory on the hard disk, type in Y for <Yes> and then the full path (a path is the branch of your subdirectory tree structure) e.g.:

```
C:\GLITE\LETS
```

If you have two floppies, you will probably want to say Y for <Yes> and then enter B:.

You can change margins and tops and bottoms of pages. You are then asked to type in the number that corresponds to your printer. There is a choice of 30. If your printer is not on this list, check the printer manual to see if it can behave like or emulate one on the list. You are also given the option to change the colours. If you don't know what to do, leave the values as they are. You can change them later, when you are running Galaxy Lite.

The final menu option will then be highlighted. This will actually install or copy the Galaxy Lite program files.

You are now ready to begin word processing.

4.2.2 Installing Write Lite

This needs installing as well with a program called LITEDISK. It will install your printer but you can also do this separately from the rest of the program. This has the advantage, that if you get the type of printer wrong or change printers, you can easily start again. What it does is to create a print control file for your particular model. You run this printer module, by running the program Printer, using, for example:

```
PRINTER C:\WRITE\PR.DEF
```

where C:\WRITE is the subdirectory where you are storing the Write Lite program files, and PR.DEF is the name of your printer control file. PR.DEF is the default name.

4.2.3 Loading the Word Processor

Loading Galaxy Lite

If you have two floppy drives:

Put your backup disk of program files in drive A:, a blank formatted disk in drive B: for work or data and then enter:

```
GLITE
```

to actually load up Galaxy Lite.

If you have a hard disk:

Change to the subdirectory where you store the Galaxy Lite program files by entering:

```
CD GLITE
```

followed by:

```
GLITE
```

to load up the program files.

An opening screen with a copyright notice reminds you that this is only an inspection copy and that you should register – Figure 4.1. Press any key to get out of this.

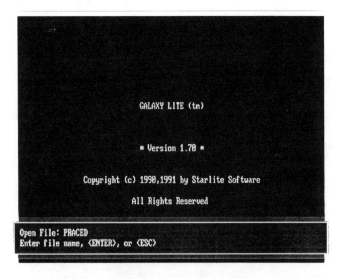

Figure 4.1: The Galaxy Lite opening screen

You then get a simple little box with:

```
Open File:
Enter file name, <Enter> or <Esc>
```

There is a blank after `Open File:`. Here you can enter the name of a file you have already written and it will load up. As you haven't written or saved anything to disk yet, just press <Rn>, which is the same thing as Enter, or <Esc>.

Loading Write Lite

If you have two floppy drives:

Put your working program disk in drive A: and a blank formatted data or work disk in drive B:.

If you have a hard drive:

Move into the subdirectory where you have stored the Write Lite program files. Do this with, for example:

```
CD WRITE
```

Whichever situation you are in, enter:

```
LITE
```

to load up Write Lite. You then get a copyright notice and the main menu screen shown in Figure 4.2. Press function key <F6> to select *File*.

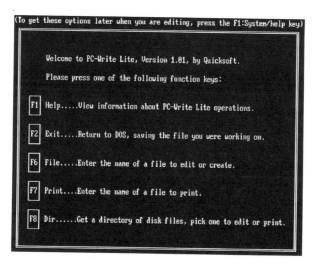

Figure 4.2: The Write Lite opening screen

At the top of the screen, you get a small single line message, saying:

```
File to load or create (Esc: cancel F8:dir):''work.doc''
```

This is actually asking you for the name of the file you are going to write. If you put in a file you have already written and stored on a data disk, it will load that up. If not, which is the situation here, it will create a new file. If you don't put in a name, it will call whatever you write WORK.DOC, its default value. Enter a name, like:

```
PRAC1
```

Write Lite will search for a file of this name, and when, not surprisingly, it doesn't find one, it will return the message:

```
File not found: Esc to retype, or F9 to create ''PRAC1''.
```

Press function key <F9> to do just that.

4.2.4 Starting to Write

This section will apply, whether you are using Galaxy Lite or Write Lite. You are now faced with a blank screen. This is your blank piece of paper and you are quite free to start writing. Do just that: it doesn't matter what it is – a poem, nursery rhyme or a piece of creative writing. Just go on typing even when you get to the end of the line – you don't need to press <Rn>. The text automatically moves itself on to the next line because Wordwrap is turned on.

If you want to make a new line or paragraph, press <Rn> twice to leave a blank line and make a new paragraph.

If you make mistakes, don't worry. This will give you practice in how to correct them.

4.2.5 Correcting Typing Errors

I deliberately wrote a little piece with some errors in it, to give you an example of how to make corrections.

```
I am going to write something or other just to practise. How about making
some mistakes to corrct. Like insrting something. Or maybe I will puot in
something I need to take oupt. Or just something that neebs ovepwriting.
```

To insert a character

A character means just one keypress – letter, number or other symbol. Move the cursor to the right of where you want to put in the character. Provided you have not pressed the <Insert> key an odd number of times since you started word processing just type in the character.

For example, use the arrow keys until the cursor is flashing on the second c in corrct. Type e, and you have correct. Move the cursor until it over the r in insrting. Type e and you have inserting.

To delete a character

Just use the arrow keys to move the cursor so that it is flashing on the character to the right of the one to delete. Press the <Del> key (the Backspace key immediately above Return) and it will disappear.

For example, move the cursor until it is on the t in puot and press <Del>. You are left with put. Move the cursor so it is on the t in oupt and press <Del> to leave out.

To write over another character

If you have put in an incorrect character which just needs to be changed for something else, without inserting or putting anything else in, move the cursor until it is on the character you want to correct.

Using Galaxy Lite

Press the <Insert> key. What this does is to put you into overstrike or replace mode. You stay in this mode until you press <Insert> again to put it back to the original Insert mode. The <Insert> key is what is called a toggle button, it moves from one thing to another, and stays where you last put it, until you make another change.

Using Write Lite

The little line of writing at the top of the screen, starts off with the word *Push* in it. This means the same as insert, that is, if you type in a new character it will push its way into the existing text. The opposite is overwrite and you get to this by pressing the <Scroll Lock> key on the top right hand part of the keyboard. The word *Push* at the top line, is then replaced with *Over*.This means that if you type in a new character, it will write over whatever character is under the flashing cursor. Over remains, until you press <Scroll Lock> again. This also is a toggle key.

Using either word processor just type the new character.

For example, move the cursor until it is flashing on the b in neebs. Press the <Insert> or <Scroll Lock> key to toggle into overstrike. Then type d to get needs. You stay in overstrike until you press <Insert> or <Scroll Lock> again to toggle back

to insert mode. To do the next change all you have to do is to move the cursor so that
it is on the p in `ovepwriting` and type `r`.

4.2.6 Saving Your Writing

When you are fed up with writing and making corrections, you may want to save or
store the file. You can then load it up and change it or print it out on another
occasion.

Using Galaxy Lite

There are three ways of doing this which will probably sound very confusing at this
stage, but you will soon get used to it and in fact, it can be very useful.

Using keys on the menu system

You can press the ordinary keys on the keyboard to get a whole menu system. You
start by pressing function key <F10> to get a menu.

This is just a single line of words at the top of the screen. Using the first letter of any
of these words will produce a pull down menu. On this occasion, type F for *File*.

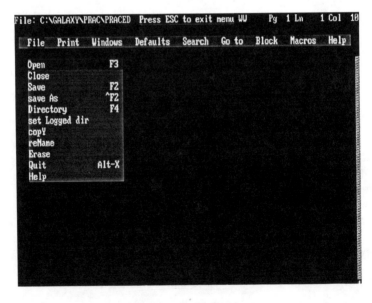

Figure 4.3: Galaxy Lite's File menu

A menu drops down beneath the word *File* as shown in Figure 4.3. Some of the
letters are underlined. Type these to select the menu choices. To save the file type S
for *Save*.

Using cursor arrows on the menu system

To get the Menu line at the top of the screen, press the function key <F10>.

You can move along this line with the <rightarrow> and <leftarrow> keys. Move to the option you want, in this case *File*. Press <Rn> to get the pull down menu. Use the <downarrow> and <uparrow> keys, until *Save file* is highlighted. Press <Rn> to select.

Using hotkeys

Hotkeys are one or two keypresses you can make, to do something quickly. You don't have to go through the menu at all. However the keypresses are rather meaningless, not nice and friendly like S for Save, and this means that you will only remember them for things that you do frequently. They only exist for the most common commands anyway.

The hot keypress for Save is function key <F2>.

Using any of these methods you will get a dialogue box, showing:

```
Filename:
```

followed by a blank. Enter a name for the file obeying DOS rules for filenames: it can only be eight letters long for the filename, followed by a period (.) or full stop, and a three letter extension and should not contain any strange characters. For my example, I typed:

```
PRAC1<Rn>
```

which was short for Practice Number 1.

There will be a whirr on the floppy or hard disk and the file will be saved.

If you want to just temporarily save a particular file in a different subdirectory than the one you set up originally, you can do this with the menu options:

Press function key <F10> to activate the menu

Press F or <alongarrow> to select File and open menu

Press L or <downarrow> to *set logged directory* followed by <Rn>.

Type in the subdirectory you want, like, for example:

```
C:\GLITE\REPS
```

Using Write Lite

You have already named the file, when you opened it. You called it PRAC1. To save it, press function key <F1> quickly followed by function key <F3>.

4.2.7 Leaving the Word Processor

Using Galaxy Lite

Use function key <F10> to get the menu line, <alongarrow> keys or F to get the submenu under *File*. Then Q for *Quit* or <downarrow> and <Rn> to highlight and select *Quit*.

The hotkey for leaving Galaxy Lite is <Alt-X>.

A message indicates that you are using shareware and tells you how many times you have used it. You are then returned to the A: or C: prompt.

Using Write Lite

Press function key <F1>, followed by function key <F2>.

Your file is saved again automatically, and you are given the main menu again. Press function key <F2> to return to the A: or C: prompt.

4.3 Making a Letter Template

A template is a basic skeleton, the background bits that you always want in any particular kind of document. For example, when you write a business letter, you might put your address in the top right hand corner of the page, if you don't have headed notepaper. Then you put your telephone number underneath that and beneath that today's date. On the left hand side you put the reference number of the people you are writing to, and under that your own, if you have one. Then leave a space or two and put in the address of the people you are writing to. You can change these positions to suit your own personal preference. In other words, what a template does is to set up the basic layout of the letter. Your address stays the same whoever you write to, and the other things act as guides, to be filled in when you write a particular letter.

You save this template or skeleton to disk. Then whenever you want to write a letter, you load it up, fill it in and write the body of the letter. You save this with a new name, using the Save As option. You now have two documents on disk: the basic letter skeleton which is used in every letter, and the particular letter you have written. The template acts rather like a blank form. You fill it in and the filled in version is the letter you actually send.

4.3.1 Making and Saving a Template

Here are some instructions for making and saving a letter writing template.

Using Galaxy Lite

Load up Galaxy Lite using the instructions given in Section 4.2.3.

When you get the opening message:

```
Open File:
```

enter the filename:

```
LETTEMP
```

Galaxy Lite goes to search for this and needless to say doesn't find it, because you haven't created it yet. It asks you if you want to create it anyway. Type Y for Yes.

You then get a blank writing screen. You want to start writing your address over on the right hand side, at about the 5th bar of the ruler grid at the top of the screen. Move along to this position by pressing the <spacebar> or <rightarrow> key several times.

Type the first line of your address then press <Rn>. Assuming that you set up Galaxy Lite so that the Tab setting was 0 which stands for automatic, you won't go to the beginning of the line on the left. You will find yourself under the first word of your address, all lined up ready to type in a new line. What the automatic tab does is to send you beneath the first non blank space on the line above, when you press <Rn>.

Type in the second, third and fourth (if you have one) lines of your address pressing <Rn> at the end of each. Then press <Rn> twice to leave a blank space beneath. The second time you do this, you will go over to the left again. Move again using the <spacebar> or <rightarrow> key up to the fifth bar on the ruler, so that the cursor is under your address and type your phone number. Press <Rn> two or three times and then move so you are under the address again. This time, type in the date, in this case:

```
29th January 1992
```

This puts the date in the correct position and you can always overwrite it with the appropriate one.

Press <Rn> two or three times again. You will have returned to the left hand side of the paper. Type in:

```
Your Reference:
```

Press <Rn> three more times. Now show where you are going to put the sender's name and address with:

```
name<Rn>
line1<Rn>
line2<Rn>
line3<Rn>
```

Press <Rn> three more times, and put in the greeting of the letter:

```
Dear Sir
```

Again, it doesn't matter if you want another greeting, you can always overwrite this one. The finished template is shown in Figure 4.4.

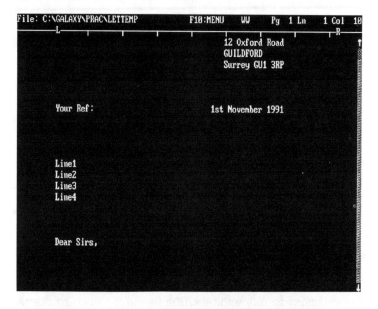

Figure 4.4: A ready-made letter template in Galaxy Lite

To save this:

Press function key <F10> for the menu then <arrowalong> until you are over *File* and press <Rn> to activate the pull down menu. Press <downarrow> until *Save* is selected. Press <Rn>.

Or press function key <F10> for the menu, F for *File* and then S for *Save*.

Or use the hotkey, function key <F2> without going into the menu at all.

Save the file with the name LETTEMP.

Using Write Lite

Open Write Lite, following the instructions given in Section 4.2.3. Give your new file the name LETTEMP. Press <F9> to open a new file of this name.

Type the first line of your address, and when you have done this, don't press <Rn> but press the key combination <Ctrl-F8>. This is the flush right key, and it should put your writing or text over on the right hand side of the page, against the right margin. Repeat the procedure for the next lines of your address.

Then press <Rn> twice to leave a line. Type your telephone number and press <Ctrl-F8> to make that flush right.

Press <Rn> twice and repeat the procedure with today's date. You can overwrite the date you put into the template.

Press <Rn> about three times. This time, write over on the left hand side, which is easy. Type:

```
Your Reference:
```

Press <Rn> twice more and then type:

```
Name<Rn>
line1<Rn>
line3<Rn>
line4<Rn>
```

Press <Rn> three or four times, and type:
```
Dear Sir
```

You may not always want this greeting, but you can easily overwrite it.

You have now written your template file, and you are ready to save it. Do this by pressing function key <F1> followed by <F2>.

4.3.2 Starting a New File With One on Screen

Once you have saved your template, it is still left sitting on the screen. To get a completely new file to start on:

Using Galaxy Lite

Press function key F10 to produce the menu bar

Press <arrowalong> until you are on *File*, and then press <Rn> to produce the pull down menu. Press <downarrow> until the cursor is on *Open* and press <Rn> to accept. Alternatively use the keys, F followed by O for *Open*.

You can also use the hot key <F3>

You will then get the message:

```
Open File: C:\GALAXY\PRAC\LETTEMP
```

or whatever the name of the last file was. Just type in the name of the file you are about to create. You don't need the C:\GALAXY bit, just type the filename, for example:

```
FUNPRINT<Rn>
```

if you are going straight on to do the next section. You then get the message:

```
File is new. Create the file? (Y/N):
```

Type Y for Yes. You then get a blank screen and can start writing.

Using Write Lite

To switch to another file, press function key <F1> followed by <F6>. You are asked if you want to make a backup of your existing file. Type <F9> to accept this or <Esc> if you are not bothered and don't want to use up disk space.

Call the new file, FUNPRINT, and press <Rn> to register.

4.3.3 Testing out Fancy Print Options

Most word processors allow you to enhance your print, or make bits of documents look special. You can do this by printing in bold, italics or by underlining. You can also make subscripts or superscripts, for footnotes or mathematics. This will not show up on the screen, but will appear when you print it out. For this reason, word processors call them printer codes.

Using both word processors

You put a code in at the beginning of the text you want to change, and another at the place where you want the change to end. You use the combination of holding down Alt and pressing another key at the same time. The other key's letter, or some other funny symbol, appears highlighted on the screen. This shows where the change is going to begin or end, but the symbol itself will not print out. This means that these shareware packages are not What You See Is What You Get (WYSIWYG) word processors, but only the newest Windows versions are anyway. Here is a sample file you can create, called FUNPRINT, to demonstrate the different codes.

This is a piece of text written to see what you can get out of your word processor and printer. To change to a fancy font you hold down Alt and press another key at the same time. To turn it off, press the same Alt-key combination for Galaxy or press <Rn> to go to another line in the case of Write Lite.

In both cases press <Alt-B> and type:

`Here is a line in bold`

Press <Alt-D> if you have Galaxy and <Alt-S> if you have Write Lite and type:

`Here is a line in double strike print`

Press <Alt-F> if you have Galaxy and <Alt-I> if you have Write Lite and type:

`Here is a line in italics`

Press <Alt-U> for both word processors and type:

`Here is underlined text`

When you get to the end of the next sentence, after the little x, press <Alt-T> for Galaxy and <Alt-H> for Write Lite and then type 2.

`Here is superscript used in maths - x2`

In the next sentence, type until you get to the end of the word `number` and then before you type the 5, press <Alt-V> for Galaxy and <Alt-L> for Write Lite.

`Here is a subscript like a footnote number 5`

Figure 4.5 shows text with attributes set for various styles.

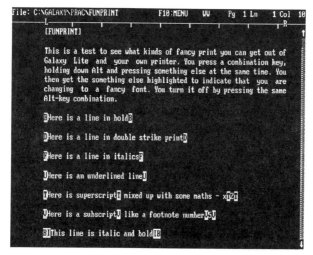

Figure 4.5: Setting text attributes in Galaxy Lite

Print out the file.

Using Galaxy Lite

To print out a file:

❏ Press <F10> to produce the menu line

❏ Press <arrowalong> to the *Print* option

❏ Press <Rn> to get pull down menu

❏ Press <downarrow> to *Print File*

❏ Press <Rn> to select

❏ Alternatively press, P, then P.

❏ Or you can use the hotkey <F9>

Using Write Lite

Press function key <F1> and soon after that <F7>. You then get the print menu, in the line at the top of the screen. It looks something like this:

```
Esc F1 F3. View F7: Copies F8:To-disk F9:Range F10-All Pages Ctrl-PgUpDn
```

Type <F10> for all pages. As you only have one page, that is not a difficult choice. You then get another message, saying:

```
Print Control File name (Esc:cancel Enter: none)
```

This allows you to put in the correct Printer Control file if you haven't managed to do this already in the installation. You can also try new ones until you get the right one. I found that typing in IBMEPSOM.PRT happened to be the correct one for my printer. It has some compatibility with the IBM Proprinter and an Epson.

I then got another funny message about omitting a colon but I just pressed <F9> to accept twice and the printing went ahead.

Otherwise just press <Rn> and your printer should get going.

If you are using Galaxy Lite and the result does not seem to do much, run the installation program again (just the middle part) and select a different printer driver.

4.4 Writing Letters and Blocking Text

4.4.1 Using a Template to Write a Letter

To write a letter, start off by loading up the file called LETTEMP.

Using Galaxy Lite

Respond to the `Open File:` prompt at the beginning of your word processing by typing LETTEMP.

When the file is loaded, change the cursor from insert to overstrike mode. When insert mode is on, the cursor is a square flashing block, when toggled to overstrike, it shrinks down to a thick line.

Using Write Lite

If you are loading up Write Lite at the beginning of your computing session, you can type:

`LITE LETTEMP`

to load straight up into LETTEMP.

Or you could load up in the usual way and get the directory with <F1> followed soon afterwards with <F8>. This shows you which files you have saved. Move the highlight bar until it is over the one you want to retrieve. Press <Rn> to do this.

Then change from Push to Over by pressing the <ScrollLock> key.

Using both word processors

Use the cursor keys to move to the date. Write over the bits that need correcting to make today's date.

If the person you are writing to has a reference, move the cursor to the right of `Your Reference:` and type it in. If they don't have a reference, move the cursor to the Y on `Your Reference` and press the space bar until it is covered up.

Then move the cursor to the N on `Name` and type in the name of the person or company you are writing to. Press <Rn>. You should now be on the L of `Line1`. Type in the first line of the address of the person you are writing to. Press <Rn> again and go on to the next line. If the address has more lines than the number you put on the template, write over the lines that you do have. Then press the <Insert> or <ScrollLock> key to toggle from overstrike to insert and go on typing the rest of the address. Because you now have insert or push on, it will automatically put in new lines.

Press <Insert> or <ScrollLock> again to toggle into overstrike and press <Rn> until you are on the D of Dear Sir. Type any changes you need to make to this.

Toggle back to insert with <Insert> or <ScrollLock>, because this is what you usually start word processing with. You are now ready to put in the body of your letter.

Press <Rn> twice to get to the first line of the written part of the letter. If you want to put a centred heading, first type in the heading itself. You may want to enhance it in some way, underline it or write it in bold. Do this in the usual way. When you have finished, press <Alt-C> for Galaxy and <Shift-F8> for Write Lite and it is automatically centred.

Carry on with the rest of the letter.

4.4.2 Saving Your Letter

The important thing is to save your letter with a different name from LETTEMP. You can do this by using *Save As*.

Using Galaxy Lite

If you are using the cursor keys, <F10> to activate the menu line. <arrowalong> until *File* is highlighted and press <Rn>.

<downarrow> until you are on *Save As* and press <Rn> to select.

To use the keypresses, <F10> to activate the menu line. F for *File*, and A for *Save As*.

Or you can simply use the hotkey, <Ctrl-F2>.

You then get a box prompting you for the filename. It gives the current filename, which is probably LETTEMP. Backspace until you have deleted this and then type in the new name. something like LETNOV11, for example.

Print out your letter using the instructions in Section 4.3.4.

Using Write Lite

To save the file with a different name, press function key <F1> followed by function key <F5>. Type in the name of the letter and press <Rn> to register.

4.4.3 Moving, Copying and Deleting Paragraphs

You can copy, delete or move whole chunks of writing. You can also call up set paragraphs from another document or write into another file. This kind of facility is very useful when you are writing letters or legal documents with standard clauses. You can knock out paragraphs or clauses that don't apply and even totally rearrange the order.

The principle is to create what are called blocks. You mark the area you want to do something with by putting a *begin block* marker at the start and an *end block* marker at the end. You then do whatever operation you want and the whole block is affected.

The best way of doing anything is by example. Start off with some word processing that has some standard clauses which won't apply to everybody you might write to. You could call up the letter template and turn it into a standard letter. Here is my example:

```
THE DAME AURORA MUSIC AND DANCE SCHOOL
New children are to bring their medical detail forms.
All children are to bring a packed lunch. Glass jars and chocolate snacks
are not allowed.
Children doing the extra dance and drama class should bring a shoe bag
marked clearly with their names.
For boys, this should contain shorts, aertex shirt and plimsolls.
For girls, this should contain leotard, cardigan and ballet shoes.
It is vitally important that we have the correct phone number for where
parents will be during the day.
```

Suppose you are sending this notice to an old pupil who happens to be a girl. She won't need the paragraphs about medical detail forms and boys' clothes, so you can delete those. Start with the paragraph about medical forms.

Using Galaxy Lite

The first thing you need to do is block the text. To begin a block, move the cursor to its first letter, in this case to the N of New. Press function key <F7> to mark the start of the block. There will be nothing to show that you have done this. Move the cursor to the last letter of the block, in this case to the space or full stop at the end of forms. Press function key <F8> to mark the end of the block. If you have colour, you will find that the blocked text is now yellow. If you have a monochrome monitor, you get high intensity video.

To delete the block

Using the cursor arrow keys, press <F10> to activate the menu bar. Press <rightarrow> until you reach *Block* and press <Rn> to select. Press the <downarrow> key until you reach *Delete* and press <Rn>.

If you use the single keys, press <F10> to activate the menu line. Type B for *Block* and then D for *Delete*.

Whatever method you use, the paragraph will magically disappear.

For practice, remove the one about boys' clothes as well.

Using Write Lite

To delete a block, move to its start, in this case, the beginning of the paragraph about New children. Press function key <F4> to start the block. Move the <rightarrow> and <downarrow> keys until you get to the end of the paragraph. As you do this, you will see that the whole paragraph gets highlighted. When you reach the end, press <F4> again and the whole paragraph magically disappears.

Use the same technique to get rid of the paragraph about boys' clothes.

You might then decide that the paragraph beginning It is vitally impor-tant... should go at the beginning under the title, instead of the end.

Using Galaxy Lite

To move a block, first mark it as a block, as you did for Delete. Move the cursor to the place you want the block moved to. It doesn't matter that you move the cursor away from the block. It has been marked out and will stay yellow, wherever you move the cursor.

Follow the same menu commands but this time select *Move* instead of *Delete*.

Using Write Lite

Go to the beginning of the block and press function key <F6>. You will see that the line at the top says, *marking*. Move the cursor keys until you get to the end of the bit you want to move. Press <F6> again. You get the message *marked* on the top line, this time.

Then move the cursor to where you want the block moved to. Press <F6> for the third time, and the paragraph will move to this new position.

There is one last vital step you need to take. You must clear the marking, or the block may move again, when you don't want it to. You do this by pressing function key <F5>.

To make the notice look better, and give you some more practice, you could copy the title so that you get it at the bottom as well as at the top.

Using Galaxy Lite

To copy a block, first mark it in the usual way. Move the cursor to the place you want the block copied to.

Go through the same menu selection procedure as you did for Delete and Move but this time select *Copy*.

Using Write Lite

Move to where you want the block to start and press function key <F3>. Then move to the end of the block. It will be highlighted, and you will get the message, *marking*. At the end, press function key <F3> again. You will now get the message *marked*.

Move the cursor where you want the block copied to. Press <F3> for the third time. You now get a copy of your original block.

Turn off the marking with <F5> or you will get it copied again in all sorts of strange places.

The final version of the notice is shown in Figure 4.6.

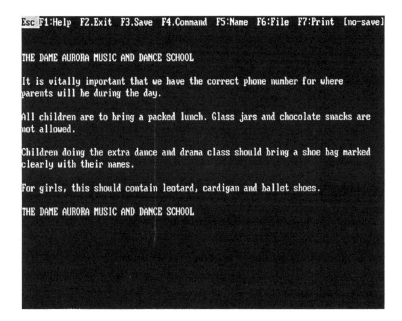

Figure 4.6: The final version of the text

4.4.4 Changing the Printing Format

Save Dame Aurora. You must always save before printing.

If you print out the notice the way it is at the moment, you will get it all at the top of the page. You can start it much further down by changing the top margin:

Using Galaxy Lite

If you are using the cursor keys, press <F10> to activate the menu. <arrowalong> until you reach *Print* and <Rn> to select. <downarrow> to *Top Margin* and <Rn> to select.

If you are using the keys, <F10> to activate the menu. P to select *Print*. T to select *Top margin*.

In all cases, you get a box saying:

```
New Top Margin: 3
```

It gives the current value, 3, as a default. Change this by entering something new, like 20 in this situation and press <Rn> to register the change. You can then go ahead and print by selecting *Print File* from the Print menu.

Using Write Lite

Go right to the very first character at the top of the first page. Make sure that *Push* is toggled on, and press <Rn> to make a new line. Move the cursor up to this new empty line and press the keys <Alt-G>. You get a funny box, which shows what are called formatting options – ways of changing the margins, both top and bottom and left and right.

Press <Esc> to get out of this and in the space right at the top of the document, enter:

```
.xt: 15
```

exactly as it is shown above, putting in the period (.) or full stop and leaving the space after the colon. This is called a dot prompt command. It is very like Wordstar. This one has the effect of leaving 15 lines at the top of your printing, instead of the usual three which is the default.

4.5 Making Forms

4.5.1 Using or Adapting Ready Made Forms

The shareware package Formgen is very useful when it comes to using and designing forms. It has several ready made forms that come with it, like invoices, bills, payments out, weekly schedules, phone message slips, membership renewal forms and a husband and wife family tree. If they are not exactly what you want, they are very easy to adapt. You can also design your own forms from scratch. You can do anything that involves boxes and lines, and you can also shade in some areas and copy them down to other parts of the form. This is a bit more fiddly. There are a couple of forms already on the disk that show how this can be done. One called MAP.FRM draws a sample street map and there is another that shows how you could use lines and shaded in boxes to provide an illustrated catalogue of spare mechanical parts. Even as a beginner, there is a lot you could use this package for.

If you know the name of the form you want to use, load up straight into it, with the command:

```
FORM PAIDOUT
```

for example. PAIDOUT is the name of the ready made form.

Otherwise, load up Formgen with:

```
FORM
```

You then find yourself with a blank form, ready for your own design.

You can, however, go on to load a ready saved form. To do this, press <Alt-F9> and a new screen appears, with a list of ready saved forms. There is a space at the bottom where you can type in the name of the one you want.

To change one of these forms, just delete or type over any writing. You will need to redraw and delete lines using the methods used to design your own forms. I'll explain how to do this later.

You can save a form, by pressing function key <F9>. If you are using an already saved form, it will show its existing name at the bottom of the screen. You can change the name to something else, if, for example, you have used a ready made form and adapted it to your own use. Press <Rn> when you have got the name you want. If you have not changed the name, Formgen will warn you that you are about to overwrite an existing form. Type y or Y for yes to do this.

To print a form, just press function key <F10>. You then get a prompt, giving you the choice of three types of printer. Look at your printer manual, to see if you have compatibility with these. In my case, the first, IBM Proprinter, was the correct one, so all I had to do was type 1 and the form printed out quite happily. It may be, that you will be less lucky, and in this case Formgen, will probably not be of much use to you. Printers can be one of the biggest problems in computing.

To load up another form, press <Alt-F9> again.

4.5.2 Designing Your Own Forms

It is worth printing out the on-disk manual, contained in FORM.DOC so that you have a record of all the commands and keypresses. The other way to do this, is to get into the package, and call up Help and then screen dump each page, if your computer will allow you to do this.

If you load up by typing FORM, you find yourself in the blank design screen. The area that shows prints out to about one third of a page, so you will probably want to scroll down to make a longer form. You can move around the form using cursor keys in the usual way but there are also quicker ways of moving from one corner to another given in the manual. You can scroll over to the right but you might have problems in printing this out.

Move to any location on the screen where you might want to write some part of the form, and type in words in the usual way. To draw a line beside it, for an answer, press function key <F1> to set the cursor to draw a single thin line. Move the cursor around, and as you do this it will draw a line. When you want to stop just press <Rn>. You can go up and down, as well as along, and this is how you draw a box. You will find that you need to turn a corner, slightly sooner than you would think, and at first, your boxes probably won't quite meet, or will be too big. Keep on practising until you have mastered the art.

Function key <F2> sets the cursor to draw a double line. You can set function key <F3> to draw a character under the cursor, anything like an x or a hyphen. All these keys can be turned off, by pressing <Rn>. When you make a mistake, press function key <F4> to rub out and go over the wrong bits. You will find that this will sometimes eat into the sides of a box, and you will then need to redraw it. To turn off the rubber, just press <Rn>.

You can draw lines for people to write answers on, to separate one part of the form from another and also to create little boxes to tick or fill in. You can put some shading on the form by pressing the <Alt> key, and while you are holding it down, typing the number 176, 177 or 178 for light, medium and dark grey. Use the numeric keypad on the right hand side of the keyboard not the numbers at the top. This will only colour one space, but you can turn on function key <F3> and the cursor will go on drawing over the screen.

When you have finished the form, save it by pressing function key <F9> and print it by pressing function key <F10>. You then get two options, given at the bottom of the screen: to save it in the standard Formgen format or in ASCII, which is what you would do it you wanted to import it into some other package, like a database. The latter is an advanced option, beyond the scope of this book, so type 1 to select the standard.

Figures 4.7, 4.8 and 4.9 are samples of some of the types of form you can produce.

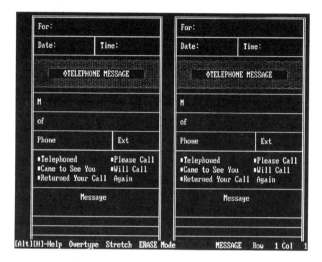

Figure 4.7: A simple telephone message form

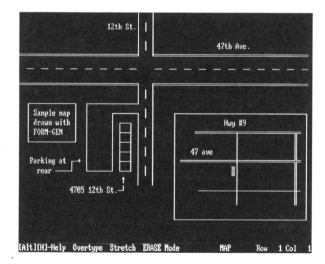

Figure 4.8: A sample map

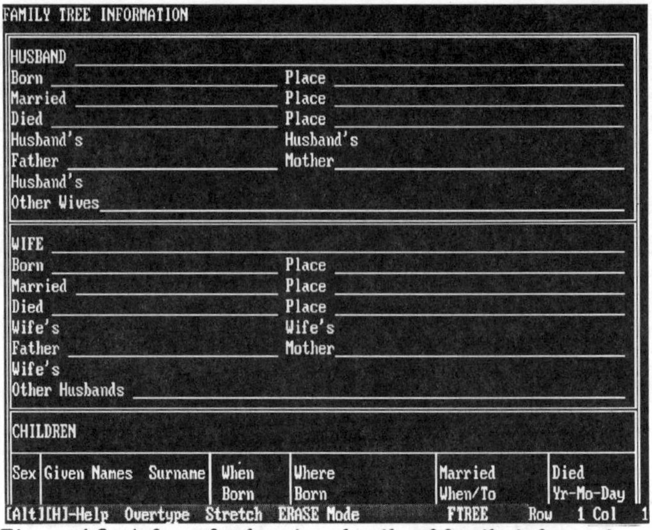

Figure 4.9: A form for keeping details of family information

4.6 Making Address Labels

It can be very useful to have all your addresses stored on the computer, so that you can print out labels. Examine your mail carefully and you will find that even quite small concerns are using this method.

Shareware has a package called Label Maker, which will do this. It is produced by a British author, Dipak Desai. What you do is create a file full of one type of label, like names and addresses, then fill these in for as many people as you are interested in. You can change or delete entries on another occasion or print all or just some of them.

There is quite a useful short document on the disk, called LM.DOC. Use your word processor to have a look and to print it out.

You need to know the filename you are going to use before you load Label Maker. This is true even when you make a new file for the first time. If you don't do this, you will get the default file, LABEL.REC, which may have things in you don't want. If you are doing names and addresses, you might want to put in everybody you know, or you might want to split them up into separate files, according to their function, files like FAMILY.REC, CUSTOM.REC or FRIENDS.REC.

So to start a family file of names and addresses and load up Label Maker, type:
```
LM FAMILY.REC<Rn>
```

The program loads and puts you into the main menu. This has four main options: create, amend, delete or print out – see Figure 4.10. You can highlight the selection and press <Rn> or type the start letter or press a function key. For now, the only sensible thing you can do is to create, so select the first option.

You get a blank 7-line form to fill in. Type in your first name and address, arranging it on the lines in any way you like. Press <Rn> at the end of each line to get on to the next one. By pressing function key <F5> you can call up ASCII graphics characters to include some decoration. A box is displayed showing what these are. Move the cursor to the one you want and then press <Rn>. After that, whenever you press function key <F6> that character appears on the form.

When you have filled in the first form, press function key <F10> to save it. You then get another blank form to fill in. Do this, and save again with <F10>. Carry on until you have put in all the addresses. After you have saved the last one with <F10> press <Esc> to show that you have finished. If you press <Esc> before saving your entry, it will be lost.

You can amend or update entries or delete them. You load up in the way demonstrated above, but select option 2 or 3 from the menu. To print out one or all the labels, select option 4. For delete and amend, you are usually looking for one entry at a time. You may want to print just one label or the whole lot. Both options are available.

When you first select option 2, 3 or 4, you come into a blank label. You can use this to type in some name or place to search on. The right name or place must be on the correct line so it is worth being systematic about how you set out your names and addresses. Press function key <F10> and Label Maker starts searching for this entry. As soon as it finds it, it stops. The box at the top left hand corner shows what numbered record you have out of how many.

There's a menu of options at the bottom of the screen. Not all of these will work in every situation. They are shown in the manual. What I found disappointing was that I could not get G for Graphics to work – it gave me a menu of picture libraries but didn't seem to produce any.

Press <P> to print out the single label you have found or <A> to print out all the labels in your file.

5

Spreadsheets

5.1 Introduction to Spreadsheets

A spreadsheet is just an electronic grid system built out of little rectangular boxes called cells. You can choose to fill these cells in different ways and this is its strength - an idea that is so simple can build up into something quite complex. You can instruct it to do arithmetic on whole rows or columns of cells and if you change the entry in just one cell it will re-do the whole calculation without any further instructions. You can take advantage of this facility in making *what if* calculations. You can try different values and the computer will automatically respond by changing the whole worksheet. Just imagine all the bottles of Tippex and all the brain stress you would need to achieve this on paper. The spreadsheet used here is As Easy As, the famous shareware package.

You either identify a cell by name or physically move to it using the cursor.

5.1.1 Naming a Cell

Spreadsheets may label their cells differently but the popular Lotus 1-2-3 and many others use letters for columns and numbers for rows.

To identify a cell by name you start with the column letter followed by the row number e.g. A6.

When you have reached Z, the column letters go AA, AB, AC......AZ, then BA, BB, BC.....BZ etc. When you reach ZZ you then go AAA, AAB....AAZ, ABA and so on.

5.1.2 Moving to Cells

The cursor keys are used to move around a single screen. <Page Up> and <Page Down> move you up and down a screen. <TAB> (the key with two arrows on it at the top left hand corner of the keyboard) moves you right half a screen and <SHIFT-TAB> moves you left half a screen.

To jump to a particular cell, say DD56, press function key <F5> for *Goto* followed by DD56.

<Home> moves to cell A1 at the top left of the screen and <End> followed by an arrow key moves you to the end of the current block.

5.1.3 Making Cell Entries

There are three types of entry you can make into cells but the general principle is that once you have finished making an entry you finalise it by pressing <Rn>. Up to this point, mistakes can be corrected by using the backspace key. You can also make an entry into a cell final, by pressing one of the cursor keys, to move to another cell.

The three different types of entry are:

Text

Just type the letters and the spreadsheet will immediately respond to the first letter and expect more text. If you start with a number followed by letters, you must show that you want to make a text entry by starting with a quote mark e.g. ' `1week`.

If you just start with a letter the text will be written starting at the left hand side of the cell. If necessary you can force it to do this by starting the text with a ' (single quote).

To put text on the right hand side, put a '' (double quote) in front of the text.

To centre the text, start with a ^ (press <Shift> and 6 in the line at the top of the keyboard).

Numbers

The spreadsheet will, if instructed, do arithmetic on these by, for example, adding up sales figures.

You can just type in numbers, but you should think about how you want them presented before you start typing. You can set the *format* in which they are to be arranged and the numbers will then be set out in the way you have requested. You can have whole numbers, different numbers of decimal places or choose the currency option. If you don't sort this out the numbers might not line up and the arithmetic may go a bit funny. For example:

786

25.14

are not lined up properly.

It is possible to change the format after you have entered numbers and you may want to do this to see them presented in a different way but it is easier to think about it before you begin.

Formulae

When you start a cell entry by typing + the spreadsheet will be expecting a formula. A formula is something that acts on a single cell or a range of cells to produce a result. You can either do this directly, e.g.+B3+B4+B5 or you can use the special functions provided by the spreadsheet like @SUM. Functions always start with the @ sign.

5.1.4 Changing a Cell after Entry

There are two ways of doing this, the first is quicker for short entries, the second better for long ones.

❏ Either move to the cell you want to change and just type the new corrected entry. Press <Rn> to finalise and the old entry will be entirely replaced with the new one.

❏ Move to the cell you want to change. Press function key <F2> for edit. You can then use the arrow cursor keys to move to the bit you want to change. Delete and backspace will work in the usual way and insert will either insert or overstrike. Press <Rn> as usual to finalise.

For the rest of this chapter I will demonstrate some of the facilities that a spreadsheet provides with a series of simple exercises.

5.2 Using a Spreadsheet to Add Up

You can use a spreadsheet to add up long lists of figures. You might well say that a calculator would be more handy: you can keep it in your pocket and you don't have to go through all that booting up, changing directory and loading up. This is very true. Both the calculator and the spreadsheet will do arithmetic completely accurately. However calculators are only as good as the figures you feed into them and if you get these wrong, the final total will be wrong too. Unless you have a calculator with a print reel attached or a screen display, you cannot see after the event exactly what you did feed in. With the spreadsheet, you can have a list of the figures together with the total, so that you can check that you did make the right entries.

If you regularly carry out large quantities of addition, you can set a spreadsheet up so that it is ready to do this, and all you have to do is to type in the figures and the answer will magically appear.

As an example, let's add up a list of whole numbers like the number of bytes used on a disk. When you type in numbers, don't put commas between the thousands. Add up 123679, 32564, 5667, 8990, 1098 and 11113.

For these examples I'll use the shareware spreadsheet As Easy As, but the basic principles will be the same with most spreadsheets.

5.2.1 Loading up *As Easy As*

If you have a hard disk drive, change to the subdirectory where you stored As Easy As, perhaps with:

```
CD \ASEASY
```

assuming that you have created a subdirectory called Aseasy and loaded the As Easy As programs into it.

If you have floppy disk drives only, put As Easy As in the A: drive. Then, whether you have hard or floppy disk, type:

```
ASEASY
```

Once the program has loaded you will see a title screen with the message:

```
[press any key to continue]
```

Do so and you will find yourself in a blank worksheet, with the cursor in cell A1.

5.2.2 Adding up the Figures

Type a heading like:

```
ADDING UP SOME BYTES
```

The message will spread across the top row of the spreadsheet. In fact it belongs to cell A1, but because the adjacent cells are empty it spreads over B1 and C1. If you had something in B1 you would only get the first nine letters of this title, the default value for the width of a spreadsheet column. You can change this width but the change takes place all the way down the column.

Use column C for putting in the figures and adding up. Leave a row below the title to make things look clearer. Move to cell C3 either by using two down and two right arrows or by keying <F5>, which means Go To, and then typing C3 followed by <Rn>.

You are now in cell C3. Put the first number in this cell:

```
123679
```

This doesn't appear in the cell itself just at the moment, but it is there in the top left hand corner beneath the cell reference, C3. You can enter it into the cell by pressing Return or using a cursor arrow key to move somewhere else. In this case use the latter by pressing <downarrow>.

The number 123679 has been entered and now appears in cell C3. At the same time you have moved to cell C4 where you are ready to make the next entry. Do this with:

```
32564
```

and then <downarrow>.

You are now in cell C5. Type:

```
5667
8990
1098
11113
```

each followed by a press of <downarrow>.

You are now in cell C9. Press <downarrow> once again, so that there is a spare row between the list of entries and the total, to make things look clearer.

To put the total in the current position, C10, you need the third kind of spreadsheet entry: a formula. This starts with a +, if you are using the individual cell references: +C3+C4+C5. You could use this for your adding up. However, it is much easier to use what is called a function, in this case SUM which acts on a complete range of cells. You start this with the @ sign which is found on the right hand side of the keyboard. You will probably need to use the shift button, although this depends on exactly what keyboard you have. Type:

```
@SUM(C3.C8)
```

What this means, is sum up all the figures in the cells running down the column from C3 through to C8, inclusive, that is, C3, C4, C5, C6, C7 and C8. The answer appears rapidly and quite magically in cell C10 when you press return.

You can do exactly the same thing using decimal numbers or money. You do, though, need to take one extra step first. To get all the numbers neatly lined up with the decimal point in the same place you need to carry out what is called a global format. This means that the spreadsheet will work to a fixed number of decimal places. We'll format for two decimal places.

5.2.3 Doing a Global Format

Start your worksheet by typing the following keys without pressing Return after each entry:

/

W for Worksheet

G for General

F for Format

F for Fixed

Now press <Rn> to accept:

```
[How many digits after the decimal(0.15) 2]
```

If you have in your addition, a number that doesn't have a decimal part, just type, say, 12 and the computer will automatically put it in as 12.00. Carry on as you did above, putting in the numbers and the formula for their sum.

5.2.4 Starting a New Worksheet

On this occasion, it is probably not worth saving your first spreadsheet. Generally, though, save your worksheet before you start a new blank one.

To start with a new, blank worksheet press the following keys in sequence:

```
/ W E Y
```

E is for Erase, Y for Yes.

5.3 Multiplication Tables

You can make a general spreadsheet which will allow you to print out some multiplication tables. What you do is to make a general outline spreadsheet, called a template. You save this, and then you can call it up and put a particular number in it.

In cell A1 in a clean new worksheet, type the heading:

TIMES TABLE SPREADSHEET

You are still in cell A1 even though the writing has spread into other cells.

Move to cell B3 by using the cursor arrow keys or using the function key <F5> for Goto followed by B3 and <Rn>. Then type:

WHAT TABLE DO YOU WANT?<downarrow>

Again this spills over into the next cells because they are empty. Because you used <downarrow> to enter this text (in spreadsheet terms, label) you are now in cell, B4. Type in:

ANSWER IN CELL E4

Move to cell B6. Type 1 and then <downarrow> to get into cell B7. Continue down the column, putting 2 in cell B8, 3 in cell B9, 4 in cell B10 and so on, down to 12 in cell B17.

Press function button <F5> followed by C6 and <Rn> to put yourself in cell C6. Type in:

times Press <Rn> to enter.

5.3.1 Copying Single Cells

You want the same word times in cells C7, C8 up to cell C17. To do this use the copy command. While in cell C6, press:

/ C

At the prompt [From C6.C6] press <Rn> because this is what you want to copy from.

The next prompt is [TO C6.C6]. In fact, you want to copy cell C6 into cells C7 to C17 inclusive. There are two ways of telling the computer this: you can either type:

C7.C17

or you can do it with the cursor keys. This method is very useful when you have a long line of cells that stretches beyond the bottom of the screen and you have forgotten the cell reference of the last one. If you use the cursor method move the cursor to C7 type . (period), move the cursor to C17 and press <Rn>.

The word times should now magically repeat itself all the way down the column.

Use the cursor keys or the function key <F5> for Go to to put yourself in cell E6. Type the label:

```
equals
```

Copy this all the way down the column, E7 to E17, just as you did for `times` in column C.

Now let's make the spreadsheet do some actual arithmetic. You want it to put B6 multiplied by D6 in column F6, B7 multiplied by D7 in column F7 and so on. Go to cell F6. This time you are going to type in a formula, so start with +:

```
+B6*D6
```

A * means multiply. At the moment you will get the answer 0 in cell F6. Don't worry, you have 0 in cell D6 so that is why you get an uninteresting result. When you do have something in that cell, the result will be much better. Now copy the formula down the rest of the column, F7 to F17, just as you did for the labels `times` and `equals`. When you have done that, move the cursor down the column, and notice the cell entry at the top left hand corner. The formula changes to match the cell you are in and this is just what you want.

5.3.2 Copying down a Fixed Cell

Funnily enough, in cell D6 down to D17, you want the same fixed number, the number you are going to put into cell E4. You want just that number or E4*1. The trouble is if you copy it down, the spreadsheet will adjust in the way it did in column F and change the number after the E. To avoid this you have to keep the E4 fixed by putting a $ in front of the E and in front of the 4. Go to cell D6 and type:

```
+$E$4*1
```

Copy this formula down through D7 to D17.

Your basic spreadsheet template is now almost ready.

5.3.3 Changing the Width of a Cell

You can improve it though by changing the width of some of the cells, so that it is better spaced. To change the width of column D, move to any cell in column D and type:

```
/ W C S
```

C stands for Change column and S for Set.

Enter 3 to make the column 3 wide. Press <Rn> to register

Move to column F and repeat the procedure to make the column 4 wide.

Your worksheet template is now ready for use.

5.3.4 Saving a Spreadsheet

Save the template with:

```
/ F S
```

F is for File and S for Store.

You are asked for the name. To save it on another drive than the current one, type the drive letter and a colon, then the file name. For example B:TABLES will save it as a file called TABLES on drive B:. As Easy As automatically puts on the extension .WKS for worksheet. Press <Rn> and it will be saved.

5.3.5 Retrieving a Worksheet

To load it up on another occasion, type:

```
/ F R
```

F stands for File and R for Retrieve.

You get a list of the worksheet files in the current directory. A blank name is highlighted. If you want to use a different directory, type it in at this point and press <Rn>. You will then get a new directory. Move the cursor keys until the file you want is highlighted, and press <Rn> to select. Once you have changed to another drive, As Easy As remembers it and always goes there to store and retrieve files, until you turn the computer off.

To make a table, all you have to do is to go to cell E4, with the cursor keys, or the function key <F5> and then type in your chosen number. The whole table will then magically appear.

An example of the completed spreadsheet is shown in Figure 5.1.

```
WHAT TABLE DO YOU WANT?
ANSWER IN CELL E4                    8

           1 times     8 equals      8
           2 times     8 equals     16
           3 times     8 equals     24
           4 times     8 equals     32
           5 times     8 equals     40
           6 times     8 equals     48
           7 times     8 equals     56
           8 times     8 equals     64
           9 times     8 equals     72
          10 times     8 equals     80
          11 times     8 equals     88
          12 times     8 equals     96
```

Figure 5.1: The completed spreadsheet showing the 8 times table

5.3.6 Printing your Spreadsheet

To print out your spreadsheet, you will need to work out the range of cells you have filled in and want printed out. A range starts with the cell reference of the top left hand corner and stops at the cell reference of the bottom right hand corner. A1 to H18 might be an example.

To print out the spreadsheet:

```
/ P P R
```

P stands for Print, P for Printer and then R for Range.

Type in the range you want printed out, or use the cursor keys to move to the start of the range, press . (period), and then move to the end of the range. Press <Rn>.

Finally type:

```
G for Go
```

5.4 Converting Centigrade to Fahrenheit

This obviously dates me a bit, but when it comes to weather temperatures, I have never really got to grips with Centigrade. To me the 80s (Fahrenheit) is a very hot day, the 50s more like typical English weather. This spreadsheet will convert any particular temperature you are interested in, and also provides a set table of corresponding temperatures so that you can get a general idea of the difference.

As usual, you start by setting up a general template or skeleton. This one is going to have a table at the bottom, with a row of sample Centigrade temperatures and a matching row of their Fahrenheit equivalents underneath. It also allows you to feed in a particular Centigrade temperature to produce the same temperature in Fahrenheit.

Load up As Easy As and get into a fresh worksheet. You should be in cell A1. Type the title:

```
SPREADSHEET FOR CONVERTING CENTIGRADE TO FAHRENHEIT
```

Enter the following labels in the cells indicated. How you get to those cells is entirely up to you:

CELL	CONTENTS
A2	YOUR CENTIGRADE TEMPERATURE
A4	GIVEN IN CELL E4
A6	IN FAHRENHEIT IS
A8	GENERAL TABLE

```
A10              CENTIGRADE
A12              FAHRENHEIT
```

The next thing to do is to put in the formula. This takes a Centigrade temperature and converts it to Fahrenheit. Press function key <F5> and E6 to go to cell E6. Type in the formula:

```
+1.8*E4+32
```

Enter the following in the cells indicated:

CELL	CONTENTS
C10	-0
D10	5
E10	15
F10	20
G10	25
H10	30

Go to C12 to put in the formula to convert the quantities you put into the table. Type:

```
+1.8*C10+32<Rn>
```

Copy this formula across cells D12 to H12 by pressing:

```
/ C
```

Press <Rn> for the prompt [Copy cells FROM C12..C12] then enter:

```
D12.H12
```

You now have the basic template or skeleton. This time improve its appearance by putting in some lines around the general table.

Go to cell A7. Type:

```
\-
```

Notice that you use the slash on the left hand side of the keyboard (the one that MS-DOS uses for its path commands). Press Return. This produces a spread of little hyphens filling the whole cell. Copy this along A9 to H9 by using exactly the same copy procedure as you used for the formula. You now have a whole line of hyphens, making a line all across the page.

5.4.1 Copying a Range of Cells

Next copy this whole line from A7 to H7, to A9 to H9. To do this use a slightly different copy procedure because you want to copy a range rather than a single cell.

Press:

/ R C V

V stands for value. Type:

A7.H7

and in response to [Output range is] enter:

A9.H9

Repeat this process to copy the line A7.H7 to A11.H11.

The template is now complete and an example is shown in Figure 5.2. Store it as CENTGRAD. When you load it up the table is automatically there with all the conversions. Use function key <F5> to move to cell E4 and type in the number for which you want the conversion. Type in another number, and the old one will be overwritten.

```
SPREADSHEET FOR CONVERTING CENTIGRADE TO FARENHHEIT

YOUR CENTIGRADE TEMPERATURE
GIVE IN CELL E4                         1

IN FARENHEIT                          33.8
-------------------------------------------------------------------------
GENERAL TABLE
-------------------------------------------------------------------------
CENTIGRADE           -5        5       15       20       25       30
-------------------------------------------------------------------------
FARENHEIT            23       41       59       68       77       86
-------------------------------------------------------------------------
```

Figure 5.2: Converting from Centigrade to Farenheit

5.5 Recipes for Different Numbers of People

Most recipes give the amounts for four people. What do you do when you are cooking for one or for six? You can use a spreadsheet to give you the quantities you need for different numbers. I have assumed that four is the standard in your recipe books- if it isn't, you need to set out the formulae differently.

What you are going to do is to set up a template or general skeleton spreadsheet. You can then use it for individual recipes, typing in the amounts, the ingredients and the standard quantities for four people. Of course, in cookery, there are some things that cannot easily be divided, like a single shallot, and you will have to use your discretion over these!

So to set up the template, load up As Easy As to start a fresh spreadsheet. You should be in cell A1. Type:

```
SPREADSHEET FOR RECIPE AMOUNTS
```

Now enter the following information into the cells indicated:

```
CELL              CONTENTS

A3                RECIPE IS
A4                TITLE IN C3
A6                INGREDIENT
C6                '1 PERSON
```

You must put the single quote mark in front of the 1 PERSON. Because this entry begins with a 1, the computer thinks that it is about to receive numbers on which it can perform calculations and if it gets anything else, like letters, it will ignore them. Putting a single quote (or double quote or hat) at the beginning leads it to expect a label or text and to treat numbers in this way. Carry on typing:

```
CELL              CONTENTS

D6                '2 PEOPLE
E6                '3 PEOPLE
F6                '4 PEOPLE
G6                '5 PEOPLE
H6                '6 PEOPLE
```

The next thing to do is set up the formulae. Go to cell C8. You can move there with the cursor keys, or by pressing the function key <F5> and then typing C8. When you use the spreadsheet you will be inserting the recipe quantities into column F which is for four people. Column C, being for one person, will need one quarter of this, or in decimal terms 0.25. So in C8, type the formula:

```
+F8*0.25
```

Remember that you need to start the entry with a + for the computer to register that it is going to get a formula. The computer uses the asterisk sign, *, as its symbol for multiply.

Then copy the cell down the next 10 rows. If you use recipes that have more than 10 ingredients you might want to make this longer. To copy it down, press:

```
/ C
```

and press <Rn> in answer to prompt [Copy cells from C8.C8]

You now get the prompt [Copy cells to C8]. You don't want to copy it on to itself. There are two ways of telling it where to copy to. You can type:

```
C9.C18
```

or you can do it with the cursor by moving it to the start of the range you want to copy to, in this case C9. Type . (period) and move the cursor down the column to C18, then press <Rn>.

You should still be in cell C8, whatever method you used. Press <Rightarrow> along to cell D8. Put in the formula:

```
+F8*0.5
```

Copy this down D9 to D18 as you did above for the C column.

Go to cell E8 and put in the formula:

```
+F8*0.75
```

Again copy it down. The formulae for cells G8 and H8 are +F8*1.25 and +F8*1.5 respectively.

You have now set up the basic recipe template. Save it as RECIPES by pressing:

```
/ F S
```

and type the filename RECIPES.

When you want to use the recipes spreadsheet, load it up with:

```
/ F R
```

Cursor along to RECIPES, then press <Rn>.

If you have a dual floppy drive, before you move the cursor along, type:

```
B:
```

You will then be shown the files on your data disk in drive B: and all loading and saving will be on drive B: during your particular computer session.

To run the spreadsheet press the function key <F5> C3. Type in the title of your recipe.

Then go to cell A8 and type in the first ingredient. Enter it by using the <downarrow> to take you to cell A9. Type in the second ingredient and enter it with <downarrow> and so on.

Then move to cell F8 and put in the quantity that goes with the ingredient name on that line. Enter it with <downarrow> so that you move to F9. Put in the next number and so on. The formulae you put in the other cells causes all the other quantities to appear automatically.

An example of the finished spreadsheet is shown in Figure 5.3.

```
SPREADSHEET FOR RECIPE AMOUNTS

RECIPE IS         MACARONI CARBONARA
TITLE IN C3

INGREDIENT       1 PERSON 2 PEOPLE 3 PEOPLE 4 PEOPLE 5 PEOPLE 6 PEOPLE

MACARONI           56.25    112.5   168.75      225   281.25    337.5
BACON                 25       50       75      100      125      150
EGGS                   1        2        3        4        5        6
PARMESAN            12.5       25     37.5       50     62.5       75
                       0        0        0                 0        0
                       0        0        0                 0        0
                       0        0        0                 0        0
                       0        0        0                 0        0
                       0        0        0                 0        0
                       0        0        0                 0        0
```

Figure 5.3: Macaroni Carbonara for one to six persons

5.6 Making a Pie Chart

You can use As Easy As to draw charts and graphs. Let's start off with a pie chart. Remember those dreadful school exercises of calculating the angles and then messing round with a protractor. With a spreadsheet you just put in the numbers and it does all the rest for you.

You can use part of an existing spreadsheet, for example the categories of expenditure on food, stationery, chemist and clothing in the final sorted household expenditure spreadsheet given in Section 5.9 or you can set up a new one specially for the pie chart. You could use As Easy As to design a form for people to fill in, like the one in Section 5.10. Then collect some information from the returned questionnaires and put it into a spreadsheet, ready to make a pie chart.

For a pie chart you need some labels and some figures to go with them. For example, in our Saturday morning computer class, six people had an Amiga, three had an Atari, four had a PC, two had Sinclair Spectrums, one had a BBC, one an Archimedes and three hadn't got anything yet. We can use this information to produce a simple pie chart.

Load up As Easy As and get a fresh worksheet. Enter the heading:

```
COMPUTERS OWNED BY OUR CLASS
```

in cell A1 and the following in the cells indicated:

CELL	CONTENTS
A3	TYPE OF COMPUTER
C3	NUMBER OF PEOPLE
A5	AMIGA
A6	ATARI
A7	PC
A8	SPECTRUM
A9	BBC
A10	ARCHIMEDES
A11	NONE
C5	6
C6	3
C7	4
C8	2
C9	1
C10	1
C11	3

You have now created the basic spreadsheet that contains the figures and labels for the pie chart. To actually make the chart, type:

```
/ G T P X
```

G stands for Graphics, T for Type, P for Pie. The labels, or words, go into the X range. These are written out in column, A, from A5 to A11. To register this with the computer, type:

```
A5.A11
```

The actual figures go into graphics range A. Select this with A to select A range and C5.C11 the column where the figures are actually stored.

It is worth putting some headings on to the pie chart. To do this, from the graphics menu, type:

```
O T F
```

O stands for Options, T for Titles and F for First. Go on with:

```
COMPUTERS OWNED BY OUR CLASS <Rn>
```

Enter S for Second which is a second line of title below the first, then:
```
AUTUMN 1991
```

You can then take a look at the pie chart. You may want to go on to print it but it is always a good idea to take a look first. Computer graphics are so powerful that you can often end up with some rather funny results you didn't plan, so glance at it before you get going on your printer. <Esc> twice to get back to graphics menu, then just type V and your pie chart should then appear on the screen - Figure 5.4.

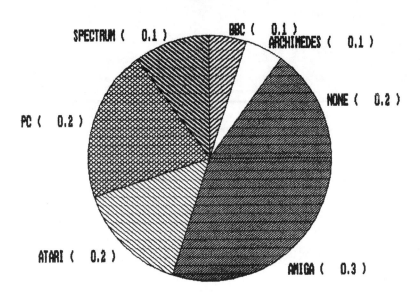

COMPUTERS OWNED BY OUR CLASS
AUTUMN 1991

SPECTRUM (0.1)   BBC (0.1)   ARCHIMEDES (0.1)

NONE (0.2)

PC (0.2)

ATARI (0.2)   AMIGA (0.3)

Figure 5.4: Viewing the completed pie chart

Older versions of As Easy As did not provide for print outs, but the latest version now has this facility. However it is limited to quite a small range of printers. You must have a graphics facility to do anything like this anyway, but unfortunately for As Easy As, you need a certain kind of graphics printer. Most modern printers have some choice of compatibility, or some standard type of printer they will emulate. You will need to consult the printer manual to find what these are, and you may have to set some kind of switch on the printer itself. As Easy As has four printer options: Pic, 9 pin Epson FX, 24 pin LQ Epson and HP Laserjet. To select one of these, from the graphics menu type P for Plot, then H for Hardware and then move the cursor to your choice.

PIC is a graphics file stored on disk, which will not result in a direct printout although you might be able to feed it into some other package and print it out from there. The other three descriptions are rather vague as there are specific laser and even Epson 24 pin printers. You will probably have to try them in turn and see whether any of them will work with your printer. My small Canon bubblejet worked on the 9 pin Epson, which is not exactly what I expected, but there you are. Other options produced one line of black overprinted machine code. Once you have found which one suits your printer you will have no further problems.

To print out the pie chart, type:

```
P G
```

P stands for Plot and G for Go.

5.7 Credit Card Repayments

As Easy As has some interesting financial functions, just like Lotus 1-2-3. One of these is @PMT. You put in the amount of a loan you have got to pay off, the interest rate and the time period over which you want to pay the loan back. It then works out how much you must pay in each time period. You can use this to plan how to pay off credit cards - a calculation that can be unpleasantly revealing. It won't allow for changing interest rates and if these do change, you will need to change the formula that carries out the calculations. It doesn't matter what time periods you use, either years, months or days but you must be consistent over all three things you feed into the function. For credit cards, monthly is ideal because you pay every month, and the interest rate is given somewhere on the statement on a monthly basis.

This spreadsheet is set up for two loans, Barclaycard and Access, but you could easily take one away or add some more. Follow the usual pattern of making a skeleton or template. Save this. Later on load it up and put in the relevant figures. You can save it with figures in as well, a bit like a blank form and a filled in one.

The skeleton has some headings and explanations written in. You put the Barclaycard and Access loan amounts in cells E4 and E9 respectively. The corresponding monthly interest rates go in cells E5 and E10. You then show how much you would pay each month to get the whole loan paid off in 6, 12, 18, 24 and 36 months.

Load up a new worksheet and in the A1 cell, type:

```
PAYING OFF CREDIT CARD LOANS
```

Enter the remaining information in the cells shown:

CELL	CONTENTS
A3	WHAT IS YOUR BARCLAYCARD LOAN
A4	ANSWER IN CELL E4
A5	MONTHLY INTEREST RATE IN E5
A7	WHAT IS YOUR ACCESS LOAN
A8	ANSWER IN CELL E8
A9	MONTHLY INTEREST RATE

A12	PAY OFF IN
C12	6
D12	12
E12	18
F12	24
G12	36
H12	MONTHS

Now you are going to put the formulae in. Use function key <F5> to go to cell C14 then enter:

@PMT(E4,E5,C12)

There must not be any spaces in the formula. Put all the dollar signs in before the column and row references, E, 4 and 5, because you want to copy the formula across the other cells in the same row, but you want the one cell where the loan amount (E4) and the one cell where the interest rate is (E5) to remain constant across all the cells. You want the number of months to vary so cell reference C12 does not have dollar signs. You will get an error message in cell C14 because at the moment there are no figures to work on.

The next step is to copy this formula across all the cells from B14 to G14. There is no heading in column B at the moment, but you are going to use that cell to put in your own choice of months so you will want the formula there as well. To copy across that row, enter:

/ C

to agree with [copy from C14..C14] and:

B14.G14

for the [copy TO]

Go to cell C16, two rows down and put in the formula for the Access card with:

@PMT(E8,E9,C12)

Copy across to cells B16.G16 as you did before.

Now, as you are going to put in figures, you need to think how the computer wants to set them out or format them, to use its own terminology. Apart from the interest rates, they all involve money. The easiest way to deal with this is to treat it as a general figure to two decimal places. Cells E7 and E9 contain interest rates, which are usually expressed as percentages. These can be formatted for percentages. Because most of the numbers are money, do a two decimal point GLOBAL format and then just format the two individual cells, E5 and E9 for percentages. A global format applies to the whole spreadsheet, unless you change it for specific cells. To do the global format first:

```
/ W G F F
```

then press <Rn> to accept [How many digits after the decimal(0.15) 2]

To do the percentage format on cell E5 and E9, use the function key, <F5> to go to cell E5. Then press:

```
/ R F P
```

P stands for Percentage.

Enter 3 to get 3 digits after the decimal point and press <Rn> to accept [Format range is E5.E5]

Repeat the procedure to do a percentage format on cell E9. The percentage format does NOT allow you to just key in the percent, say 1.85 or 2. You have to key these in as full decimals, 1.85 is 0.0185 and 2 per cent 0.02. All that the percentage format does is to then write it out as 1.85% or 2%. It won't do a wonderful mathematical conversion for you.

Because we started by globally formatting the whole worksheet to two decimal places, one further problem remains: the cells containing the months will also produce numbers with two decimal places. We can get round this by formatting the range of cells in row 12 containing the months, using:

```
/ R F F
```

Put in 0 when prompted for decimal points to ensure we get whole numbers the range C12. G12.

You might want to add up the monthly instalments so that you can see exactly how much you can pay altogether. To do this, go to cell C18 and type the formula:

```
+C14+C16
```

Don't forget to start with a + to alert the computer to the fact that you are going to be putting in a formula, and just use cell references rather than the @SUM function. Copy the formula through to C18.G18 and put the heading TOTAL in A18. You could then go on to multiply the monthly amounts by the different numbers of months for pay back. The answer can be an unpleasant surprise. No wonder the credit card companies make such good profits!

Your template is now complete, and you can save it, perhaps with the title, CREDCARD.

When you want to put in an entry, press the function key <F5> to go to cell E4. Type in the Barclaycard loan amount. Press <downarrow> to enter it and to move down to cell E5. Type in the interest rate, say 0.0185 or 0.02 for 1.85 or 2 per cent. <downarrow> three times to enter it and move to cell E8 and type in the appropriate loan amounts and interest rates for the Access loan. There should now be figures all across the table at the bottom as shown in Figure 5.5. If you want to try a different number of months, go to cell B12 and put in your chosen number.

```
PAYING OFF CREDIT CARD LOANS

WHAT IS YOUR BARCLAYCARD LOAN?
ANSWER IN CELL E4                        2001.74
MONTHLY INTEREST RATE IN E5                 1.850%

WHAT IS YOUR ACCESS LOAN
ANSWER IN CELL E8                         573.32
MONTHLY INTEREST RATE IN E9                 2.000%


PAY OFF IN              6        12        18        24        36 MONTHS

                   355.56    187.54    131.77    104.04     76.65

                   102.35     54.21     38.24     30.31     22.49
```

Figure 5.5: Loan repayment calculations

5.8 Testing Foreign Language Vocabulary

You can use a spreadsheet to learn and test foreign language vocabulary. Umlauts and accents present some problems so be prepared to ignore these. As for ancient Greek, forget it! You learn your vocabulary by typing in the foreign words, together with their answers. You can then make the answers disappear off the screen, type in what should be the answer, and compare it with the hidden answer using a useful little text function, called @EXACT. Things do have to be exactly the same, though, including upper or lower case letters, so keep the caps lock on. It will not allow for another word which means the same. However when you are doing language learning, you tend to have one version written down, so for your own use, this is not such a problem.

Start a new worksheet. In cell A1 type the title:

TESTING GERMAN VOCABULARY

For French and German, you not only have to remember the word but also the case as well. In French it can be masculine or feminine, Le or La. In German it can be neuter as well, so that the choices are Der, Die or Das. Put the articles in the A column, the actual German word in column B and the English equivalent in column C. Each column comes with a default width of 9, which will not be large enough for the foreign word and its equivalent so it is worth changing. The article (der, die or das or le or la) is only two or three letters but you also need a space between the article and the word in the next column. Words get left justified or positioned on the left side of the column. Change column A to 4 wide, columns B and C to 15. To change the width of column A, go to any cell in that column and press:

```
/ W C S
```

then the number you want, in this case 4 and then press <Rn>

Repeat the process to make columns B and C 15 wide. Then you can start putting in your vocabulary.

Enter:

DAS in cell A3, GIFT in cell B3 and POISON in cell C3

```
 F1:Help 2:Edit 3:Macro 4:Abs | READY! | 5:Goto 6:Window 7:Wp 9:Calc F10:Graph
 A:F2: @SUM(A:F3..A:F50)

[ A ]...A/.............B/.............C/.......D/.......E/.......F/.......G/.
  1|TESTING GERMAN VOCABULARY
  2|                                                            0          0
  3|DAS GIFT            POISON                                  0          0
  4|DIE FAMILIE         FAMILY                                 0          0
  5|DAS KIND            CHILD                                  0          0
  6|DIE STADT           TOWN                                   0          0
  7|DIE ECKE            CORNER                                 0          0
  8|DER DOM             CATHEDRAL                              0          0
  9|
 10|
 11|
 12|
 13|
 14|
 15|
 16|
 17|
 18|
 19|
 20|
    Free: 99% [338k]    Auto |              |      .  Num Cap   .   6:30:36 pm
```

Figure 5.6: Entering the vocabulary

This is an example, with German vocabulary, but you can use any words you want. Go to cell A4 and put in the next article, German noun and English equivalent across the row. Carry on down the columns until you have put in all the vocabulary you want as in Figure 5.6. You might want to print the worksheet out in its current form so you have a copy to take round with you and learn.

We now need to hide the German words away out of sight, over to the right so that you are left with just the English in column C. To carry out your test you write the German article in column D and the noun in column E. The computer will compare these with the hidden answers. To do this, go to cell F3 and type in the function:

```
@EXACT(A3,D3)
```

Copy this down the F column, for as many cells as you are likely to have words. If you are a hard worker, it could be as many as 50. You should still be in cell F3.

Go to cell G3 and enter:

```
@EXACT(B3,E3)
```

Again copy this down the column, G.

What @EXACT does it to make an *exact* comparison of the two cells you put in the bracket. This means that if you have anything different, it will not regard the match as exact. Any extra spaces or punctuation marks, slightly different spelling or difference in use of capital letters (what we call being case sensitive) will result in the answer 0 or *not exact*. If the match is correct it gives out the answer as the number 1. This is rather useful because you can add up the answers and this will give you the number of correct entries you have made. To do this, go to cell F2 and type:

```
@SUM(F3.F50)
```

This example uses F50, but you can put in the last cell in your row of vocabulary. Copy this formula across to cell G2.

You might wish to save the worksheet at this point.

When you want to test yourself, remove the German answers by moving a whole range of cells (columns A and B) away over to the right, to, say, columns M and N. To move the whole range type:

```
/  M
```

and enter A3.B50 in answer to [move cells from] and reply M3.N50 in response to [move cells to].

The two columns disappear out of sight, but are still there as you can see if you move over to the right. You can now test yourself by putting the article in column D and the word in column E. Do not forget to use upper case throughout if that is what you used for the original entries. Your count of correct answers should build up in cells

F2 and G2 as you go through typing in correct entries. The finished spreadsheet with hidden cells is shown in Figure 5.7.

```
TESTING GERMAN VOCABULARY
                                                    3          4
            POISON      DIE     GIFT                0          1
            FAMILY      DIE     FAMILIE             1          1
            CHILD       DAS     KIND                1          1
            TOWN        DER     DOM                 0          0
            CORNER      DER     ECKE                0          1
            CATHEDRAL   DER     STADT               1          0
```

Figure 5.7: Testing German vocabulary

5.9 Sorting out Household Expenses

As Easy As has good sorting facilities which you can use to monitor your household expenses. Try as I might, I never manage to keep an up to the minute account of the state of my current account, for any length of time. The way round this is to write the amount of cheque payments in the front of my cheque book. Whenever I pay by Switch, I tuck the receipt into my wallet. Once a fortnight or once a month, I take these out and put them on to my expenses spreadsheet. It doesn't matter whether I do cheques or Switch first or which receipts I take out. As Easy As will sort them into date order for me.

As usual you start with a template or skeleton. You can then fill this in every month and save it with a new name.

Open a new worksheet. In cell A1 type:

CHEQUE AND SWITCH EXPENDITURE FOR SEPTEMBER 1991

Enter DATE in A3 and SHOP in B3

Shops generally have names that are longer than nine characters, so widen column B to 20. To do this enter:

/ W C S 20

Then enter: CODE in C3 and AMOUNT in D3

This worksheet has two kinds of numbers: dates and money. These will both need formatting. There are several choices of date formats so choose the one you like - the one here is day, month in writing and then year. For money, do a general two decimal fixed format - if you do the currency format you get dollars put in everywhere. To format for dates use:

```
/ R F D
```

and press <Rn> to select date type 1

You then get a prompt saying [Range is D3.D3]. At this point, type in the range you want to format, in this case:

```
A4.A50
```

Then do the currency format with:

```
/ R F F
```

press <Rn> for two decimal places and enter D4.D50 for the range.

You will need to widen the column to 10 to take the date entry. Unfortunately putting in dates is a bit awkward. As Easy As (and Lotus 1-2-3) like dates in the form of number of days from the 1st January 1900. Fortunately, you don't actually have to calculate this yourself but you do need to put the date in a function. This returns the number of days from the turn of the century, but since you have set a date format, the date will be written in that way. To put in the first entry, move to cell A4 and put in the date function:

```
@DATE(92,1,11)
```

or whatever the date happens to be.

You must put the last two digits of the year first, followed by a comma, then the month number and a comma, and the day number. Obviously you don't want to type out this function every time you put in a date, so copy this down column A. To do this enter:

```
/ C
```

and press <Rn> to register you want to copy from cell A3.

You then get the prompt [Copy cell to A3.A3]. In fact, you want to copy it to A4 to A50. To do this, type:

```
A4.A50
```

You now have the first entry date all the way down the column. To put in a new date, if it is different from this, press function key F2 to edit the date function. Move the left arrow key until it is on the day number you want to change. Use the usual editing keys to overwrite, delete or insert extra numbers. Press <Rn> when you have finished to register the change.

Your skeleton or template is now complete and can be saved with a title like SPENDSKEL.

To start making entries, restore it to the screen and start filling it in. Move to cell B4 to put in the first shop name, say SAINSBURYS, <rightarrow> to enter this and move to cell C4. This is where the expenditure codes go and you will need to choose codes that suit your own spending patterns and the way you want these broken up. I use C for Children, CL for clothes for me, S for Stationery, B for Books, CH for the Chemist, F for Food and FH for Healthfoods. Write the code down on an index card or in your diary, so that you know what they all mean a month or so later.

CHEQUE AND SWITCH EXPENDITURE FOR SEPTEMBER 1991

DATE	SHOP	CODE	AMOUNT
11-Sep-91	SAINSBURYS	F	27.19
09-Sep-91	GAP	C	17.99
05-Sep-91	SAINSBURYS	F	23.45
25-Sep-91	WATERSTONES	B	11.99
15-Sep-91	SAINSBURYS	F	17.95
12-Sep-91	BOOTS	CH	27.99
22-Sep-91	SAINSBURYS	F	19.42
01-Sep-91	BOOTS	CH	9.89
03-Sep-91	MARKS & SPENCERS	F	12.78
11-Sep-91	DEBENHAMS	CH	3.99
16-Sep-91	SAINSBURYS	F	21.34

Figure 5.8: Expenditure for September - initial entries

Finally in cell D4 put in the amount, which should neatly format itself into two decimal places, even if you put in a whole number and nothing else.

Do all the rest of your entries. If you are taking slips of paper out of your wallet and then going through your cheque book after that, it is most unlikely that they will be in date order. The end result will be something like Figure 5.8.

The next thing to do is to sort them, so that they are in date order. In case you don't get the sort quite right, save the raw data first. To do this enter:

/ F S

then SPENDSEP as a file name - SEP is the month. Do whatever is appropriate for your expenses.

After that, you are ready to do the sort. Enter:

/ D S

then press <Rn> for D-Range.

Put in A4.D24 to select the range to sort, the whole spreadsheet, not just the column that you are sorting on. This one stopped at 24, because that was the last entry on this particular spreadsheet. You just put in the cells where you have data, below the titles. Everything in the range will get sorted, blanks included. Make sure you leave out titles and blank lines and totals or you will get some funny results.

CHEQUE AND SWITCH EXPENDITURE FOR SEPTEMBER 1991

DATE	SHOP	CODE	AMOUNT
01-Sep-91	BOOTS	CH	9.89
03-Sep-91	MARKS & SPENCERS	F	12.78
05-Sep-91	SAINSBURYS	F	23.45
09-Sep-91	GAP	C	17.99
11-Sep-91	SAINSBURYS	F	27.19
11-Sep-91	DEBENHAMS	CH	3.99
12-Sep-91	BOOTS	CH	27.99
15-Sep-91	SAINSBURYS	F	17.95
16-Sep-91	SAINSBURYS	F	21.34
22-Sep-91	SAINSBURYS	F	19.42
25-Sep-91	WATERSTONES	B	11.99

Figure 5.9: Expenditure for September sorted into date order

Enter P for Prime key then A4.A24 for the date column you want to sort on. You then get a prompt of [Ascending or Descending] with a default value of A. Press <Rn> to accept Ascending and then G for GO.

Your spreadsheet should now appear in date order as shown in Figure 5.9. You can use this to do a reconciliation against your bank statement. Put in an @SUM function at the bottom of column D to get your total expenditure. This appears almost instantly and can be unpleasantly revealing.

Save this as say DSPNDSEP. The D in front shows that it is sorted by Date Order.

You can then go on to do another sort by category. Do this in exactly the same way but make the P for Prime key C3.C24 (or anything with C in it instead). You can save this as say CSPNDSEP, for sorted by category.

5.10 Making Forms with a Spreadsheet

You don't have to have arithmetic or maths in your spreadsheet at all. The spreadsheet provides a grid of columns that can be used to line up written information. It is ideal for any tabular material, like sports results, but you can also use it for making forms, where you want to do a certain amount of lining up.

The example given here is a form that children fill in when they come to their first workshop. The instructions seem quite complicated when you see them written down, but are much simpler when you are actually whizzing round a screen. Start up a fresh worksheet and enter the following information:

COMPUTER WORKSHOP FORM in cell D1, SURNAME in cell A3 and CHRISTIAN NAME in cell D3.

This puts in the text for the first two questions on the form: SURNAME and CHRISTIAN NAME. After that, it goes down a row and goes to the right of where the writing stops. Since writing spills into the next cell if it is more than nine characters long, this might actually be two cells to the right of where the writing started. The next step is to fill one or two cells with dashes. Since these are one row below the writing they provide a line to guide where the user will put his or her answer. You fill two or even three cells if a longer answer is expected. Cell B4 is where the first of these starts. To fill it with dashes all the way across, all you have to type is move to cell B4 and enter:

\-

The slash is the one you use for MS-DOS subdirectories on the left hand side of your keyboard. Press <Rn>. Move to C4 and repeat, then do F4 and G4.

The next row of questions is made in exactly the same way. Use function key <F5> to go to cell A6 and enter DATE OF BIRTH and key AGE into cell D6. AGE and DATE OF BIRTH only needed one cell of dashes in C7 and E7 <Rn>.

After that move to cell A9, and the enter:

WHAT DAY DO YOU COME (CIRCLE THE CORRECT ONE) TUES SAT

This spills right across the spreadsheet. Text only spills over in this way if you do not fill the cells it happens to cover. If you do put something in these cells, the spreadsheet will save all the text but it will only actually display enough to fit the original cell, that is generally only nine characters, and at that point it will just cut it off, however nonsensical the result may be.

The next entry is in cell A11, leaving one empty row as a gap between the questions. Here you put:

```
DO YOU HAVE A COMPUTER AT HOME?
```

There is the usual dash line in the row beneath it. The next question is:

```
WHAT MAKE IS IT?
```

Because people often feel a bit bewildered when they first come to a workshop and can't remember what it is they have got, there is a little reminding prompt in cell A16 of:

```
Some makes are BBC, Amiga, Atari, PC, Spectrum
```

The next bit of the form goes on to give people some more answers to ring. These are either Yes or No for four computer activities. Enter the following in the cells shown:

CELL	CONTENTS
B18	HAVE YOU DONE THE FOLLOWING
B20	WORDPROCESSING
B22	LOGO PROGRAMMING
B24	BASIC PROGRAMMING
B26	GAMES

You then need to go to a cell over to the right of where the longest piece of text spills over, in this situation E20. In here, you put:

```
Yes No
```

and in cell G20:

```
Ring choice.
```

The row beneath this entry is blank to space out the entries and make them look better. The next step is to copy the whole range of six cells, from E20 in the top left hand corner to G21 in the bottom right hand corner, on to the range, E22 to G23. To do this, you use the Range Copy command:

```
/ R C
```

and press <Rn> for Value.

At the prompt [Value range is G20.G20] type in the copy from range:

```
E20.G21<Rn>
```

The next prompt is [Output range is G20]. All you need to do here is to put in the cell entry of the top left hand corner of the copy to range, in this case E22, so type:

```
E22 <Rn>
```

and the two bits of text will magically copy down to the two rows below.

You can now copy the four row range, E20 to G23 down to E24 to G27, using exactly the same procedure.

The rest of the form uses all the techniques that have been given above.

IF YOU PLAY GAMES etc goes in cell A30

YOUR ADDRESS goes in cell A48

PHONE NUMBER? goes in cell A53

Dashed lines go in cells D33, E33, F33, D36 to F36, D39 to F39, D42 to F42, D45 to F45 and also in C49 to F49 and C54 to D54. The numbers for the games go in cells C32, C35, C38, C41 and C44.

Be careful when you type in these numbers. If you type just 1., the computer will treat the . as a decimal point and will expect something after it. Start it with the double quotes mark, '', so that it gets treated as text.

The finished form is shown in Figure 5.10. Save it so that you can use it on a future occasion.

To print it out, the worksheet runs from A1 to G55. It is possible that your version is a bit different because it is quite easy to miss rows as you set it up. Enter:

```
/ P  P  R
```

and at the prompt [Range to print], type in:

```
A1.G55 <Rn>
G
```

5.11 Time Manager Spreadsheet

You can use your spreadsheet for a Time Manager. You put in the tasks you have got to do, the date by which you have to complete them, and the kind of priority they need. You could also put in the type of activity - it is no good phoning someone up in the middle of the night, whereas you might get your letters written at this time. You

                            COMPUTER WORKSHOP FORM

SURNAME   CHRISTIAN NAME
          ------------------   ------------------

DATE OF BIRTH   AGE
                 ---------   ---------

WHAT DAY DO YOU COME (CIRCLE THE CORRECT ONE) TUES SAT

DO YOU HAVE A COMPUTER AT HOME?

WHAT MAKE IS IT?

Some makes are BBC, Amiga, Atari, PC, Spectrum

          HAVE YOU DONE THE FOLLOWING

          WORDPROCESSING   Yes No   Ring Choice

          LOGO PROGRAMMING   Yes No   Ring Choice

          BASIC PROGRAMMING   Yes No   Ring Choice

          GAMES   Yes No   Ring Choice

IF YOU PLAY GAMES, WHAT ARE YOUR 5 FAVOURITE GAMES?

                    1. ---------------------------

                    2. ---------------------------

                    3. ---------------------------

                    4. ---------------------------

                    5. ---------------------------

YOUR ADDRESS?

PHONE NUMBER?

Figure 5.10: Using a spreadsheet to produce a form

can just put the events in as they occur to you and get the spreadsheet to sort them out into date and priority order. You might say that some things have no end date and put these activities into a type of their own. For simplicity, you could also give them a quite distant end date, like one or two months ahead.

Start a new worksheet in the usual way, and in cell A1, put in the heading:

```
TIME MANAGEMENT SPREADSHEET
```

Starting at A3 put in the column headings in the cells indicated:

CELL	CONTENTS
A3	ACTIVITY
B3	TYPE
C3	PRIORITY
D3	DATE

You need to widen the date column to 10 to accept the date format using:

```
/ W C S
```

At the prompt [Enter column width 1.72] enter 10. You will need to format the date and also widen the activity column in the same way as the column width:

```
/ R F D
```

then 1 for D-M-Y.

You are then prompted for the range you want to format. In case you have a lot of activities you have got to do, it is worth formatting quite a long way down, so type in:

```
D5.D50
```

You will still be in cell D3.

In cell D5 type in the date function:

```
@DATE(91,9,18)<Rn>
```

adjusting the figures for whatever date it happens to be. It should come up on the screen as a proper date. You don't want to type this formula in every time you put in an entry, so it is better to copy it all down the column and edit it when you want to put in a different date.

To copy it all the way down the column, use:

```
/ C
```

and at the prompt [FROM D5.D5] press <Rn> to accept.

At the next prompt [Copycell to D5.D5] type in:

D6.D50

The date copies all the way down the column. To put in a different date, type the function key <F2> for edit, change the numbers, and press <Rn> to enter. You can't use the cursor keys to enter and move away.

```
TIME MANAGEMENT SPREADSHEET

ACTIVITY              TYPE      PRIORITY DATE

PHONE AMY BAKER        T         A        18-Sep-91
WRITE BANK             W         B        25-Sep-91
WRITE AUNT             W         C        18-Oct-91
BUY PRESENT            SH        C        25-Dec-91
NEW JOB                P         C        01-Jan-92
RING SALLY             T         A        17-Sep-91
SCHOOL TROUSERS        SH        A        08-Sep-91
PAINT LOUNGE           P         B        01-Nov-91
WRITE PAPER            W         A        22-Sep-91
ORDER SHAREWARE        T         B        14-Sep-91
CANCEL MILK            T         B        15-Sep-91
BOOK HAIRDO            T         C        10-Sep-91
```

Figure 5.11: Initial entries in the Time Manager

You have now completed the skeleton worksheet. Save it and then you can start putting in some entries as Figure 5.11. Then you can sort it out, into date order, by priority. The letters A, B and C are used for priority, with A being the most urgent. The primary sort key is date, the secondary key is priority. You could sort it the other way round if you want, first by priority and then by date. To sort enter:

/ D S

then press <Rn> for D Range.

You then put in the range you want to sort. Be careful to put in all the columns that go together and to only put in the rows containing information. If you put in titles and blanks, they will be sorted too and that may look a bit funny. For my example, the filled in range is:

A5.D24

then press:

P for P1-key. Make sure you are in the D column and press <Rn> to accept

<Rn> to accept A for Ascending

S for S(2)-key for second

C5 or any cell in the C column, the column to sort on

<Rn> to accept A for Ascending

G for Go.

The sort should magically occur. You can see the results in Figure 5.12.

You print it out with:

```
/ P P R
A1.D24>
G
```

```
  F1:Help 2:Edit 3:Macro 4:Abs | READY! | 5:Goto 6:Window 7:Wp 9:Calc F10:Graph
 A:B18:
[  A ]..................A/.......B/.......C/........D/.......E/.......F/.....
   1│TIME MANAGEMENT SPREADSHEET
   2│
   3│ACTIVITY              TYPE      PRIORITY DATE
   4│
   5│SCHOOL TROUSERS       SH        A        08-Sep-91
   6│BOOK HAIRDO           T         C        10-Sep-91
   7│ORDER SHAREWARE       T         B        14-Sep-91
   8│CANCEL MILK           T         B        15-Sep-91
   9│RING SALLY            T         A        17-Sep-91
  10│PHONE AMY BAKER       T         A        18-Sep-91
  11│WRITE PAPER           W         A        22-Sep-91
  12│WRITE BANK            W         B        25-Sep-91
  13│WRITE AUNT            W         C        18-Oct-91
  14│PAINT LOUNGE          P         B        01-Nov-91
  15│BUY PRESENT           SH        C        25-Dec-91
  16│NEW JOB               P         C        01-Jan-92
  17│                                         18-Sep-91
  18│                                         18-Sep-91
  19│                                         18-Sep-91
  20│                                         18-Sep-91
      Free: 99% [339k]    Auto |            |     Ovr Num Cap   .    8:09:01 pm
```

Figure 5.12: Sorting by date then priority

5.12 Monthly Weather Statistics

Spreadsheets are ideal for carrying out statistical analysis. They can work out averages and give you maximum and minimum values. The example given here is a weather spreadsheet. You put in the daily temperatures for a given month and the computer then calculates average, maximum and minimum. It doesn't matter if you don't have a reading for every day of the month, the computer can still do its calculations and it can also tell you how many days of observations you have.

As usual the first thing you do is to make a general skeleton or template. You can then call it up and fill it in for the individual months.

Get yourself into a fresh worksheet. Start off in cell A1 and type:

```
AVERAGE AND MAX AND MIN TEMPERATURES FOR
```

Goto cell A4 and enter:

```
''MON'
```

Be sure to put the '' in front of MON. This right justifies the text entry in any cell. It will have the effect of lining the text column heading above the figures, which are automatically right justified. Go on with the other days of the week.

```
CELL            CONTENTS
B4              TUES
C4              WED
D4              THURS
E4              FRI
F4              SAT
G4              SUN
```

Leave five rows below this for entering figures. Put a line in underneath this by going to cell A11. <Rn> Type:

```
\-
```

Copy this across the rest of the row with:

```
/ C
```

Press <Rn> to answer the prompt [Copy cells FROM A10..A10] then go to cell G10 and press <Rn>.

Enter the following details in the cells indicated:

```
CELL            CONTENTS

B12             AVERAGE
B14             MAXIMUM
B16             MINIMUM
E2              NUMBER OF DAYS
```

All the headings are now in place, so the next thing to do is to put in the formulae and functions. Enter the following:

CELL	CONTENTS
G2	@COUNT(A5.G9)
D12	@AVG(A5.G9)
D14	@MAX(A5.G9)
D16	@MIN(A5.G9)

@AVG is a very clever function. It ignores any cells that happen to be blank in the range you have given it. This means that you just get the average of the figures you have actually put in. @COUNT counts up the number of cells which do have entries other than blanks.

Because you have no figures in the spreadsheet, at the moment there are only zeros. This is your basic skeleton or template so save it with a name like WEATTEMP.

Then when you want to put some figures in, call it up, put the month name in cell F2 and enter your figures. You can do just part of the month if you want. Then save the filled in worksheet with a new name, like NOV91WEA. You can call NOV91WEA up another time, to put in some more figures. An example of the finished spreadsheet is shown in Figure 5.13.

AVERAGE	AND MAX AND MIN TEMPERATURES FOR			DECEMBER 1991		
				NUMBER OF DAYS		9
MON	TUES	WED	THURS	FRI	SAT	SUN
	9.1	7.8	-2.1	3.4	5.6	
		-1.2	-2.1	-0.6	5.2	

AVERAGE	2.788888
MAXIMUM	9.1
MINIMUM	-2.1

Figure 5.13: Keeping an eye on the weather

5.13 Leaving As Easy As

Make sure you have saved anything valuable before you leave As Easy As. Then enter:

```
/ E Y
```

Databases

6.1 What are Databases?

You probably don't even think about it, but there are databases all around you. A database is just a computerised store of information and in an information age, there is no shortage of facts and figures. You could say there is rather too much and it changes too fast. Phone up a mail order company and the assistant may say: "Yes, you ordered a disk drive unit from us in December 1989". All you have done is to give your name and perhaps a customer number. A visit to the hairdresser produces a: "Yes, you had a short bob last time with a small fringe". Has my hairdresser really got such a good memory? I only go every six months and it is a large town company. The secret is their new database. The receptionist asks for my surname and initials and in seconds she has a record of all the treatment I have ever had.

Those dreadful mailshots that keep on coming in the post are the product of databases. Selling data is big business. The big mail order catalogue firms keep a record of how much you spend and the type of goods you buy. This gives them a profile of your lifestyle and tastes so that they can direct their advertising more closely. Buy some luxury goods and you will be for ever inundated with advertisements for exclusive, limited range facsimile grandfather clocks.

There are specialised databases for lawyers and doctors. Researchers and journalists can key in the subject areas they are interested in, and out comes a bibliography of all the past articles in newspapers and journals. It is quite likely that your local library has a computer which will show whether its books are on the shelf or on loan.

Banks produce vast amount of database information. They keep details of the amount in your account, how much has gone out and when. A year or two ago, a couple were murdered on a coastal walk. The murderer stole and used their cash point cards and this gave the police a database record of where he had been at particular times.

Databases are now being used for tourist information. You can press buttons to locate museums and galleries, the main shopping areas, restaurants and other attractions. The National Gallery in London has just started an on screen gallery guide. You can key in the painting you want to see and it will display a map of how to get there. This kind of database can be highly visual, with colourful pictures and symbols.

At the moment, we still get quite a lot of our information from books, but in the future we will probably be much more likely to look at a screen.

What is the attraction of databases? One is that the information can be very immediate: you access exactly what you want very quickly. Suppose you want a past article in a newspaper. You would have to rustle your way through whole piles of paper and if you get in as much of a mess with newspapers as I do, you would be covered in black typeface. You would also have the problem of where to store them all. Use a database and all you do is type in CHILDREN and COMPUTING and you will be told that in the past five years there were 63 articles in the Guardian covering the two combined subjects. You can then produce a print out of the relevant dates.

A computerised database is also much more flexible in the way in which it can do searches. Without it, information can only be stored in one way. For example, suppose you want to order a book. Before computerisation, bookshops used to get monthly copies of Whitakers, which listed all the books currently published in the UK. The books were listed by title and by author, in alphabetical order. This was fine if you knew either the title in full or the author. But suppose you are not that organised. All you know is that there is a book on PC-FILE but it is about some other things as well and PC-FILE is not the first word.

Without the computer, you are stuck. The computer, on the other hand, can search through whole titles very quickly and can pick things out in the middle. Suppose you want a book on dBase IV, a big commercial PC database package. Under the old system, it would be fine if that was how the title started. But often it isn't - there can be variations like *Getting to know dBase IV* or *Using dBase IV*. With the computer, you set up the search term, DBASE and it will find everything that has that word anywhere in its title. It also does this extremely quickly, often in a matter of seconds.

A third advantage is that it is very easy to update a computer. Once you have written and published a book, it cannot be changed and it begins to get out of date. You can't scrub out one paragraph and put in the correct version. A database tends to be a more ongoing operation, and it is very easy to change the odd little bit so that it can constantly be kept up to the minute.

6.2 How Databases Organise Information

Databases do not store information in a higglety pigglety fashion like all the old scribbled on envelopes in my handbag. The information is highly structured and carefully thought out. You take a group of similar things, like people, or factory goods and keep the same kind of information about each of them. The things, be they people or stock, are called entities. Mrs. Jones is an entity, Mr. Jones is an entity, little Johnny is an entity. Each human being in the database is an entity. If you run an electrical goods shop, a particular make of washing machine, say a cream Electrofig 4050X is one entity, a Moulibar 670S is another and so on.

You then have to decide what you want to know about each of these entities. This will depend partly on what you can find out about them and also on what you will want to ask your database. For human beings, it will be things like name, surname, address and date of birth. If it is a hospital, it will include which department they are visiting, when they visited it, what operations they have had and the name and address of their G.P. If you are running a school, you will want to know what class they are in and what grades and assessments they have achieved. For stock items, you will want to know the cost price, the selling price, the number actually in stock, the number below which you will want to re-order, the name and address of the supplier, where on the shelves they are kept and things like that.

Each of these individual items of information is called a Field. School class, geography exam mark, hospital ward, patient number are all fields. The combined information you keep about each entity is called a Record. The whole thing ends up like filling in a standard form for each person or stock item. In fact, commercial database writers will produce forms for the computer screen that look much like all the forms that we are constantly filling in in this modern age. You may leave some of the entries blank because you don't know the answers, but the form will force you to give a certain kind of very structured information.

Now there are some messier databases. The police use what the jargon calls a text based database. This means that they can put in a whole load of little bits of hearsay about a whole host of potential criminals, things like *had a red pimple on her nose*, or *was wearing a brown, yellow and purple kilt*. They can actually get the computer to search through very unstructured chatty prose, looking for a man with a boil on his nose or leg. The computer can do this much more quickly than a human reader. However, databases do work much more quickly and efficiently if the information is more structured, so messy text is a last resort.

How about creating your own databases? The professionals will say that databases are not for beginners. This is not true. You can create your own very simple, standard databases with relatively little trouble. Books will give you guidance on well used types of databases like names and addresses of customers or how to handle your stock items. Part of the reason for professionals wanting to keep it to themselves (apart from making money) is that most commercial databases require a lot of time, money and effort before you get them going. This is partly because there are usually so many people, items of stock or whatever else you are dealing with. It takes a lot of effort to get all the information into the computer in the first place, and if you haven't properly planned what you are going to get out, you may have wasted a lot of effort. Home databases are likely to be so much smaller that effort is not so wasted.

However having said this, you will probably find that your first database does not work the way you want it to, probably because you only think after the event what you really want to get out of it. For this reason, it is worth doing a small practice run with just a few entries. This way, you will learn your lessons before you have invested too much time. In fact, building your own small database is probably one of the very best ways of learning how they work. Your errors will tell you more than the bits you get right.

What kind of package should you use? Like word processors, there is no shortage of candidates. In the reviews, you will find them divided into flatfile or relational databases. Flatfile databases are the simplest. They will hold information about one kind of entity only, in a single database (you can, of course, use your package to build several different databases). So you must restrict yourself to just human beings or electrical goods and not try to mix them together. You can hold a lot of information about your one entity, or in jargon have a large number of fields. For many purposes, this will be quite enough and this is probably true for most home databases.

A relational database holds information about several entities, all at one time. So it can hold information about customers, about stock items and about the names and addresses of suppliers all quite separately. When you want to make relationships between the entities, about the stock that a customer has bought, or the address of the supplier of that item of stock, you can make links between the different entities. You can't do this with a flatfile database, but you can, of course come out of one database and go into another one, although this will be much slower.

The largest commercial packages are relational. They also have their own programming languages but you don't have to use these yourself and they usually provide standard, easier ways of doing things. dBase (now in Version IV) used to be the market leader, but its company, Ashton-Tate has recently been taken over by Borland, another giant software company, so its future looks much more uncertain. So much effort has been put into dBase over the years and so many professionals are involved, that it will probably NOT die an instant death, but for a newcomer it does not seem entirely the best place to go. Borland's own product, Paradox might be a better alternative. Some people swear by Smart. However, whatever the ins and outs of the future large database market, any well established product will always get some kind of support.

On the home or small business front, there are plenty of candidates for the flat file database race, Rapidfile or Cardbox being possibilities. However shareware has a very good answer in PC-File, now in Version 5. It is produced by a company called Buttonware and has been a great success. It is a friendly, professional little package which can do some powerful things if you wish to expand. According to the press, the next version, number 6, will not be issued on shareware so get in quick! PC-File is supposed to be compatible with dBase, so you can always expand into something bigger at a later date.

6.3 Designing Your Own Databases

Databases can be for beginners, but whatever the level, every database should begin with careful planning. Forget the computer and bring out the paper and pencil. You need to consider:

❑ What are your entities? If you are storing names and addresses, then your entities will be people. If you are doing stock control, the entities will be the various items you keep in stock, each title of book if you are a bookseller or each type of electrical goods if you are running an electrical shop. In a recipe database, each entity will be a recipe, for chicken chow mien or beef stew, for example.

❑ The next thing to consider is what you will want to ask the computer about the entities. What sort of searches will you want to do for particular categories of information? For example, will you want to find all your customers living in a particular town or city, London or Glasgow perhaps? Will you want to mail shot customers who have spent above a certain sum of money or chase up ones who haven't paid up within a month? How are you going to search out your recipes? Will you hunt for all the recipes whose main ingredient is beef? Will a recipe have only one main ingredient or several.

❑ The answers you get will be vital in determining what your fields, or particular items of information, will be. If you are going to search for something, it should have a field of its own. If you want to get lists of all the customers in a particular town, make *Town* a field on its own, don't just make it part of a long and messy address. *Amount spent last year* or *Amount spent so far this year* could be another field. *Main ingredient 1, Main ingredient 2* and *Main ingredient 3* could be fields for your recipe database. This is the most difficult part of planning your database and you should think about it very carefully. You can usually change the fields in the early stages of setting up a database but once you have started to put some actual information in, this can be very difficult.

❑ You need to consider whether you can actually get the information for the fields you have planned. It is no good chasing unpaid up customers, if your accounts are in such a mess that you can't tell how much anyone has paid (if this is the case, abandon operations and attend to your accounts before the tax man gets you). However you might decide that you will reform your ways and that in future you will make sure you do have this information. Thinking about using a computer can make you look quite carefully at your present procedures and may lead to re-organisation. This may be more useful in some cases than the actual computerisation.

❑ The next thing to do is decide the length and type of each field. Most databases allocate a set length to each field and if the actual data put into a field doesn't fill it up, the computer will pack it out with blank spaces. What is the longest entry that is likely to go into a particular field? Not just the longest now, but the longest you might ever have. If there is one that is very much longer than all the others, you could end up with a lot of wasted space. In this situation, it might be better to have one cut off or shortened entry than masses of filled in blanks. Suppose that most Christian names are not more than 15 letters long but one individual happens to be called Arabella Eliza Appledora Partitita. Rather than using 34 characters for all the entries, it might be better to quietly say: "sorry, if your name is that long, you will just have to be Arabella to us".

The type of field depends on your database package. Most have character or numeric fields. Numeric fields are numbers, but if you are using, say, identity numbers that you will not want to do any arithmetic on, you can call them character rather than numeric. If you leave them as numbers your computer may decide to do some uncalled for arithmetic. If you have numeric fields you will usually be asked how many decimal places you want. For money, this is 2.

Another type of field is the date field. Less common are what are called memo and logical fields. Memo fields are where you put the messy things that you can't structure. For example, in a book collection database, you might want to keep a mini review of each book. These will be so different and subjective that there is no way you could structure them all: *It was fab - spine chilling and hair raising - the most appalling writing I have ever come across - had me tickling my sides.* The trouble with this is that you can't do very effective searches, so in database terms you should see them as extra messy information. If you want to search for funny or horrifying books, it might be better to give them some more regular coding, and set up a field for type of book, with H for horror, F for funny and so on. Logical fields are for either true or false, or yes or no. They can be very useful for things like whether a customer has paid yet or not. When you do a search you can pick out all the customers who have not paid and send them reminder letters.

You are now ready to start creating a database on the computer. The first thing you have to do is to set up the database structure, the basic skeleton of field names, lengths and types that you will later fill with actual information.

When you have done this you feed in the actual data or information. If you are running a business and have a database of any size, this can take a lot of time, perhaps two or three full time days, or even a week, of hard computer work.

You may then want to make, what are called in database language, reports: set ways of getting information out of the database. These can be on the screen or printed out. The package may allow you to design your own special layout. You may also want to use the computer to design what are called data entry forms, making forms like the paper ones you fill in all over the place.

The next section will show how you would design some particular databases. Full instructions are then given for using the main shareware package, PC-File, to set up one particular database. You are left to put the rest in for yourself, following the same pattern.

6.4 Setting up a Database

The database package I shall be using is the famous shareware PC-File. It tends to change its look from version to version, so if you have a earlier one, things may be a bit different. It is described in the shareware guide as being for hard disk drives only but it runs quite happily on a twin drive floppy.

The database used is a relatively simple one, a list of all the books you own or perhaps keep in a bibliography. As usual, you decide what the entity is - here it is an individual book. It is assumed that you do not have two copies of the same book, a not unreasonable assumption in the home. If you do have two identical copies of the same book you could call them say *Treasure Island 1* and *Treasure Island 2*.

What sort of things will you want to ask the database about your books? *Title* and *Author* are obvious ones. You might want to know where you store them, particularly if you have a large library. Call this field *Location*. Don't type out the whole location in full, it is easy to make spelling mistakes. Make a code and write it down on a card so that you know exactly what your codes are. It might look like this:

B1	Top shelf in bedroom
B2	Middle shelf in bedroom
B3	Bottom shelf in bedroom
A	Attic
S1	Sitting room - top right hand shelf
S2	Sitting room - middle right hand shelf
S3	Sitting room - bottom right hand shelf
S4	Sitting room - top left hand shelf
H1	Top shelf in hall

Draw a clearly marked plan so that you know where they all are.

Another thing you will want to know is what type of book it is. You might decide to divide your books into say fiction, poetry, history and chemistry. You may want to classify them as reference or easy to read, things like that. Get some more cards and write out some more codes. For example:

FW   Fiction - Western
FH   Fiction - Historical
FR   Fiction - Romance
FD   Fiction - Detective
CD   Computer - Databases
CS   Computer - Spreadsheets
CW   Computer - Wordprocessors

You can use more than two letters and it is worth trying to use ones that will make some sense. You could call this field, *Type*.

You may want to know when the book was bought and how much it cost, particularly if you are a second hand fiend. You could call these fields, *Dategot* and *Pricepaid*. In this situation you might record when you sold it and for how much. Call these fields, *Datesold* and *Pricesold*. If you do this, you will want to either leave *Location* blank or perhaps put something in like G for Gone.

You may want to know when you read the book (if you did!). This field could be called *Dateread*. A record of where you got the book from, either a shop or a present from a friend, might be useful. You could call this field *Origin*.

When you have finally decided on all your fields, the next step is to draw up a list of their names and to decide on their types, either character, numeric or date, and how long the field length should be. Make a table like the one below.

Fieldname	Type	Length
TITLE	Character	25
AUTHOR	Character	25
INITIAL	Character	1
PUBLISHER	Character	20
ISBN	Character	11
DATEPUB	Date	8
LOCATION	Character	2
TYPE	Character	2
DATEGOT	Date	8
PRICEPAID	Numeric	7 with 2 decimal places
DATESOLD	Date	8
PRICESOLD	Numeric	7 with 2 decimal places
DATEREAD	Date	8

Dates are handled in a standard way by most databases and have a set length. Money is dealt with by making a numeric field with two decimal places. Numeric fields have a length which covers both decimal places and the point. A length of seven with two decimal places, leaves four figures before the decimal point - maybe a little optimistic for most people's book collections and certainly for mine. You can always live in hope and it is worth allowing for totals which could be in the thousands if you are a keen book collector.

In your own database, only put in the fields you are interested in and add any extra that you can think of as being important to you. Remember that your database is only going to be useful if you keep it up to date. If you put vast quantities of information in for each record (the details about one particular example of an entity) you will probably give up in despair and defeat the whole purpose. Keep it as simple as you can, allowing for the fact that you actually want to get something out of it. Many home databases, like diaries and time organisers, never quite get brought up to date. But never mind, you will have learnt quite a lot about databases and the way the world is going, which will not be a waste of time.

Having made up a table of fields, *data types* (the jargon word for whether it is character, numeric or date) and lengths, you are now ready for the next part, actually building up the database structure and then putting in some entries.

6.5 Hobby and School Databases

A database can be made out of any information that can be structured in some way. In fact, planning a database is a wonderful way of making yourself look at some chosen subject in more detail and you can learn a lot in the process.

For example, take the topic of animals. The entity in this case would be *animal*. What kind of things would you want to know about animals? What sort of questions would you ask the database? You might want to know what kinds of animals are found in Europe or in Africa, the kinds of things they eat, the sort of land they live in, called terrain. The biological species they belong to, like insects or mammals, how long they live and whether they are an endangered species.

This might lead to the following table of fields, types and lengths.

Field	Type	Length
Animal	Name	Character 30
Group	Character	2 (use a code)
Country	Character	20
Continent	Character	2 (use a code)
Food1	Character	10
Food2	Character	10
Food3	Character	10
Terrain	Character	3 (use a code)
Rarity	Character	1 (Just Y or N)

There are probably animals, countries of the world and types of food that occupy more than 30, 20 and 10 characters respectively. There is always something somewhere that is exceptionally long. However you can always cut them off and there will still be enough characters to see what the names really are. There are three food fields, because some animals have a major diet of more than one type. You can't cover everything that every animal eats so *Food1, Food2* and *Food3* are meant to cover the three most important items. You could have more, if you felt it was interesting. In fact, the biologist would make a much better job of this than the database expert!

Using codes is a good idea because it saves disk space, cuts down the typing and prevents spelling mistakes that will stop your searches working properly. You could use, say, E for Europe, AF for Africa, NA for North America, SA for South America, AU for Australasia and AS for Asia.

Terrain could be W for wooded, M for marshes, SW for saltwater, RW for river water, T for towns and so on. When you invent your codes write them down. You can do this on file index cards or put them in a special file to go with your project. If you don't, you will come back to your database several weeks later and wonder they are all about.

Geography provides good material for making databases. You can put in all the countries of the world. The kind of fields you might have would be name of country, continent, population, land size, capital city, currency, main language spoken, prime minister and type of government. The list is endless. Pick out the ones that interest you. Some atlases provide material that is already well classified and can easily go straight into a database. The Economist Atlas is ideal in this respect. It is necessary though to keep the same unit of measurement, say thousands or millions. Britain has a population of about 55 million, but a small country might only have a population of 1287. Expressed in millions this is 0.001287. Expressed in thousands, the respective population figures are 55000 and 1.287. The arithmetic can get quite hairy, so watch out!

You can store historical information on a database. Your fields could be year, event1, event2, event3 (each year is only allowed up to three exciting events, but you could extend this), king or queen on the throne. Make the event fields quite long, say about 40 or 50 characters. In fact they could be even longer but if you set that as the field length, you would waste a lot of disk space. Once you have set up your database, you can add to it as you learn more history. You could look up all the events that occurred during a certain king or queen's reign or all the events that occurred during certain years. In this case search for events that occurred after the beginning date and before the end date.

6.6 Creating a Database

This example database is a record of my video recordings. The starting point was the information I would want to get out of it. I decided that I would want to know:

❏ What is on a particular tape.

❏ Whether a tape has spare room for another recording.

❏ Where I can find a particular program.

❏ Where I could find a program to fill a particular amount of time. For example, I might have half an hour to spare or it could be more like two hours.

❏ What type of programs I have stored in case I'm feeling choosy.

❏ A list of all the episodes of the same series, like all the Rupert programs.

❏ A list of all the programs recorded more than six months ago, to see whether I might clear them out.

This gave me a better idea of the kind of information I would want to feed into my computer so that I could decide what fields to create.

I concluded that I would want to keep information on the number of each tape. This meant I had to decide how to classify them. In the end, I used colour labels, with red for social science, yellow for art, green for science and blue for my son William. I classified my tapes by letter and number, so W1, W2, W3 and W4 were my son's tapes. A1, A2, A3 and A4 were the arts and so on.

I decided I would take the reading of the point on the tape where the program started, where it ended and the length of the program. In fact you only needed one of the last two for any individual program, but the end position was useful if you wanted to go on to record another program.

I developed a code to classify the programs, like F for Film, N for Nature, H for History, S for Science, P for Politics. I also used a logical field, called *Keep*. If this was true, it meant that I wanted to save the programme permanently. Another logical field was *Watched*, which told me whether or not I had got round to viewing a program. Logical fields are a bit like ticking a box. They can only take Y or N or T or F, Yes or No, True or False.

Last but not least, was the title of the programme. It is a rule of database construction, that every record can be uniquely identified, which means one or two fields are always different for every record in the database. Since you can watch several versions of a particular programme, this needs to be both Title and Date together. The field or fields which identify a record are called the key. You can build an index on any field that you use for a lot of searching and this will make it quicker to recover information.

If you have a hard disk, start by creating a directory called PCF, Change Directory (CD) into this and install PC-File using the INSTALL.COM program.

Load up PC-FILE by typing:

```
PCF
```

PC-FILE passes through a large number of screens.

You are asked:

```
Which drive for the database?
```

You get the prompt B or C depending on whether you have dual floppies or a hard disk. If it is correct, press <Rn> to accept, otherwise change it.

You are asked:

```
Which path for the data?
```

This is only relevant if you have a hard disk, and want to store your data in some subdirectory away from where the program files are stored. If you don't want to do this, or have floppies only, just press <Rn>.

```
Select an existing database or give a name for the new database.
Type a name or number, or select with cursor keys.
```

Beneath is a directory of existing databases. If this is the first time you have used PC-File, the only entry will be Jim Button's ready made PEOPLE.

To create a new database enter its name into the blank. I typed in VIDEO and pressed function key <F10> for complete.

PC-File searches for a database called VIDEO and, not surprisingly, finds it hasn't got one. As a result it comes up with a message, **like:**

```
C: PCF\VIDEO is a new file. Do you want to define it?
Yes
No
```

Figure 6.1 (overleaf) shows this screen.

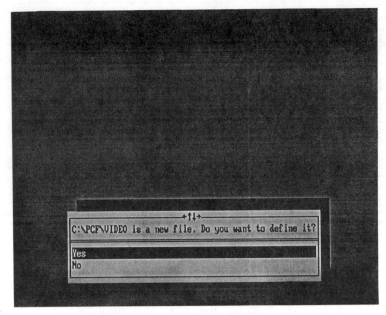

Figure 6.1: Naming the new database

Yes is highlighted so press <Rn> to accept.

This says:

There are two ways to define a database

Fast and Paint (it explains what these are).

Which method,
Fast
Paint

On this occasion, select Fast. It is highlighted, so just press <Rn>.

Enter the field names in their relative positions. You can place the names anywhere on screen.

I put in:

TITLE
DATE
TAPENO
STARTPOS
ENDPOS
LENGTH
CATEGORY
KEEP
WATCHED

If you make a mistake you can move around with the cursor keys and amend it. Press <F10> when the list is complete.

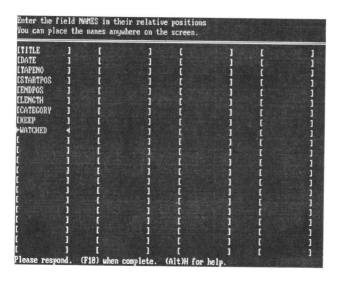

Figure 6.2: Entering the database fields

Enter the display length (1-65) for each field.

These went 25, 8, 4, 4, 4, 4, 3, 1, 1 respectively. A date field must be 8 characters. I decided that I would measure length in minutes to avoid mixing hours and minutes.

Press <F10> when done – see Figure 6.3.

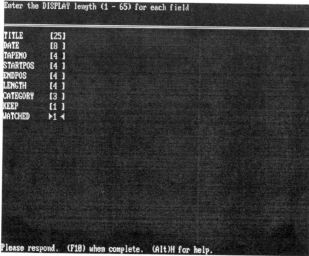

Figure 6.3: Setting the field lengths

Then you are asked to enter the type of field. These should go C, D, C, N, N, N, C, L, L.

If you have numeric fields you will get a further menu - Figure 6.4. asking you how many decimal places you want. Press <F10> to accept the zeros.

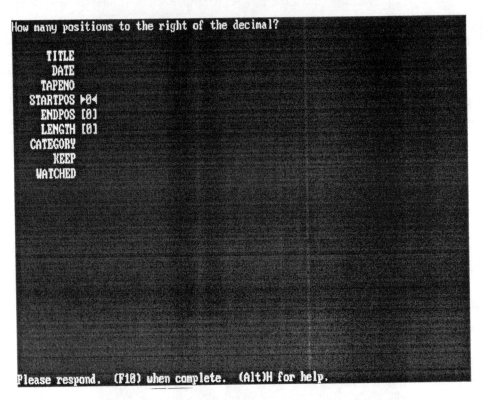

```
How many positions to the right of the decimal?

    TITLE
     DATE
   TAPENO
 STARTPOS ▶0◀
   ENDPOS [0]
   LENGTH [0]
 CATEGORY
     KEEP
  WATCHED




Please respond.  (F10) when complete.  (Alt)H for help.
```

Figure 6.4: Indicating the number of decimal places in numeric fields

`Are any of the fields Window Fields?`

You use these for *messy text*. There is none here, so press <Rn> to accept No, which is highlighted.

`The fields will be accessed from left to right and top to bottom as you`
`drew them on the screen.`
`Would you like to change this sequence?`

This is your opportunity to change the order. Press <Rn> for no, or cursor and <Rn> for yes.

You get a list of your fields. You can mark those which you want to index, that is ones you will use for frequent searches. For me TITLE and TAPE NO and DATE seemed good answers, so I put an x in the relevant space. <F10> to complete.

The indexes are built up, with various messages. Press <Rn> to give them the same names as the fields (this makes more sense later) and <Rn> if you are happy with ascending order.

```
Please reply
Database Description
```

You can write a few words to give a fuller description of your database. I typed in

```
Keep a record of video recordings
```

anything that makes it clearer.

You have now set up your database and are ready to start entering data. You are given the Main Master Menu.

```
F1 A Add a new Record (Highlighted)
F8 U Utilities
F9 M Menu of smart keys

Q Quit this database
```

Type A or <F1> to add new records and follow the instructions given in section 6.7.1

6.7 Searching a Database

Most of your work with databases will be looking up information that has already been stored. You will also want to modify or change existing entries, make new entries and delete old ones that are out of date. When you want to look up a database, think what kind of information you want out of it. You will probably want to look up the same sort of thing on different occasions and develop routines - a series of key presses - that do this for you. Once you have worked them out, write them down on an index card or at the beginning of a paper file and eventually you will get to a stage where you do them quite automatically.

To have a look at the whole database

Load up PC-File in the usual way. You will be asked for the drive and path in the same way as when you create a database.

This time, you have a database to open up. A directory of databases is shown on the screen. Type the number of the required database in the blank space and then press function key <F10> to accept.

You should now be in the Main Menu shown in Figure 6.5. You will often return here when travelling through PC-File. It allows you to do some more advanced things, but as a beginner, the choices you will use most are <F1> or A to add new entries, F or <F2> to find an entry, R or <F6> for reports and Q for Quit.

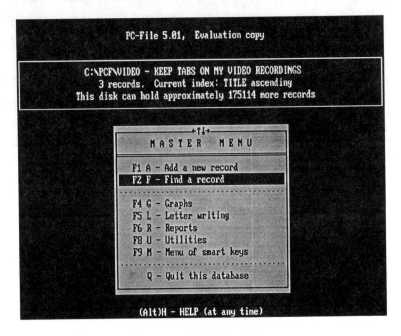

Figure 6.5: PC-File's main menu

6.7.1 To Add New Entries

Press key A or function key <F1> from the Main Menu. You then get a screen with your field names and blank spaces. Fill in the spaces with the data of your first additional record. You can cursor around and change them. When you have got them correct, press function key <F10> to accept.

Then comes another little menu, with Yes, No, X for Yes always or Q for Quit. X for "Yes always" means that you won't get this message on your following entries. This can be useful if you have a lot to do. If you accept the entry, you get another blank screen. Fill in the next one in the same way.

When you have finished, just press <F10> on a blank entry to go back to the Main Menu.

6.7.2 To Look for a Particular Record

You will often want to find a single entry, maybe just to look at it, or to amend or delete it. To do this, press F or function key <F2> at the Main Menu.

The first thing that happens, is that you get another menu offering a simple search (this is the highlighted entry). You can go to a given numbered record in the database, start at the beginning, go to the next record or choose + or -. This gives you the whole or part of the database in a simple table form, one record written across the screen per one line.

If you select the highlighted option, a form with your fields is shown with asterisks beside each one. Fill these in with one or two details of the record you are searching for. Just part of a title will do, something that should identify it. Press <F10> when done, and your entry should appear.

You get a long, thin menu over on the right hand side that allows you to amend or modify the entry or delete it. It also allows you to go to the next or previous entry or to do another search. Pressing + will produce a table setting out the records that follow your chosen one. You could have selected this form of presentation, from the search menu.

6.7.3 Making a Report Format

A database report is just a way of getting information out of the database. This information can be structured in whatever way you want and you can choose just selected fields. You create a general report format - you may want to produce several of these, save them, and call the general format up on another occasion, to fill it with actual information out of the database.

For example, for my video collection, I might just list the Title, Startposition and Tapenumber in one report format. In another report format, I may want to show all the fields.

You need to set up a report format. This is slightly hard work, but once you have done it, it is easy to call up and fill in.

To make a report format, select R or <F6> from the Main Menu. You get the screen shown in Figure 6.6. This allows you to choose existing reports. This time you want to make a new one so just press <F10> while the cursor is on blank. A new menu shown in Figure 6.6 offers Page Format, Row Format, Mail Label, Free Form and Commands. Row Format is highlighted so for the first Report, select this. It will put the records along a single row, one below the other.

```
Which report format?  (Leave BLANK to CREATE or MODIFY a format)
Type a name or number, or select with cursor keys
▶       ◀
 [1]  PEOPLE1  Mailing Labels for People database
 [2]  PEOPLE2  One Person per Page for People database
 [3]  PEOPLE3  Phone Directory for People database
 [4]  PEOPLE4  Rolodex Cards for People database
 [5]  PEOPLE5  3" by 5" Cards for People database
 [6]  PEOPLE6  Envelopes (1 at a time) for People database




Please respond.  (F10) when complete.  (Alt)H for help.
```

Figure 6.6: Choosing the report format

You then get a screen, saying:

`Number of columns to print from left to right.`

You are then given a list of your fields. Use the numbers 1, 2, 3 and so on, to list the order in which you want the column headings to appear, starting with 1 at the left hand corner. If you don't want to include a field in your table, leave it out by not giving it a number. The usual <F10> to accept.

The prompt is `Permanent title Line.`

This is the heading for your report. It stays fixed, so it needs to be something rather general, like `What's on a tape` or `Animal details`. This will allow you to use it as a framework for quite different collections of records.

`Would you like to save this report format?`

`Yes` (highlighted)
`No`

Press <Rn> to save it.

You are asked for a Report Description. This can be some kind of explanation which makes its purpose a little more obvious than the more limited title.

```
Enter a name for the format.
```

A simple eight letter filename is what is required here. This is the name it will be saved under. I used TAPE.

A message to tell you it is being saved.

A Report Menu, Figure 6.7, allows you to set margins, type of print and whether you want to save it to disk, print it out or show it on the screen, or change the defaults. The bottom entry, A, will produce a report of all your entries. If you only want some selected out, change this to S.

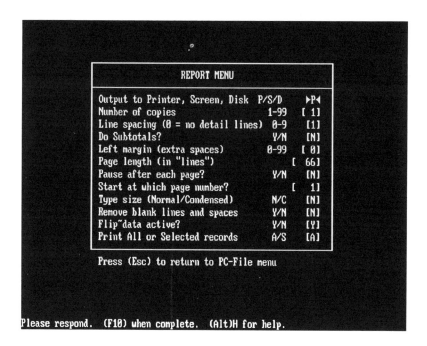

Figure 6.7: The Report menu

The usual <F10> for done.

If you selected S, you will be asked whether you want to make a simple or complex search. See the instructions on making an actual report to see what to do.

6.7.4 Putting Data into a Report Format

Select R or <F6> from the Main Menu. Once you have created at least one report format, you will get a menu like the opening database one, showing what reports you have created and saved. Type the number of the one you want, in the blank space.

Press <F10> to select in the usual way.

You then get a menu like Figure 6.7 in the last section, making a report format. Selecting S will display a further menu, for the type of search you want to do. For your first one, do a simple search. You get a blank form, with asterisks, like searching for a single entry. Put in what you want to search on, like SOOTY, if you want a report of all the recordings of SOOTY.

Press <F10> for done and your report should then appear, in whatever form you gave in the menu. A sample finished report is shown in Figure 6.8.

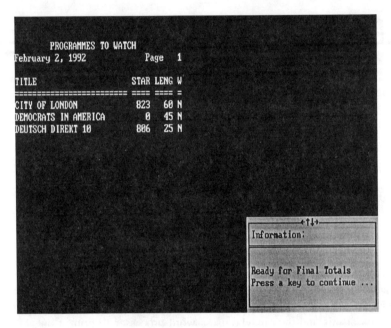

Figure 6.8: A sample report

A complex search lets you use criteria like all recordings before a certain date or programmes that last for more than half an hour. A box allows you to fill in entries like:

```
LENGTH > 30
```

for programmes more than 30 minutes long.

7

Getting to Grips with Logo

There is a version of the Logo programming language available on shareware called Ladybug. It is not a full version: it has very little in the way of list processing (word handling), but does provide a reasonably full coverage of the graphics commands. It is based on the Apple II version written by Terrapin Inc. You can use most of the graphics procedures given in the major books on Logo such as:

❏ *Learning with Logo* by Daniel Watt

❏ *Discovering Apple Logo* by David R. Thornburg.

I'm going to use it for demonstration here because it allows you to get a good taste of Logo graphics and would cover most of the Logo work done at school in maths projects. You do need a graphics screen to get much out of it, but apart from this, the memory and MS-DOS requirements are quite modest. Like most shareware it is not presented in a very friendly way but there is a long user manual stored on the disk in the LADYBUG.DOC file. Use the utility LIST (see Chapter 3 *DOS in a Nutshell*) to have a look at this and then maybe use a word processor to print it out. Most of the manual seems OK but one exception is the reference to some of the function keys.

Because you are producing graphics or picture material, if you have a CGA screen, you must load up GRAPHICS.COM from MS-DOS before you run Ladybug Logo. If you use floppies, copy it on to the Ladybug program disk or better still write a batch file (see Chapter 3).

7.1 Getting Started

To load up Ladybug Logo, type:

```
LADYBUG
```

You are then asked if you have a monochrome screen (y/n). This is rather a silly question because if you have, there is not much use in loading up a graphics programming language. Monochrome literally means one colour, i.e. black and white, or yellow and brown, but it mainly means you haven't got a screen capable of producing graphics. Press <Rn> as instructed.

After that you get a blank screen with a cursor and a question mark at the top. Type in:

```
DRAW
```

to put yourself into turtle graphics.

You now find a little *turtle* triangle in the centre of the screen and are ready to go ahead.

7.1.1 A Few Simple Commands

The turtle draws by making a *snail trail* as it moves along. You can make it go forwards or backwards and left or right. It can also lift its trail and move without drawing. In the Logo spirit, I like to start with as little as possible and leave the child to do his or her own exploring. So begin with:

```
FD 30
```

FD is short for forward. It must have a space after it and then a number. In this example I have used 30. These are 30 turtle steps and you can leave it to the beginner to find out what this means by trying out different numbers. Pressing <Rn> makes the computer register the command, and the turtle walks a line vertically up the screen.

Try:

```
FD 10
```

and the turtle walks further up the screen, a third as far again to be precise.

The next command is to do a turn. This can be either left or right. This time try:

```
LT 30
```

LT is short for left, RT for right. Again you must have a space, followed by some number. The turtle now points over to the left, although still upwards.

Try some more turns like:

```
LT 110
RT 65
```

and see where the turtle is pointing.

Then go forward a bit more, with say:

```
FD 20
```

You have now met the very basics of Logo. At this point you can take the turtle back to the start position with the command:

```
HOME
```

and then:

```
CS
```

to clear the screen.

You can now leave the beginner to draw his or her own picture with the FD, LT and RT commands and various numbers. It is the spirit of Logo to invent these and to develop a feel for what this means in terms of distance and direction. Adult mathematicians may have their own view of what turns mean but it is much more fun for them to keep quiet and let children discover it for themselves. Not knowing angles and degrees, they can get a real intuitive understanding of turning in turtle *rounds* and moving a distance in turtle *steps*.

Logo is a wonderful expression of spatial awareness and it can be very helpful for children to think about the kind of turns they make when walking round the house or garden or up or down the town. When they are away from the computer, get them to work out how they would walk out a square or even more of a challenge, how they would walk out a circle.

But for the moment, just explore the movements and draw anything, the more irregular the better. One word of warning though – one of the limitations of Ladybug is that it does not let you rub anything out, so turn your mistakes into something interesting.

If you have a CGA screen, provided you have loaded up GRAPHICS.COM you can screen dump your picture to the printer. If you have VGA, this may work without having to load up GRAPHICS.COM. To do this press <Shift> and hold it down while at the same time, pressing <Print Screen>. After a few seconds' wait, the printing should begin.

It is quite likely that you will walk the turtle off the screen. Never mind, it will just wrap round and appear at the opposite side. This can sometimes add further interest to your pictures. You can stop it happening by typing:

```
NOWRAP
```

and to turn it on again

```
WRAP
```

With Logo there is no need to hurry to move on to the next stage. Its strength lies in the fact that you can do all kinds of things with just a few very simple commands. So stay with the simple for as long as you find it interesting.

When you want to come out of Ladybug type BYE and you will be returned to the MS-DOS prompt.

7.2 Getting Used to Logo's Main Commands

Try to measure how tall and wide the screen is, in turtle steps. To do this don't take a ruler, but let the turtle walk a little bit, then a little bit more and so on, until it reaches the edge. You might go something like this:

```
FD 50
FD 10
FD 2
```

Only one command shows up on the screen at a time, so keep a record on paper of how far you have gone. For the teachers among you, this is called iteration.

Do some similar experiments with the turns. What number of *rounds* do you need to use so that you are facing down not up? If you are an adult, don't supply the answer – it is more fun for a child to work it out for himself.

Particularly if you have a group of children, it is worth getting some acetates and some blue tack or string to stick them to the front of the computer screen. Draw some obstacle courses or other tracks on them. Make the paths reasonably wide so that the turtle can travel along them, but not so wide that there is no challenge. Like most things in Logo it is a matter of trial and error. Children may want to invent some themselves. Examples would be going down the Thames, going through a maze or a street map of your town or village or the route to school. Just trying to get along the track is quite fun or you could provide a competitive element, by seeing who can do it in the fewest moves.

7.2.1 Your First Procedure

You can teach the turtle how to do things. You give each set of instructions any name you like and then all you have to do is to type in the chosen name, and the turtle will carry them out. Each named set of instructions is called a *procedure*.

To make a procedure you start with the command TO, then a space and then give it your chosen name. You can start with something silly, like:

```
TO BLOB
```

then put in five or six commands, anything will do. For example:

```
RT 45<Rn>
FD 30<Rn>
LT 50<Rn>
FD 20<Rn>
RT 70<Rn>
```

It is very important that when you get to the end of your list of commands, you type:

```
END
```

If you don't do this at the end of a procedure, funny things will happen and the computer won't do what you planned.

When you have done this, type:

```
BLOB
```

and the turtle will draw out your set of commands, just like that!

Turn through some angle, and do BLOB again.

```
RT 28
BLOB
```

Try:

```
REPEAT 10 [BLOB]
```

Be careful to use the square brackets in this example.

It is fascinating to watch a really boring little pattern like BLOB repeat itself on the screen and in doing so, often produce a really intriguing shape as shown in Figure 7.1.

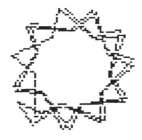

Figure 7.1: The Blob at work

If you are very adventurous, you can make procedures within procedures.

For example:

```
TO REPBLOB
REPEAT 10 [RT 22 BLOB]
END
```

I'll show you how REPEAT works shortly.

Type:

```
REPBLOB
```

and see what you end up with – Figure 7.2.

Figure 7.2: Variation on a Blob

7.2.2 Making Shapes

The next major breakthrough is to start making regular shapes like squares, rectangles, hexagons and circles. It is fun to try and work out how to do this yourself.

A square has four sides all the same length but what angle do you have to turn through?

Try:

```
FD 80
RT 60
```

Repeat this three times (just type out the commands another three times). The shape doesn't meet, it doesn't turn enough.

Try again – this time turn through 80 degrees. It's a bit better but it still doesn't get there. Try something even bigger, like 100 degrees. This time there is the opposite problem, you get there too soon. So it looks as though you need something in between. What do you think it might be?

In the early stages of doing Logo you will probably want to write out a long list of instructions, step by step. For example, you might go:

```
FD 50
RT 45
FD 50
RT 45
FD 50
RT 45
```

After a while, you may notice that you are doing the same thing over and over again, in this case FD 50, RT 45. You could use REPEAT and rewrite the long list as

```
REPEAT 3 [FD 30 RT 45]
```

Keep the spaces, Logo is very fussy about this and make sure you use the square brackets. Don't force REPEAT on yourself, if it seems difficult and you prefer your longer lists, stick to them.

When you have got the shapes you want by trial and error, turn them into procedures. For example:

```
TO TRIANGLE
REPEAT 3 [FD 30 RT 120]
END
```

makes a triangle with sides length 30. Type:

```
TRIANGLE
```

and there it is, drawn out on the screen.

Suppose you want to change it, to make it larger with sides of length 50. You can do this with the EDIT command. Type:

```
EDIT TRIANGLE
```

You now move into a new screen, what we call the editing screen. It has some writing at the bottom, the turtle has disappeared and the instructions of the procedure TO TRIANGLE are written at the top. You can add extra instructions or change what is already there. This is called editing. You move round with the cursor keys until you get to the place where you want to insert or delete something. In this case you want to change the 3 in FD 30 to 5 so you have FD 50 instead. Move the cursor so that it is flashing under the 3. When you move into the editing screen, it is in what you call overwrite mode, so that if you type anything it writes over the existing characters. This is what you want to do in this situation, so type 5 to replace the 3.

If you want to put in something extra move the cursor one character to the right of where you want to add something. Press the <Insert> key – any characters you then type will be added, instead of writing over what is already there. Once you move away again with the cursor keys, it goes back to overwrite, so you need to press insert *every time* you want to add something new. This is different from most word processors, where you stay in insert or overwrite until you toggle the insert key and then stay with the opposite until you change again.

When you have finished making your changes, press function key <F9>. You then return to the turtle draw screen.

Type:

TRIANGLE

again. This time the turtle draws a larger triangle. Try some other changes. From now on you should do all your Logo programming by writing procedures. It makes it easy to make changes and try them out and as you will see soon, you can save them and use them another day.

Go on to make some more shapes. In case you don't want to work it all out for yourself, here is a list.

```
TO SQUARE
REPEAT 4 [FD 10 RT 90]
END

TO RECTANGLE
REPEAT 2 [FD 20 RT 90 FD 50 RT 90]
END

TO TRIANGLE
REPEAT 3 [FD 50 RT 120]
END

TO HEXAGON
REPEAT 6 [FD 20 RT 60]
END

TO DECAGON
REPEAT 10 [FD 10 RT 36]
END
```

It can be quite fun to try and work out the triangle yourself but it is quite difficult and the result will probably surprise you. Mathematicians will probably think that as the angles of a triangle add up to 180 and as it has three sides, you turn through 60 degrees. These are what you call interior angles and it is the exterior angle that the turtle turns through, which is 180 less the interior angle, in this case 120.

There is some interesting maths in all this. The number of sides times the angle of turn is 360 in all cases.

7.3 Saving and Loading Procedures

It won't be long before you have made some interesting procedures that you will want to save and use again later. You don't save procedures one by one like you do with BASIC programs or the separate letters or documents from your word processor. Instead you save a collection of different procedures all at one time, called a workspace, and you can give it a suitable name. If you have procedures that need to be called at the same time, like having squares and circles to make a picture, make sure that they are saved in a single work space.

As an example, save a workspace called FIXSHAPE. It contains shapes of a fixed size – later on you will learn how to make more general procedures, where you can make shapes any size. Key in the procedures, TO SQUARE, TO TRIANGLE and TO HEXAGON.

Then type:

```
SAVE ''FIXSHAPE
```

All three procedures will be saved in a workspace called FIXSHAPE. Ladybug automatically puts on the extension .BUG so the file is called FIXSHAPE.BUG.

Type:

```
CAT
```

This gives you a directory listing of the files on your Ladybug disk. There are several files ending with the extension .BUG, ready made procedures that Ladybug has already given you. Among them is your newly saved file, FIXSHAPE.BUG.

Next time you have a Logo session, call up your saved procedures by typing:

```
LOAD ''FIXSHAPE
```

The three you saved should be there and you can run them straightaway by typing in their respective names followed by <Rn>. To look at them written out, type:

```
EDIT ALL
```

There are the procedures, shown up on the Edit screen. You can change them if you want to. You can also add to them. Type:

```
TO DECAGON
REPEAT 10 [FD 30 RT 36]
END
```

Press <F9> to accept the changed procedures and then type:

```
SAVE ''FIXSHAPE
```

You had called up the original FIXSHAPE with its three procedures. You have now added a further procedure, DECAGON. When you type `SAVE ''FIXSHAPE` you instruct Ladybug to save all the procedures that you have called up or made during your current Logo session and to call this workspace or collection of procedures, FIXSHAPE. Having made an additional procedure, you now have four in your workspace and these are put into the file FIXSHAPE.BUG. Since you have called this workspace by a name you have used before, Ladybug just writes over the file of that name. In this case it doesn't matter because you are writing the same previous three procedures all over again and you are adding a fourth as well. If your new set of procedures had been completely different you would choose a different filename.

7.3.2 Ready Made Movements and Shapes

If you are working with young children or handicapped people, you can write the procedures yourself and perhaps give them the names of the letters or characters on the keyboard. For example, TO SQUARE could be called S. All the person has to do is to press the key S, and, hey presto, the turtle draws a square on the screen. R could produce a rectangle, T a triangle and B a *bee hive* hexagon.

You could write simply ready made move procedures to move a set distance in a set direction. For example:

```
TO U
FD 50
END

TO R
RT 90
FD 50
LT 90
END

TO L
LT 90
FD 50
RT 90
END

TO D
BK 50
END
```

Save them all in a single workspace and each time you use Logo load it up so that they are all available.

7.3.3 Using Shapes to Make Pictures

Now you have learnt how to make the basic shapes, you can use them to build up pictures. It can be quite rewarding to set yourself up with some simple projects, like drawing a house. You may make several attempts before you get there, but you could say that achievement is not worthwhile without some trial and error beforehand. In my workshop, one little boy, Simon, spent several weeks working out how to make a spider, and when we had done that, the next challenge was the web. Sometimes the parents get more involved than the children. One dad produced the most beautiful sunflower. This is very much the spirit of Logo – choose an idea that appeals to you, (the choice is almost limitless) and work on it. When you get to the end you will feel very satisfied. If you don't get to the end, your mistakes may have given you some more ideas.

Logo provides the best of programming, the chance to be creative, to develop your own idea and the chance to solve a problem and to feel delighted when you have finally cracked it.

Here are some ideas to whet your appetite:

A house

This is definitely not an architect designed house, just a square with a triangle on top for the roof – Figure 7.3.

```
TO SQUARE
REPEAT 4 [FD 50 RT 90]
END

TO TRIANGLE
REPEAT 3 [FD 50 RT 120]
END

TO HOUSE
SQUARE
FD 50
LT 90
TRIANGLE
END
```

It doesn't really matter what size the square and triangle are, but they should have sides of the same length. If the square and triangle you saved in the FIXSHAPE workspace had the same sized sides, you can call that up with:

```
LOAD ''FIXSHAPE
```

and then all you have to do is to type the last procedure, TO HOUSE.

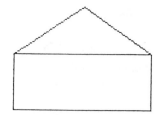

Figure 7.3: The result of HOUSE

Beehive

One hexagon is easy enough. Just use the hexagon procedure from the workspace, FIXSHAPE. But how do you fit them together to make a beehive?

Castle

The castle is made out of two towers with a rectangle in between. You can draw a tower by doing one type of rectangle with some ins and outs at the top. This will take you back to your starting position with the turtle pointing upwards. You don't draw the rectangle from here, but from the opposite corner. You can make a procedure to move through a horizontal distance with:

```
TO MOVE
RT 90
FD 50
LT 90
END
```

You need a tower procedure and a rectangle for the body of the castle between two towers. The tower is 50 wide, the rectangle is 100. Here is the rectangle procedure:

```
TO RECTANGLE
REPEAT 2 [FD 60 RT 90 FD 100 RT 90]
END
```

The tower is an upended rectangle but along the top it needs some in and outs to give it a castle shape. In all the procedures the turtle is left facing upwards which may mean an extra turn at the end. This is a good habit to get into, because it makes it easier to fit procedures together.

```
TO TOWER
FD 80
REPEAT 2 [REPEAT 2 [RT 90 FD 10] REPEAT 2 [LT 90 FD 10]]
RT 90
FD 10
RT 90
FD 80
RT 90
```

```
FD 50
RT 90
END
```

Finally, all these procedures are built up into Castle – Figure 7.4:

```
TO CASTLE
TOWER
MOVE
RECTANGLE
MOVE
MOVE
TOWER
END
```

Figure 7.4: An Englishman's home

Tree

Trees can be made out of a triangle for the leafy part and a thin rectangle for the trunk or with two or three triangles for a fir tree.

Straight sided letters

These can provide some interesting challenges. Figures 7.5 and 7.6 are some examples. The letter A needs a TRIANGLE procedure with sides length 50.

```
TO A
RT 30
FD 50
TRIANGLE
RT 60
FD 50
RT 60
```

```
FD 50
END

TO  E
LT  90
FD  60
RT  90
FD  40
RT  90
FD  30
BK  30
LT  90
FD  40
RT  90
FD  60
END
```

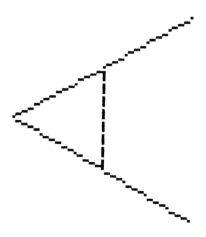

Figure 7.5: The result of TO A

Road signs

Make the outline of a road sign. Later on you will learn how to make circles, but for the moment stick to ones made out of triangles, rectangles and squares.

7.3.4 Making Different Sized Shapes

So far you have made just one size of shape, for example, a square with sides length 40. You can change this by moving into the Edit screen, changing the 40 to say 50, and pressing <F9> when done, but then all the squares are bigger.

Figure 7.6: The ouput from the E procedure

The next big breakthrough in Logo is to make shapes that allow you to put in a different size each time you use them. Start with a square and let the word SIZE stand for the length of each of its equal sides. So the procedure goes:

```
TO SQUARE :SIZE
REPEAT 4 [FD :SIZE RT 90]
END
```

Logo requires you to put a colon sign in front of the word SIZE – this shows that it is what is called a variable and can stand for different values on different occasions. To make the turtle actually draw a square, you now need to put in a number after typing SQUARE followed by a space (Logo is fussy about spaces).

Type:

```
SQUARE 30
```

You get a small square. Go on and type:

```
SQUARE 40
SQUARE 50
```

and so on. A quite interesting pattern begins to emerge.

You can do exactly the same thing for shapes that have two different numbers, like the length and breadth of a rectangle. Find some suitable names like LONG and WIDE. The procedure for RECTANGLE now becomes:

```
TO RECTANGLE :LONG :WIDE
REPEAT 2 [FD :LONG RT 90 FD :WIDE RT 90]
END
```

To run it, you type two different numbers when you call up the procedure, with spaces in between.

```
RECTANGLE 50 30
```

If you have noticed that RECTANGLE 30 50 would work just as well but that you would have a WIDE that was bigger than LONG. You might prefer to use:

```
TO RECTANGLE :SIDE1 :SIDE2
```

and to rewrite the procedure accordingly.

You can use a similar procedure for the pictures you made in the previous section, for example:

```
TO HOUSE :SIZE
```

where SIZE stands for the side of the square bottom and roof triangle, or:

```
TO TREE :SIZE
```

where SIZE stands for the length of the triangle that forms the main part of the tree.

7.4 How to Make a Circle

You could argue that, at the moment, your Logo world is rather a square one, not a curve in sight. The next big breakthrough is to make a circle and to use parts of it, what the mathematically minded call an arc.

It can be quite fun to try and work out how to make a circle yourself. Remember Logo involves walking forwards or backwards and turning. What instructions of this variety will produce a circle? Those who have got used to the mathematical idea of a circle being the path you draw when you keep a fixed distance from a fixed point are likely to be too stuck to have the kind of lateral thinking that leads to the answer. This, if you like, is one of the joys of Logo. It is a new spatial way of thinking and there is plenty of room for exploration, although I can't give you more than a few hints here.

So how do you make a circle? Try a decagon,

```
TO DECAGON
REPEAT 10 [FD 5 RT 36]
END
```

On 10 occasions you turn through 36 degrees and this means that you have gone through 360 altogether, that is, all the way round. Try:

```
TO TWENTAGON
```

```
REPEAT 20 [FD 3 RT 18]
END
```

This time, on 20 occasions, you turn through 18 degrees, which again is 360 altogether or all the way round. Look at twentagon – looks like a circle, doesn't it. This is, in fact, the principle of making a Logo circle. It is really just a straight sided figure but there are so many sides that it looks like a circle. The final version could be:

```
TO CIRCLE
REPEAT 360 [FD 1 RT 1]
END
```

Turning through 2 degrees, 180 times, would do as well.

The Ladybug disk has some circle and arc procedures already saved for you. To load these up, type:

```
LOAD ''CIRCLES
```

and then:

```
EDIT ALL
```

to see what procedures are on offer. The main ones are:

```
RCIRCLE :SIZE
LCIRCLE :SIZE
RARC :SIZE
LARC :SIZE
```

The R and L stand for right and left. Try out different numbers to get a feel for the different sizes of circle.

```
RCIRCLE 10
RCIRCLE 20
RCIRCLE 40
RCIRCLE 70
RCIRCLE 100
```

and so on.

An arc is part of a circle. The procedures RARC and LARC are quite funny. The larger the number you feed in, the longer and flatter they are.

Test them out by making the procedure TRYARC:

```
TO TRYARC
RARC 10
PU
```

```
HOME
PD
RARC  20
PU
HOME
PD
RARC  30
PU
HOME
PD
RARC  40
END
```

The results can be seen in Figure 7.7.

Figure 7.7: TRYARC in action

The two commands here you haven't met before are PU and PD for Pen Up and Pen Down respectively and should speak for themselves.

You can make a quite interesting fern shaped plant by combining this with a similar set of left handed arcs with:

```
TO FERN
TRYRARC
TRYLARC
END
```

Try doing some turns and then doing RARC or LARC.

```
TO PATTER
REPEAT 12 [RT 30 RARC 70]
END
```

Use EDIT PATTER to go into the edit screen and change the 30 after RT 30 to say 45, press <F9> for done, and see what happens. Change the numbers again to 120, 150 and 180.

Try messing round with little sets of instructions like:

```
RARC 70
RT 180
RARC 70
```

This might give you some ideas for some shapes you can make. Try:

```
TO PETAL
RARC 70
RT 90
RARC 70
END
```

Put this together to make the flower in Figure 7.8 with:

```
TO FLOWER
REPEAT 6 [PETAL RT 150]
END
```

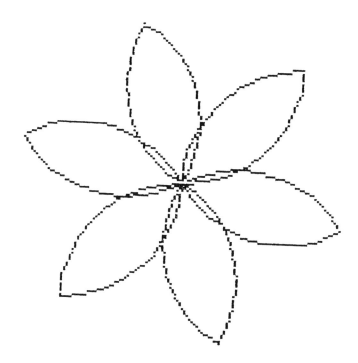

Figure 7.8: The result of TO FLOWER

Edit FLOWER and try some different turns, say 90 or 120 or 82. You get some quite interesting patterns. You can make waves across the screen with:

```
TO WAVE
REPEAT 5 [REPEAT 2 [RARC 50] RT 180]
END
```

7.4.1 Making Pictures using Circles

Circles open up an even larger world of pictures. Below are some procedures for making spectacles, sunflowers, spiders, a face and a car, all using circles or parts of circles. The spirit of Logo is to find some theme or project that interests you and to set yourself a problem – how do I make the turtle draw that shape? I have given you procedures for my final end products but some rather funny things happened along the way and sometimes these early versions give you further ideas for new projects or patterns.

Load up Ladybug's ready-made circle procedures with:

```
LOAD ''CIRCLES
```

Then add some procedures that allow you to move up or down, left or right, followed by a number so that you can move through different amounts.

```
TO RMOV :SIZE
RT 90
FD :SIZE
LT 90
END

TO LMOV :SIZE
LT 90
FD :SIZE
RT 90
END

TO DMOV :SIZE
BK :SIZE
END

TO UMOV :SIZE
FD :SIZE
END
```

Save all the procedures again into a new workspace with the command:

```
SAVE ''CIRCPIC
```

The movements are now combined with the ready-made circle procedures. Call CIRCPIC up again when you want to make a picture using them. You can add triangles and squares if you want these in your pictures as well.

Make the spectacles in Figure 7.9 with:

```
TO SPECS
LCIRCLE 70
RMOV 30
RCIRCLE 70
END
```

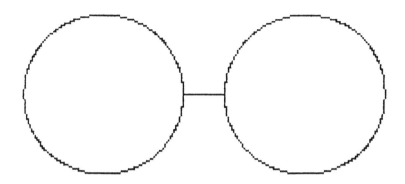

Figure 7.9: TO SPECS

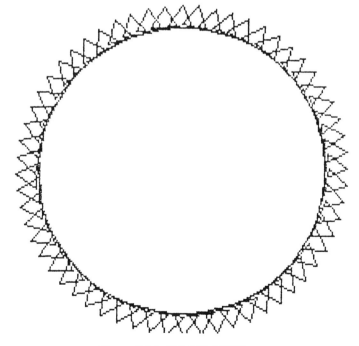

Figure 7.10: TO SFLOWER

For the sunflower in Figure 7.10, you need to put in a triangle procedure.

```
TO SFLOWER
REPEAT 60 [FD 12 TRIANGLE 20 LT 6]
END
```

The spider in Figure 7.11 goes:

```
TO SPIDER
REPEAT 4 [REPEAT 36 [RT 1 FD 1] LT 90 FD 40 BK 40 RT 90]
REPEAT 36 [RT 1 FD 1]
REPEAT 360 [LT 1 FD .25]
REPEAT 4 [REPEAT 36 [RT 1 FD 1] LT 90 FD 40 BK 40 RT 90]
REPEAT 36 [RT 1 FD 1]
END
```

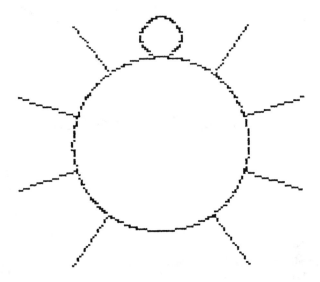

Figure 7.11: Logo Spider

My face in Figure 7.12 started off as a seeded potato. It then became rather boss eyed with a distinctively lop sided mouth in various different places. The final version had a slightly one sided mouth but most people don't have completely regular features.

```
TO FACE
RCIRCLE 80
PU
RMOV 40
PD
RCIRCLE 10
```

```
PU
RMOV 60
PD
RCIRCLE 10
PU
DMOV 30
LMOV 50
PD
LT 230
LARC 60
END
```

Figure 7.12: The face that launched a thousand chips

When you have put this procedure in, save it by typing:

```
SAVE ''FACE
```

This way you get all the movements and circles you need to make the face as well as the face you make out of them, a bit like the old lady who swallowed a fly.

The car in Figure 7.13 also started in a rather strange way as two unjoined lollipops. Repeat these several times and you have a pattern. Eventually I got the circles empty and joined together. I could have used these shapes to make models for a chemistry lesson.

The possibilities are endless.

```
TO CAR
RT 90
REPEAT 2 [FD 42 PU FD 8 LMOV 10 PD RCIRCLE 10 PU RMOV 10
FD 10 PD]
FD 42
LT 90
FD 30
LT 80
FD 30
RT 80
FD 20
LT 90
FD 80
LT 70
FD 20
RT 70
FD 40
LT 90
FD 30
END
```

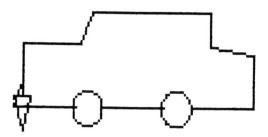

Figure 7.13: One for the road

7.5 Egg Shapes

So far all our circles have been round, or if you are a stickler for accuracy, more or less round. Sometimes though, you really want to make a squashed down circle, like the top of a birthday cake or a squashed in egg shape. The fancy mathematical word for these shapes is an ellipse.

Ladybug has a command called SETSCRUNCH which allows you to do this. It changes what is called the aspect ratio, the height of the screen in relation to its width. It is normally set at 1, the default value, the value the computer takes, unless you tell it to do something else.

You can use Setscrunch to change the aspect ratio, draw a figure in that ratio, use Setscrunch again to change the ratio and then draw another figure with this new value. The old figure will be left unchanged.

Setscrunch needs to be followed by a number. According to the manual, this should be anywhere between 0.1 and 10. I found that when I tried 0.1, Ladybug complained and said it was too small.

Experiment with different values of Setscrunch and draw circles to see what happens. Call up the ready made CIRCLES procedures stored in the workspace, by typing:

```
LOAD ''CIRCLES
```

and then try things like:

```
SETSCRUNCH 0.5
RCIRCLE 50
```

and:

```
SETSCRUNCH 2
RCIRCLE 50
```

0.5 gives you a squashed in circle, a sort of egg shape, whereas 2 gives you a squashed down circle, something like the top of a cake. As the circle gets squashed down it gets wider and wider and is likely to wrap round the screen. Try RCIRCLE 10, 20 and 30 and see what happens.

Experiment with some more values then go back to the default value with:

```
SETSCRUNCH 1
```

Draw a circle, say: RCIRCLE 70. Does it look completely round? No, not really. What value of SETSCRUNCH would be better? I personally found that 1.2 was nearer the mark.

The aspect ratio changes the shape of other figures as well: squares, rectangles and hexagons. Load up your saved workspace with all the basic shapes and try different values of SETSCRUNCH. You will notice that a square is not a square. Keep the same SETSCRUNCH and make a rectangle. Then turn RT 90 and draw the same rectangle. This time it comes out on its side and looks a bit different.

You can make pictures with ellipses, just as you did with circles. Load up CIRCPIC to get the standard circle routines and the movements you added yourself. My example is a birthday cake with candles on it – Figure 7.14.

```
TO BIRTHDAY
SETSCRUNCH 3
```

```
RT 180
FD 50
RHCIRCLE 40
FD 50
RCIRCLE 40
REPEAT 5 [PU RMOV 13 PD CANDLE]
END
```

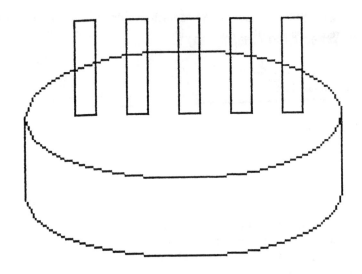

Figure 7.14: Happy Birthday

It was necessary to add two new procedures, one to draw half a circle and one to draw a candle.

```
TO RHCIRCLE :R
REPEAT 18 [RCP :R]
END

TO CANDLE
REPEAT 2 [FD 60 RT 90 FD 5 RT 90]
END
```

7.6 Knowing Exactly Where You are Going

The whole spirit of Logo is to move from one place to another, just as you would in real life. From where you are standing now, you could turn a bit, move forward a bit, do another turn, forward a bit more and so on. You turn or move forward from the position you are actually in at the moment. If you were already pointing right and you turned right through 180 degrees you would be pointing to the left. Try it with the turtle: RT 90 to turn right, then RT 180. You are now pointing left. You turned right from your last position. The next few commands given in this section use fixed or absolute instructions. When you use:

```
SETHEADING 180
```

you always turn to point vertically down the page and this would have happened wherever you had started off from. Try some more for yourself to see what it does.

SETHEADING 0 always sets the turtle heading vertically up the screen,

SETHEADING 90 sets it facing directly to the right

SETHEADING 270 to the left.

SETHEADING 360 is just the same as SETHEADING 0.

This command can be useful when you have lost your direction and want to turn somewhere very specific.

SETX, SETY and SETXY work like a co-ordinate system in maths. X measures along, Y measures up. Right in the centre of the screen, X is 0, Y is 0. As you go along the screen from left to right, X moves from -200 to +200. As you move from bottom to the top, Y moves from -150 to + 150. Try some for yourself.

SETXY -200 100 takes you to the top left hand corner, leaving a turtle trail in the process.

SETX 200 will then move you horizontally straight along to the top right hand corner. It leaves the Y value unchanged, at 100.

SETY -100 will then move you vertically down to the bottom right hand corner, leaving X unchanged at 200.

SETX changes the X co-ordinate only, SETY changes the Y co-ordinate only, SETXY changes first the X, then the Y co-ordinate.

Again, these commands can be useful when you know exactly where you want to go. You can also use them to make procedures so that you can go to a fixed spot on the screen and then perhaps draw some shape in each spot. To make your own simple grid of nine spots on the screen, type in:

```
TO A1
PU
SETXY -160 40
PD
END

TO A2
```

```
PU
SETXY 0 40
PD
END
```

Create procedures for A3, B1, B2, B3, C1, C2 and C3 using the following values:

```
           SETXY
A3         160  40
B1        -160   0
B2           0   0
B3         160   0
C1        -160 -40
C2           0 -40
C3         160 -40.
```

To get to any of these nine positions, just type the relevant procedure name, say A1 or B3. I chose names that worked like the co-ordinates of a simple grid.

7.7 Making Music

You can also make music with Logo. It divides the notes up into octaves. Middle C to upper B is called octave 4, higher C up to the next B is called octave 5, lower C to B below middle C is octave 3. You use the letter names, C, D, E, F, G, A, B for the notes. A with a plus (+) afterwards makes it a sharp, a minus (-) a flat.

A crotchet is length 4, a minim 2, a semibreve 1 and a quaver 8. L stands for length, O for octave. If you don't give the computer instructions it will take octave 4 (middle C to upper B) and length 2 the crotchet, as the default values. In other words, it will take these values until you tell it to do something else. Then if you want it to go back to these values, you must give it instructions. You use O4 for octave 4 and L2 for crotchet. Notice that it is capital O for octave not a zero.

You make music with the PLAY command followed by a space and then a square bracket. Try:

```
PLAY [CDEFGAB]
```

You can use procedures, just like you do for pictures or writing and if you make mistakes, edit or change them until they are correct. I have made some samples to show you how to do it. There is Frere Jacques, which is a good example of repeats, Hot Cross Buns and the Holly and the Ivy.

```
TO FRERE
REPEAT 2 [PLAY [F G A F]]
REPEAT 2 [PLAY [O4 l4 A B- l2 O5 L2 C]]
REPEAT 2 [PLAY [L8 O5 C D C O4 B- L4 A F]]
REPEAT 2 [PLAY [L4 F C L2 F]]
PLAY [L4]
```

```
END

TO HOLLY
PLAY [G L8 G G L4 G O5 E]
PLAY [D O4 B G L8 G G L4 G O5 E]
PLAY [L2 D L8 D C O4 B A L4 G B]
PLAY [L8 E E L4 D L8 G A B O5 C]
PLAY [O4 L4 B A L2 G L4]
END

TO HOTCROSS
PLAY [O5 D O4 D L2 G O5 L4 D O4 D L2 G]
PLAY [L8 O5 D C O4 B A G A B O5 C]
PLAY [L2 D O4 D L2 G L8 B B B B]
PLAY [L4 B A L8 G A B O5 C L2 O4 A]
PLAY [L8 O5 D C O4 B A G A B O5 C]
PLAY [L4 D O4 D L2 G L4]
END
```

7.8 Using Colour

If you have a colour monitor, you can add colour to your Logo pictures. You have a choice of 16 backgrounds. You type in BG, which is short for background, followed by a space and then a number. Try:

```
BG 4
```

Your whole screen should turn a bright red. The numbers for the other colours are given below.

0	Black	8	Grey
1	Blue	9	Light Blue
2	Green	10	Light Green
3	Cyan	11	Light Cyan
4	Red	12	Light Red
5	Magenta	13	Light Magenta
6	Brown	14	Yellow
7	White	15	High Intensity White

If you don't set a background colour, the computer will give you black, the default value – what you get anyway if you don't do anything about it. In other words, the default background colour is 0.

You can draw with different coloured lines and fill in or paint shapes and pictures. You don't get a choice of 16 colours for drawing and painting. You have a choice of two separate palettes, each with four different colours. If you change your mind and shift to the other palette, everything you have done is changed to the new palette's colours.

Palette	Colour	
0	0	same colour as background
	1	Green
	2	Red
	3	Brown
1	0	same colour as background
	1	Cyan
	2	Magenta
	3	White

So you are left with an effective choice of just three colours, since 0 is the background colour.

To draw coloured lines, you use PC for Pencolour, then a space, then a number 0, 1, 2 or 3.

Painting gives the same choice of colours as drawing. Again, you have a choice of two palettes, but when you've made your choice you are stuck with it for both drawing and painting. What painting does is to start wherever the turtle is, and to fill the surrounding area with colour, until it reaches a border. If there is no border it will colour the whole screen right to the edges. This means that you need to make sure the turtle is sitting inside a completely closed drawing. If there are any gaps you will lose everything and get just a coloured screen. When you draw shapes in Logo, the turtle tends to end up on the edge of what you've drawn, so you need to take it inside before you paint the shape.

Here is a procedure to produce a square, drawn in a red pen, and painted green. It is called COLSQUARE.

```
TO COLSQUARE
PALETTE 0
PC 2
REPEAT 4 [FD 100 RT 90]
PU
RT 30
FD 10
PAINT 1 2
LT 30
BK 10
PD
END
```

Type COLSQUARE and you should get your coloured square. This procedure chooses PALETTE 0 and selects pencolour 2, which is red. Then in the REPEAT 4 line it draws a square with a red line. At the end of this stage, the turtle is sitting on the edge of the square. To colour the square it moves the turtle inside the square. First there's a PU for penup, because you don't want to leave a mark as it moves into the square. Then it moves right and forward a little bit, inside the square.

The PAINT command has two numbers after it. The first is the colour it is actually going to be painted in, the second is the border it is going to fill up to, in this case the colour you drew the square in, which was red.

Use EDIT COLSQUARE to change PALETTE 0 to PALETTE 1. Type COL-SQUARE to run the procedure again, and see how this time you get the other choice of colours, because you now have a different palette. The square is drawn with a magenta line and painted in cyan.

You can then try out some different background colours with, for example:

BG 14

and then some other numbers to see what effects you get.

You can build these colour commands into all your shape procedures and all your Logo drawings. The procedure is to choose a palette right at the beginning, then to set the pencolour out of your three effective choices. Put in the instructions to draw whatever shape or object you are interested in. Provided it is a completely closed shape, with no gaps in the lines that draw it, you can paint it in. Use PU to lift the turtle from the screen and make some movements to get inside the shape. Then use the command, PAINT *paintcolour bordercolour* to actually do the painting. The second number should be the same as the colour of the line you drew the shape in because this is where the painting border will be. After that, move the turtle back again to where it finished drawing and put the pen down with PD.

7.9 Animation or Moving Logo

Logo can be used to make moving pictures. Use the palette command to set a paint palette, even if you are using black and white then use Pencolour 1, 2 or 3, anything other than 0, and draw a figure. Then pause for a moment, and draw the same figure in exactly the same position – only this time in Pencolour 0, the background colour. Drawing background on background produces a blank screen.

The trouble is if you draw the picture in one colour and then blank it out by drawing it again in the background colour, it all happens so quickly that you don't see anything at all. You need a pause in between but one problem with Ladybug Logo is getting the computer to wait. There is a WAIT command in the manual which ought to do exactly what you want, but it doesn't seem to work. The way round this is to take the pen up and draw an *invisible* shape and then put it down and do the next drawing in the animation sequence. A square worked quite well.

The procedure below is supposed to represent a flying bird. There are two basic wing positions, made out of inverted V shapes. They are carefully designed so that you end up in the middle, at the same position you started from with the turtle pointing vertically upwards in the usual way. This means that when you draw the shape again, in the background colour, it fits on top of the old one and effectively rubs it out. The wing shapes were made in the procedures, WING1 and WING2 sown in Figure 7.15.

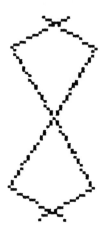

Figure 7.15: The ouput from WING1 and WING2

The BIRD procedure made one flying movement, consisting of WING1 drawn in a contrasting colour, WING1 drawn in the background colour to effectively rub it out, then PENUP for the *invisible* square, followed by PEN DOWN and WING2 in contrast and background colour.

The procedure FLY went through 20 sets of flying movements.

```
TO WING2
RT 120 FD 40
LT 90 FD 30
BK 30 LT 90
FD 40 LT 60
FD 40 RT 90
FD 30 BK 30
RT 90 FD 40
LT 60
END

TO WING1
RT 60 FD 40
RT 90 FD 30
BK 30 RT 90
FD 40 RT 60
```

```
FD 40 LT 90
FD 30 BK 30
LT 90 FD 40
LT 120
END

TO BIRD
PALETTE 0
PC 1
WING1
PU
REPEAT 4 [RT 90 FD 30]
PD
PC 0
WING1
PC 1
WING2
PU
REPEAT 4 [RT 90 FD 30]
PD
PC 0
WING2
END

TO FLY
REPEAT 20 [BIRD]
END
```

7.9.1 Making a Clock

You can use a similar *waiting* technique for making a clock. It doesn't take very long to draw an *invisible* square so it is better to make a circle instead, because that goes much more slowly. You want to go round and round for a minute and you can get this by drawing one complete circle and timing it with a stopwatch to see how long it takes. On my computer it took exactly 38 seconds, but I have an old portable which is slow. Then make it draw more than one circle and time it again. Change it until it takes one minute. This time procedure was called ICIRCLE, for invisible circle. I ended up with (this time I was using a faster 386SX):

```
TO ICIRCLE
PU
REPEAT 555 [FD 1 RT 1]
RT 165
PD
END
```

The RT 165 is one last turn so that the turtle ends up pointing the way it started.

To make the clock itself, you draw a minute hand that takes one hour to get round. Every minute it wipes out the old hand, and draws in a new one, 1/60th further round.

This means that it will turn through six *turtle rounds* each time the hand is redrawn. Here is the clock procedure lasting for just five minutes.

```
TO CLOCK
PALETTE 0
PC 1
FD 60
BK 60
REPEAT 5 [ICIRCLE PC 0 FD 60 BK 60 RT 6 PC 1 FD 60 BK 60]
END
```

If it works, and if you don't mind having your computer tied up for an hour, change the 5 after the REPEAT, to 60.

7.10 Writing Stories

Ladybug's strength is its graphics, the turtle and the drawing commands. If you look at books on Logo, you will tend to be disappointed if you try and follow the sections on what is called list processing, the things you can do with words. For example, in Ladybug you cannot pick out the first or second word in a list or pick words out at random.

But if you keep life very simple, there are a few things you can do and they can give you quite a lot of fun. You can make your computer write stories but you need to go into the text screen. When you load up Ladybug, you usually type in the word DRAW and then you move into the screen with the turtle, what Ladybug calls the graphics screen. In fact, right at the start of this chapter you arrived in the word or text screen, and immediately changed into the drawing or graphics screen. So if you are loading Ladybug up for the first time, don't type DRAW.

If you are already in the graphics or drawing screen, change to the text screen, by typing:

```
NODRAW
```

You can write on the drawing screen but it will only show one line at a time, and a second line will just write over the first, which isn't much use if you want to show a long story.

To write something on the screen, just use PRINT followed by square brackets containing whatever it is you are going to write. For example:

```
PRINT [THIS WILL APPEAR]
```

To write a story, make a procedure with several lines of PRINT statements:

```
TO STORY
PRINT [THERE WAS AN OLD FAIRY]
```

```
PRINT [WHO LIVED IN A WOOD]
PRINT [IN A LITTLE OLD HOUSE]
PRINT [BESIDE A STREAM]
PRINT [ ]
END
```

If you want a blank line, leave a space inside the square brackets. This can be useful if you go on to write another paragraph, and you want to leave a gap at the end of the first one.

Once you have made the procedure, you can get the story to write on the screen by just typing:

```
STORY<Rn>
```

Here is another story:

```
TO MORESTORY
PRINT [AN OLD GOBLIN CAME ALONG]
PRINT [HE WAS WEARING GREEN]
PRINT [WITH BROWN SHOES]
PRINT [ ]
END
```

You can put the two stories together to make a longer one, with the procedure:

```
TO ADDSTORY
STORY
MORESTORY
END
```

You can also put in bits that get repeated more than once. For example, here is CHANT, which we can make appear twice in the new BIGSTORY.

```
TO CHANT
PRINT [I AM A WICKED FAIRY]
PRINT [SCREAM SCREAM SCREAM]
PRINT [ ]
END

TO BIGSTORY
STORY
CHANT
MORESTORY
CHANT
END
```

7.10.1 Having a Chat With the Computer

Ladybug allows you to use print statements with the word REQUEST in them. This waits until you put something into the computer and then whenever it sees the word

REQUEST, Ladybug prints out the word you put in. If you use REQUEST again it waits until you type in another word, or the same one again if you are not feeling very imaginative. Try it out with:

```
PRINT SENTENCE [YOU TYPED IN] REQUEST
```

Nothing happens until you type in a word. The computer then comes out with YOU TYPED IN followed by whatever word you entered. There is one odd thing though. Notice the word SENTENCE in front of the square brackets. It seems to be necessary to put this in if you want REQUEST to work. In fact, you don't have to use just one word for REQUEST, you can put in a whole collection, and it may be that this is what SENTENCE allows you to do.

You can build up PRINT, SENTENCE and REQUEST so that the computer seems to be talking to you. Here is an example:

```
TO CHAT
PRINT [WHAT'S YOUR NAME]
PRINT SENTENCE [HELLO THERE] REQUEST
PRINT [TYPE SOMETHING YOU LIKE]
PRINT SENTENCE [I'M GLAD YOU LIKE] REQUEST
PRINT [HOW MANY BROTHERS AND SISTERS DO YOU HAVE]
PRINT SENTENCE [YOU SAID YOU HAVE] REQUEST
PRINT [WHAT ARE THEIR NAMES]
PRINT SENTENCE [THEIR NAMES ARE] REQUEST
END
```

Starting BASIC programming

8.1 What is BASIC?

BASIC is a major programming language. It stands for Beginners All-Purpose Symbolic Instruction Code and was founded by Professors John Kemeny and Thomas Kurtz at Dartmouth College, USA in the mid 1960s. Professionals tend to be ridiculously snobbish about it but around half the programming that is done, is in some kind of BASIC.

It has one great advantage for the home computer user – it tends to arrive with MS-DOS, so it won't cost you anything extra. If you use C or PASCAL, languages that are considered more *professional*, you will have to purchase a compiler and these can be quite expensive. If you can learn BASIC, you should have little difficulty in learning other languages.

Modern BASICs have improved. They are more structured, have more strange logic, and can come in compiled versions which means that their programs run much faster, thus meeting many of the criticisms of the experts.

When you use software like word processors, spreadsheets, databases or games, what you do is to load in a set of programs that someone else has written. These will have been written in a programming language, often in this day and age, in C. When you program yourself, you are doing much the same thing except that, being single handed and still learning, you cannot hope to achieve quite as much as vast teams of trained programmers with ready made libraries of code. In the early days of personal computing, you needed to write your own programs. Now there is so much excellent software around, it is quite unnecessary. The only reason for doing your own programming is that you enjoy it. Programming can stretch your mind in much the same way as doing crossword puzzles or learning a language.

Occasionally you will write a little program that really does do something that you can't get on commercial software. However, these days, you could probably have met the same need by using a spreadsheet or database. You can adapt these for your own use and the more sophisticated ones provide their own programming languages. These have the advantage that the actually package already contains a lot of its own processing power which saves a lot of coding.

Never force programming on children who don't want to learn. By the time they grow up, most programs will write themselves. It is much more important that children:

❑ Learn how to use big software packages to their full capacity.

❑ Use computers as a time saving tool in projects, mathematical and statistical work and in information gathering and retrieval and learn to be critical about the way in which software is presented.

When they are grown up, all they will need to do is to plan out a program, and the coding will occur automatically.

Having said all that, if you do enjoy programming, you can get a lot of pleasure and satisfaction when you finish a program. You will present yourself with a set of puzzles and when you find the solution, you will feel pleased. Programming can be very creative, because you have to plan and design your own code. You will look at ready-made commercial programs in a new light and you will learn something about how computers work.

BASIC is a high-level programming language. This means that it uses special words or commands that look a bit like the words used in ordinary English. Low-level languages, like Assembler, use code words like LDA, and are concerned with the internal workings of the computer's main processor. This means that they may use 25 lines of code to achieve what you can do in one line of BASIC. You really do get to know exactly how a computer works but at a price in terms of time!

High-level languages can be interpreted or compiled. All languages, including Assembler, have to be translated into 1s and 0s, which is the only thing the computer can understand. This is called machine code. With an interpreted language, this translation is done while the program is running, line by line. This means that interpreted languages run relatively slowly. With a compiled language, when you have written your program, you put it through a compiler, which does the translation in one go. You can then run the compiled version straightaway.

If you have mistakes or bugs in your program, in an interpreted language, it will run until it comes across a mistake. You can then alter this and try running it again. With a compiled language, you are running a compiled version. The bug means that it will stop or go wrong. If you are lucky you will get a useful error message to tell you what is wrong. You then have to go into the original program to amend it and then compile it again before you can try another run. This means that it is more tedious to correct mistakes when you are programming a compiled language.

BASIC used to be an interpreted language, but now there are many compiled versions, one of these being called Quickbasic. The BASIC with MS-DOS will usually be GW-BASIC or BASICA, but if you have the latest version of MS-DOS, Version 5.0, you will get the newer, QBASIC. This has some improvements over GW-BASIC and also has a more modern, mouse driven screen on which you actually write your programs. It is derived from Quickbasic but is different in that it is interpreted, not compiled.

8.1.1 Loading up BASIC

Find where your BASIC is stored, using DIR to see what is on your MS-DOS disks. It is possible that your particular dealer bundle does not have BASIC, so don't get too excited until you are sure you have got it. If you have a hard disk, load BASIC in the usual way. If you are just going to use it very occasionally, you can leave it in the same place as the rest of your MS-DOS. If you think you might be a regular user, create a separate subdirectory, called BASIC, and load in the program files with BASIC.* and any demonstration programs you are given, with *.BAS. BASIC programs are stored with the extension, .BAS.

If you have GW-BASIC and floppy only drives

Insert the disk with BASIC on it in disk drive A: and type:

```
BASICA
```

If you have GW-BASIC and hard disk drive

Get into the subdirectory where you store BASIC and type:

```
BASICA
```

For QBASIC, just type:

```
QBASIC
```

8.1.2 The Opening Screen in BASIC

If you have GW-BASIC

You get a screen showing the type of BASIC you have got and the version, something like COMPAQ BASICA v3.3 and various copyright statements. At the bottom of the screen, there is a list of what the function keys do. This is the main

BASIC screen where you put in all commands and where all programs will run. You are now ready to start writing a program.

If you have QBASIC

You get a screen with a menu bar along the top. You can operate this by using <Alt> plus various other keys or by using your mouse.

There is a Welcome box in the middle with a copyright notice. Press <Esc> to get rid of it. You then have a blank screen. This is what is called the Editing Screen and is where you will type in your programs and correct or edit them. They are run on another screen, which you will find is rather less pretty, at least until you do something more exciting with your programs.

8.1.3 Your First BASIC program

If you have GW-BASIC

As your very first step type:

```
PRINT "IBM"
```

To get the quotes mark press shift and the 2 key at the top of the keyboard. Now press the Return key. What happens?

You get the bit inside the quotes mark, shown on its own on the screen. If you leave out the quotes mark, it will not work. Try some more, like:

```
PRINT "BASIC PROGRAMMING"
```

and then:

```
PRINT "COMPUTER"
```

Try some more of your own not forgetting to press Return at the end of each line.

What you have been doing so far, is to use the PRINT command in what is called the *direct mode*. As soon as you press Return it prints out whatever is inside the quotes.

What would happen if you wanted to make it do the same thing again? You would have to do all the prints and quotes all over again, one at a time. If you write it out as a program though, you can make it repeat itself again and again, without having to put all the PRINTS and quotes in. Every time you run the program, it will do a repeat performance. You can save a program on disk and use it another time. It is slightly harder work setting up a program in the first place, but as soon as you want to do something more than once, it is well worth it.

To start your first program, type:

```
10 PRINT "IBM"
```

The only difference is that now you have started with a number, in this case 10. However, this time when you press Return, nothing happens. This is now a program and it won't do much until you run it. You do this by typing:

```
RUN <Return>
```

or by simply pressing the <F2> function key, which has exactly the same effect.

What happens?

Go on and type:

```
20 PRINT "BASIC PROGRAMMING"
```

Press function key <F2> to run the program. What happens?

Notice that it prints out BASIC PROGRAMMING, the bit in quotes from our second line number 20, but before that it prints out IBM, the bit in quotes from the first line number 10, as well. Add the third line:

```
30 PRINT "COMPUTER"
```

Press function key <F2> to run it. All the lines are carried out again. This is what is useful about programming, it will do things time and time again, every time you run it.

If you have forgotten what your whole program looks like, type:

```
LIST <F1>
```

and the whole program is listed out. To do this quickly, press the function button <F1>.

You could ask why the line numbers were called 10, 20 and 30 and not 1,2 and 3. Try adding:
```
15 PRINT "PC"
```

Press function key <F2> to run it. Line 15 is the last line you typed in, and you would expect to see:

```
IBM
BASIC PROGRAMMING
COMPUTER
PC
```

but in fact, you get:

```
IBM
PC
BASIC PROGRAMMING
COMPUTER
```

What the computer did was to put the new line 15 between line 10 and line 20. Press function key <F1> to list the program. You will see that the computer has automatically put the program in number order.

When you write programs, use numbers 10 apart and then you have spare numbers that you can use if you want to put in extra things later on.

If you have Q-BASIC

Type:

```
PRINT "IBM"
```

It doesn't matter whether you type PRINT in capital letters, little letters or a mixture of both. Make sure you use the quote marks. Press Return and the cursor has now moved on to the next line. If you used any little letters in the PRINT, they will be turned into capitals.

This is actually a small program. You can now run it.

Using the mouse

The mouse runs a red cursor. Take it up to the menu at the top, put it over the Run bit and click the left mouse button. A drop down menu appears with the top choice, Start, highlighted. Move the mouse cursor over this and click the left mouse button again, to select it. This will run your program.

Using keys

Press <Alt-R> to select the Run menu. This means that you hold down the <Alt> key with one hand, and while you are doing this press the R key. You get a menu, with the top choice, Start, highlighted. Press <Rn> to register this choice. You could have typed S, without a <Rn> instead.

Using a hot key

A hot key press is a quick way of going somewhere by just pressing one or two keys. You don't have to go to the menu, you can just press hot keys while you are in the Editing screen. To run a program, type:

```
<Shift-F5>
```

and your program will instantly run.

Hot keys are useful for things you do very frequently. They tend to be more meaningless than menus and if you don't do things often, you will find it difficult to remember them.

Whatever method you used to run QBASIC

You go into another screen, containing various bits of junk from your past activities, and you will see:

```
IBM
```

This is what your program does. It puts on the screen whatever is contained in the quote marks, following the PRINT statement.

Underneath you will see the message:

```
Press any key to continue
```

Do this, and you will return to the Editing screen.

Add another two lines to your program, by typing:

```
PRINT "BASIC PROGRAMMING"
PRINT "COMPUTER"
```

Run the program again to see what it does.

8.1.4 Correcting Typing Mistakes

If you have GW-BASIC

Soon enough, you will make some mistakes in your typing. Changing mistakes is called editing.

If you notice you have made a mistake, before you press Return at the end of a line, use the <backspace> key to rub out backwards towards the mistake and type it in correctly.

Often you won't realise you have made a mistake until after you have pressed Return and gone on to a new line. Or you may try to run your program and find that it doesn't work and that the computer comes up with an error message, like *Syntax error*. In these situations you can either type:

```
EDIT 30
```

or whatever the line number is, after which the line will appear on the screen with the cursor flashing on it. Alternatively you can use the cursor keys to move to the line you want to change. Move the <rightarrow> or <leftarrow> cursor keys until the cursor is flashing on the character or number you want to correct. Press the <Delete> key to delete it or just type in the new character you want to replace it with.

If you want to put something extra in, take the cursor to the character which is immediately after or to the right of where you want to put a new letter or number. Press the <Insert> key to put yourself into insert mode and type in the new letter or letters.

Then you must press Return to register the change. If you move away to another line with the cursor keys, the change will not be registered and you will have to start all over again.

If you have QBASIC

Use the cursor keys to move to the place where you made the mistake.

To insert a letter, move to the right of where you want it to be and just type it in.

If you want to write over a letter, move to the letter you want to change. Press the <Insert> key to put it into overstrike or replace. It will stay like this, overwriting everything, until you press it again, and toggle it back to Insert.

To delete a character, move the cursor over that character, and press the <Delete> key.

Suppose you want to put in a new line of program, in the middle of what you have already written, for example, PC before the word BASIC PROGRAMMING. In GW-BASIC, this was done with line numbers. In QBASIC, you need to put in a new line, exactly where you want it. You can use line numbers in QBASIC but you don't have to, so you might as well do without.

To make a new line move the cursor to the end of the line above where you want to put the new line, in this case at the end of PRINT "IBM". Just press <Rn> and you will get a new line, provided you have not toggled the <Insert> key into overstrike.

Type:

```
PRINT "PC"
```

Run the program again and see what happens.

8.1.5 Leaving BASIC

You have now finished your first programming session. To leave BASIC and get back to the A: or C: prompt:

If you use GW-BASIC

Just type:

```
SYSTEM
```

If you use QBASIC:

Move the mouse cursor to the menu bar at the top, put it on *File* and click the left mouse button to get a drop down menu. Move the mouse cursor down until it is on the *Exit* and click the left mouse button to select. You then get a dialogue box telling you that your loaded file is not saved, with a cursor on Yes for *Save it Now?* Don't bother to save this program so move the cursor to *No* and click the left mouse button.

Alternatively press <Alt-F> to select the File menu. Move the cursor down until *Exit* is highlighted or type X to select *Exit*. You get a dialogue box stating that your loaded file is not saved. Type N for No.

8.1.6 Print Statements are Everywhere

PRINT statements appear all over the place in almost every program. Here are some examples, to let you see what they do and to give you some ideas of your own. DO NOT type these in, they are just examples.

PRINT statements could be used to write a story. If you really want to write one, a word processor would be a much more sensible way of doing it. Here though is a PRINT story that might entertain a young child:

```
10 PRINT "In the beginning there was a wicked witch"
20 PRINT "who lived all on her own in a tumbledown"
30 PRINT "cottage by the side of a wood"
```

Run it, and you just get the story part, not all the PRINTS and quotes.

PRINT statements are used to give instructions at the beginning of programs like quizzes or adventure games. For example:

```
10 PRINT "YOU ARE IN THE MIDDLE OF A DARK WOOD"
20 PRINT "SURROUNDED BY TALL TREES. OVER ON THE"
30 PRINT "LEFT THERE IS A CASTLE WITH A LARGE OAK"
40 PRINT "DOOR, YOU CAN GO SOUTH OR EAST OR WEST"
```

or something like:

```
10 PRINT "THIS IS A MULTIPLE CHOICE QUIZ PROGRAM"
20 PRINT "ABOUT ENGLAND. YOU GET 20 QUESTIONS AND"
30 PRINT "YOU GET A SCORE AT THE END. THERE ARE"
40 PRINT "5 POSSIBLE ANSWERS TO EACH QUESTION"
50 PRINT "AND YOU ARE ASKED TO GIVE YOUR ANSWER"
60 PRINT "IN THE FORM A, B, C, D OR E IN CAPITAL LETTERS"
```

PRINT statements can be used to write out menus. You will need some different programming to actually be able to choose something, but more of that later. To just write out the menu you would use:

```
10 PRINT "1. DEMO GAME"
20 PRINT "2. NOVICE GAME"
30 PRINT "3. HARD GAME"
40 PRINT "4. IMPOSSIBLE GAME"
50 PRINT "5. QUIT GAME"
60 PRINT "MAKE YOUR CHOICE BY PRESSING A NUMBER (1-5)"
```

QBASIC variations

With most of the programs in this and the next chapter the main difference is the lack of line numbers and you can assume that all you need to do is leave these out for the program to work as shown. Any major differences in the structure will be indicated in detail.

You will certainly see PRINT again!

8.2 Putting Things Into the Computer

8.2.1 Computing is Interactive

Computing is usually what is called interactive – when you are running your computer, you press a mouse button, push the joystick or type on the keyboard, and what you do makes the computer behave in different ways. On the other hand, a television programme does its own thing whatever the watcher does or does not do.

Often when a computer is running it will ask questions and wait for your answer. For example:

```
Are you sure y/n?
```

and you type in y or n.

8.2.2 Your first Input Program

You are going to see how to put questions in your programs. Try:

```
10 PRINT "What is your name?"
20 INPUT Yourname$
30 PRINT "Your name is ";Yourname$
```

Run the program and see what happens. What is your name? appears on the screen, followed by a flashing cursor and then the computer stops.

The program is waiting for you to do something. This is the effect the BASIC command INPUT has. On this occasion it is going to take your name and put it into a box which it will call *Yourname$*. Answer the computer by typing in your name – for me that is BARBARA, then press Return to register it. The computer then comes up with Your name is BARBARA.

Try running the program again and put in a different name. Notice that *Yourname$* can stand for different names at different times. What is the computer doing? It is making a memory box and giving it the label *Yourname$*, a bit like the lockers at the swimming pool.

The lockers usually have numbers for labels. One day you put your clothes in one locker, another day in another one. On the same day a particular locker will hold different people's clothes at different times.

This happens to the computer's memory box holding *Yourname$*. Every time you run this program and put in a different name, the computer takes the old name out of the box and puts the new one in.

Exercises

❏ Write a program that asks your occupation and then tells you what your job is (memory box – *job$*)

❏ Write a program that asks you what the weather is like and then tells you that today the weather is whatever you put in (memory box – *weather$*)

❏ Write a program that asks you what your favourite food is and then tells you that your favourite food is bad for you (memory box – *food$*)

❏ Write a program that asks you for your address and then tells you where you live (memory box – *address$*)

8.2.3 Strings and Numbers

The dollar sign on the end of the memory box label name is vital. Just to demonstrate what happens if you leave it out try the following.

If you have GW-BASIC

Type:

```
EDIT 20
```

to change line 20 of the program. Cursor along until it is on the dollar ($) sign. Press <Delete> to get rid of the it and <Rn> to register the change.

Then edit line 30 and take the $ off the end of Yourname as you did for line 20. Be careful to press Return to register the change. Your program should now look like this. Press function key <F1> for list to check that this is the case.

```
10 PRINT"What is your name?"
20 INPUT Yourname
30 PRINT"Yourname is ";Yourname
```

Press function key <F2> to run the program again, and when the computer stops, put in a name, just as you did before. This time, the computer comes up with an error message, that you must redo from start. This time put in a number – it seems a bit funny putting in a number for a name but it works.

If you have QBASIC

When you have run the program, press any key to return to the Editing Screen. Move the up, down, right and left arrow keys, until the cursor is sitting on the $ sign at the end of Yourname. Press the <Delete> key to delete it. Do the same for the *Yourname$* on the next line.

Use the mouse, keys or hotkey to run the program again. Try putting in your name as you did last time. You stay in the Run screen, and get the message *?Redo from Start*, with the cursor waiting for you to put something in. Type in a number. This time the computer accepts it and tells you that your name is that number.

Remember: If you want to put a word into your memory box you must use a label name which has $ at the end. This is what is called a string variable – it tells the computer to expect a word, or in computer terms, text. Leave the dollar sign out and it will expect a number. It will then be prepared to use the number sign to do some arithmetic. Here is a program to show you how it manages this.

8.2.4 Using Numbers to do Arithmetic

Start off a new program:

If you have GW-BASIC

Type NEW to start a new program.

If you have QBASIC

With the mouse move the mouse cursor so it is on *File*. Click the left mouse button to pull down menu. Move the mouse cursor so it is on *New*. Click the left mouse button to select.

Alternatively press <Alt-F> to pull down the menu under file. Move cursor down to *New* and press <Rn> or press N for *New*.

You get a dialogue box, like you did when you left QBASIC in Section 8.1.6. Don't bother to save the last program. Move the mouse cursor to *No* and click the left mouse button or just type N for *No*.

You then get a clear Editing Screen.

Type in this program:

```
10 PRINT"What is your age?"
20 INPUT Age
30 Days = 365*Age
40 PRINT "You are ";days;" days old"
```

Try running it and put in your age. Because there is no dollar sign at the end of the memory box label, the computer expects a number. In line 30 it does some arithmetic on this (* means multiply). It will multiply your age by 365, the number of days in the year – this is roughly the number of days you have been alive.

This is one occasion where you do not put a $ character on the end of the variable. Try the following:

If you have GW-BASIC

Type EDIT 20 and add a $ onto the end of Age, press <Rn> to register the change, then use EDIT 30, put a $ on the end of Age and <Rn> to register the change. Press function key <F2> to run the program. Put a number in for your input. What happens now?

Type mismatch means that it can only do the arithmetic in line 30 on a number and *Age$* is not treated as a number. You put a number in, but because of the dollar sign on the end of *Age$* the computer thinks of it as a word and refuses to do arithmetic on it

If you have QBASIC

Press any key to return to the Editing Screen. Use the cursor arrow keys to move to *Age* in the second line of your program. Put a $ on the end of Age so it reads *Age$*. Do the same thing for *Age* in the next line, the line that does the arithmetic.

Try running the program. You get a dialogue box, with the error message *Type mismatch* and at the same time the *Age$* in the arithmetic line is highlighted. The clever Editing Screen has spotted your mistake and pointed it out to you. You can call for Help to see what is wrong. In this case select OK by pressing <Rn>. Delete the $ in INPUT age$.

If you try running the program again, you can put in a number but you will always get the answer 0 for the number of days. This is because the computer treats *Age$* and *Age* as two completely different variables. Since you haven't actually put anything into *Age*, it treats it as 0.

In both cases

Be very careful when you are using INPUT in your programs. Do you want to put in text (words) or a number?

Exercises

❏ Write a program to input a number (memory box – *number*), to add 12 to it and then to put the answer onto the screen (use the PRINT statement)

❏ Write a program to ask how much money you earn (memory box – *money*) per week and to tell you how much you get in a year (keep it all in pennies for now)

❏ Write a program to input three numbers (memory boxes – *firstno, secondno, thirdno*), to add them together and then to output the result

❏ Write a program that asks for the month, first by name (memory box – *monthname$*) then in number (e.g. February = 2) and then multiplies the month number (memory box – *monthno*) by 30 to give you the number of days in the year so far and prints this to the screen (memory box – *daysno*). This doesn't give you a completely correct answer, that kind of challenge will come later.

8.3 Doing Things Again and Again

What happens when you are made to do the same thing over and over again, like doing the same sort of work day after day. You get bored and when you are bored you tend to make a mess of things.

Computers don't get bored. They can do the same old thing over and over again – and they do it just as well the thousandth time as they did it the first. That is why computers are now doing some of the more boring jobs in factories. Computers also do things very quickly.

Try this program.

```
10 FOR N=1 TO 5
20 PRINT "HELLO"
30 NEXT N
```

Run the program – what happens?

It comes up with Hello five times on the screen. What you have here is called a FOR...NEXT loop – a loop because the computer goes through it several times. The first time it comes to line 10 it takes N as 1, then goes to line 20 and puts the first Hello on the screen. Then it goes to line 30 which tells it to take the next N. This makes it loop back to line 10 where the next N will be 2. It prints another Hello and goes to 30 again, which loops it back to 10 to pick up the next N which is 3. When it has picked up the last N which is 5 it prints Hello but this time when it gets to line 30 there are no more Ns – it has picked up the last one so it does not loop back. In this program it stops – in other programs it may go to line 40 and 50 and so on.

Can you work out how you would change the program to make it print Hello on the screen eight times?

So far you have had just one line of program in the middle of the loop. You can have as many as you want. You could use this to print out notices for a charity event or a party invitation. Try:

```
10 FOR N=1 TO 10
20 PRINT "THE CHRISTMAS CRIB SERVICE"
30 PRINT "IS ON SATURDAY DECEMBER 14TH"
40 PRINT "AT 2.30 PM ST. MARY'S CHURCH"
50 NEXT N
```

Run the program. The notices should run all over the screen. The trouble is that there is no gap between them. You can get round this with the line:

```
45 PRINT:PRINT:PRINT
```

Each PRINT leaves an empty line so you get a nice gap between the invitations.

You could turn these into real printed out invitations. Add the lines

```
47 LPRINT "------------------------------------------------"
48 LPRINT
```

and edit or change all the PRINT statements in the other lines so that they read LPRINT instead. The dotted line in line 47 gives you a cutting line so that you can cut between the invitations more easily. If you want some number of notices or invitations other than 10, change the FOR N = 1 TO 10 in line 10 to whatever value you want.

You will probably want to save your notice so that you can print some more at a later date. To save a program, you need to give it a filename which is up to eight characters long, doesn't begin with a number and doesn't use spaces or funny signs. Give it a name that will make some sense several months later, then when you look back at your disk you will know what program it was. For the moment, use CRIBSERV.

If you use GW-BASIC

To save it to the same drive or subdirectory as the BASIC programming language, type:

```
SAVE "CRIBSERV
```

If you have a double floppy disk drive and want to save it on drive B:, type:

```
SAVE "B:CRIBSERV
```

If you use QBASIC

Use the menu at the top of the screen, and select Save under the *File* Menu.

Try using this program to write a general invitation to a party you are going to hold.

So far we have made exactly the same thing happen again and again. However it is possible to make something slightly different happen each time you go through the loop. For example, start a new program and then:

```
10 FOR N=1 TO 5
20 PRINT N
30 NEXT N
```

This time it prints something different each time it goes through the loop because it is told to print *N* which has a different value each time the computer goes through the loop. You could add to this and get the program to set out some multiplication tables for the kids.

Change line 20 to:

```
20 PRINT N; " x ";2;" is ";2*N
```

Try running it and see what happens. You get the first five entries of the 2 times table. To get more entries change the 5 in line 10 to, say, 10.

To get the 3 times table change the two 2s in line 20.

You can play around with this program to write out more tables.

So far we have always gone up in 1s. However you can go up in other *steps* or even come down.

Start a new program and type in:

```
10 FOR N=1 TO 20 STEP 4
20 PRINT N
30 NEXT N
```

Run the program and see what happens. Then change the 4 in line 10 to -1 and see what happens. Try some more.

8.4 Making Decisions

In Section 8.2 I said that computing is interactive and showed how you could build this into your programs using the INPUT command. When you used that command, the program would stop in the middle and wait for you to put something in. When you put in names or ages, it would print them on the screen or do arithmetic on them, and because you had fed in different words or numbers, the results were different.

When you run a commercial program it often starts with a menu. If you key in, say, the letter W, the computer loads up a word processor but if you press S it loads in the spreadsheet. Something completely different happens in response to what you type in. This is what is called branching. If you type in W, the computer travels down the word processor branch and if you type in S it travels down the spreadsheet branch.

The menu is a little program that goes something like this. Don't type it in.

```
10 PRINT"Type in W or S"
20 INPUT LETTER$
30 IF LETTER$="W" THEN LOAD WORDPROCESSING
40 IF LETTER$="S" THEN LOAD SPREADSHEET
```

But do try this program:

```
10 PRINT "1 or 2"
20 INPUT ANSWER
```

```
30 IF ANSWER=1 THEN PRINT "I LOVE YOU"
40 IF ANSWER=2 THEN PRINT "I DON'T"
```

Run it, and when it stops and gives you a flashing cursor, try putting in 1. Run it again and this time try 2.

Here is another program to try. First of all clear any previous program from memory typing NEW in GW-BASIC or using the File menu and *New* in QBASIC.

```
10 PRINT "Please give your age in years"
20 INPUT AGE
30 IF AGE>18 THEN PRINT "You can vote" ELSE PRINT "You can't vote"
```

This time there is a condition, whether the age is greater than 18 (this is what the symbol > means). If the condition is true, or the age is greater than 18, then the program will print: You can vote. There is another new thing in this line as well, the ELSE. This means that if the condition isn't true, you get a different statement printed out: You can't vote. Try running the program, putting different numbers in for the age to see what happens.

Decisions can be very useful when you want to write quiz programs. Start a new program and type in:

```
10 PRINT"THE CAPITAL OF FRANCE IS"
20 PRINT"(A) BONN"
30 PRINT"(B) PARIS"
40 PRINT"(C) LONDON"
50 PRINT"Answer A/B/C"
60 INPUT ANSWER$
70 IF ANSWER$="B" THEN PRINT"WELL DONE. CORRECT" ELSE PRINT "WRONG"
```

When you use ELSE, it is important that the whole IF....THEN.....ELSE goes on the same line.

Exercises

❏ Write a program that asks for someone's age and tells them that if they are over 40 they should be thinking about a pension.

❏ Add a bit more to the program above so that it also tells them that if they are over 65 they can retire.

❏ Write a program to ask for someone's waist measurement. If it is over 73 cms tell them they are fat.

❏ Do your own multiple choice question.

❏ Ask someone if they like computers, Y or N (capitals). If they say yes tell them they are excellent, if no they are behind the times.

❏ Write out a menu with three pudding choices, icecream, gateau and fruit salad. Tell them that the last is a healthy choice whereas the other two are not.

8.5 The Computer Makes Some More Decisions

The computer is very good at testing you. How old are you? If you are over 18, you can drink alcohol in a pub, if you are under 18, you can't. Here is a program to tell you whether you can drink in a pub or not.

```
10 PRINT "HOW OLD ARE YOU?"
20 INPUT AGE
30 IF AGE>18 THEN PRINT "YOU CAN DRINK IN A PUB"
40 IF AGE<18 THEN PRINT "YOU CAN'T DRINK IN A PUB YET. HARD LUCK"
```

Try running it putting in different numbers. What happens if you get 18? The answer is nothing, because the test only looks for numbers greater than 18 or less than 18, not 18 itself. Put an equal sign in after the 18 in AGE>18 so that it reads AGE>=18, and this problem will be remedied.

A common test in many games programs will be whether you want to go on playing a game or not. Put on your caps lock to type in the following program and to run it. Start a new program.

```
10 PRINT "DO YOU WANT ANOTHER GO?"
20 PRINT "TYPE IN Y/N IN CAPITALS"
30 INPUT GO$
40 IF GO$="Y" THEN PRINT "WE'RE GOING TO PLAY AGAIN"
50 IF GO$="N" THEN PRINT "GAME OVER. GOODBYE"
```

Normally, of course, if you entered Y for Yes, the program would run again. In this case, to make the programming easier we just put in a message.

What happens if you don't put your caps lock on when you run the program? Try putting in a y or n in lower case and see for yourself. If a program reacts differently when you use a different case of letter i.e. lower rather than upper or vice versa, it is called case sensitive. Fortunately, when you type in GW-BASIC programs or run most modern programs they are not sensitive. The old BBC Basic was, and it is quite painful going back to it. You can get a bit sloppy when programming is not case sensitive.

You can change your program to make it case insensitive. Edit line 40 to look like this:

```
40 IF GO$ = "Y" OR GO$ = "y" THEN PRINT "WE'RE GOING TO PLAY AGAIN"
```

Make a similar change to line 50 so you end up with "N" OR "n".

Ideally, you should remove the line that asks you to put the answer in capitals, as it doesn't matter any more.

Try running the program again to test what happens if you use the lower case y or n.

Allowing for the fact that people will not want to worry about using upper or lower case keys, is what is called being user friendly. When you write programs, you have to allow for the fact that the user may be very stupid.

Another kind of test the computer can do is to make sure that people use a password before the program will run. When I am at work, I first type in my user name BEDWARDS and then I am asked to type in my password. This changes every month or so. I type it in by pressing the relevant keys but I am not allowed to see what I am typing on the screen. This just stays blank. But the computer receives what I type and checks to see if it is correct. Not showing the password on the screen means that no one can stand near me and learn my password by seeing it on the screen. If the password is correct, I get a menu of all the programs I am allowed to use at work: my spreadsheet, database and so on. If not, no programs for me. I have to start again.

Here is a program which allows you to put in your password, and then checks to see if it matches one that the computer has stored in the program itself. In this program, what you type will appear on the screen. The password in this program is BARBARA but you can put your own name in *password$*. People tend to be very unoriginal when they select their passwords and choose names of their friends, children or towns they have lived in.

```
10 PRINT "PLEASE ENTER YOUR PASSWORD"
20 INPUT PASSWORD$
30 IF PASSWORD$="BARBARA" THEN PRINT "YOU CAN PLAY NOW"
40 IF PASSWORD$<>"BARBARA" THEN PRINT "YOU GOT IT WRONG. BYE BYE"
```

In line 40, the symbol <> means does not equal.

As you saw in the last section, tests like this are very good for writing quiz games. Ask a question like *Who is the Prime Minister of England?* The user gives an answer and you want to test this to see if it is correct or not. Supposing you just let them type in a name for their answer. You want to compare it with the correct one. The string would have to be exactly the same, letter by letter and space by space to pass the test. Someone could type in the right answer but put the surname and christian name the wrong way round, put two spaces between them or put in a different mixture of capital and lower case letters. Though the answer would really be correct, it would come out as wrong. This is why it is usually best to write your quizzes as multiple choice tests so that the user only has to type in one letter. So try this:

```
10 PRINT "WHO IS PRIME MINISTER OF ENGLAND"
```

```
20 PRINT "IS IT (A) MARGARET THATCHER"
30 PRINT "IS IT (B) MICHAEL HESELTINE"
40 PRINT "IS IT (C) NEIL KINNOCK"
50 PRINT "IS IT (D) JOHN MAJOR"
60 INPUT ANS$
```

You could now add:

```
70 IF ANS$="D" THEN PRINT "JOLLY GOOD, YOU ARE QUITE RIGHT"
```

Now you could write three more lines of program for what happens if you give the answers A, B and C:

```
80 IF ANS$="A" THEN PRINT "YOU ARE WRONG"
90 IF ANS$="B" THEN PRINT "YOU ARE WRONG"
100 IF ANS$="C" THEN PRINT "YOU ARE WRONG"
```

See how similar these three lines are. In fact you could replace them with just one line. The same thing happens whichever answer you give so you could put it another way by saying:

```
80 IF ANS$<>"D" THEN PRINT "YOU ARE WRONG"
```

This is quite a good method because it lets you press silly keys as well as the possible answers. There are even neater ways of dealing with tests but more of that later.

Note to parents: IF THEN ELSE would be better but the logic of coping with IFs can be quite difficult, particularly in the early stages of programming. Children are often happier seeing them written out in lots of statements and I think they should be allowed to do this. They should write in the way that they understand. We don't expect them to start writing English in full literary style, we are just happy seeing them writing and expressing themselves. The elegance can come later.

8.6 More Ways of Putting Things into the Computer

You have already met the BASIC command INPUT. Try a little program to have another look at how it works.

```
10 PRINT"How old are you?"
20 INPUT AGE
30 PRINT "You are ";AGE
```

Run the program and see what happens. It carries out the first instruction and then waits for you to put something in. Type in your age. While you do this what you type is echoed on the screen but it does not do much else until you press Return. Do this and the computer tells you how old you are.

There are times when you don't want to have to key something in and then press Return before the computer will go on. Imagine trying to play a shooting game where you had to keep on pressing Return. You would never hit anything. What you want here is instant action and that is where INKEY$ comes in handy.

INKEY$ reads the first key that you press. If you go on pressing keys, it won't notice anything beyond the first key press. It is very useful for a quick response to pressing a single key but wouldn't be much use for putting in long names or even your age if you have reached double figures. You don't want your 10 or 11 to be treated as 1.

INKEY$ is a string value. So any key you press will be treated as a string, even if it is a number and you must use the string sign if you want to make something equal to INKEY$.

If you run a program which contains INKEY$, when the program comes to that very point, it reads into INKEY$ whatever key is being pressed at that very split second. If a key is not being pressed it says INKEY$ is a blank or null string. It will not wait until the moment that you do press a key. The only way of handling this is to make the program run round and round in a circle, until a key is pressed. What happens then is that the computer keeps on reading INKEY$ time after time, and every time nothing has happened and it gets a null string, it goes back and reads INKEY$ again. Lewis Carroll would have loved it.

If you have GW-BASIC

This is done in line 30 in the program below. Try it out. Start a new program and then type in:

```
10 CLS
20 PRINT "Press any key...."
30 A$=INKEY$:IF A$="" THEN GOTO 30
40 PRINT "Your key was ";A$
```

Run the program. The message *Press any key* appears on the screen and then nothing happens at all until you do actually press a key. What line 30 does is to test for a key. It actually takes the value of the keypress at the very second when it reaches this line of the program. If no key is pressed at this moment, INKEY$ gets the value of empty or what is known as the null string and is shown with two quotation marks squashed together. The second half of the line tests for this value, and if it finds that INKEY$ did come up with the null string, it sends the program back to the beginning of the line and makes it test for another keypress.

It then goes on to line 40, and shows the value of the key that you did press.

If you have QBASIC

You need a slightly different program. The PRINT statements are the same, but because you generally don't use line numbers you need to deal with INKEY$ a little differently.

Start a new program and enter:

```
CLS
PRINT "Press any key"
DO
A$=INKEY$
LOOP WHILE A$=""
PRINT "Your key was ";A$
```

The LOOP WHILE sends the program back to the DO. As long as you are not pressing any keys, INKEY$ reads as "" and you loop back again. The line A$ = INKEY$ puts the value of INKEY$ into a new string, called *A$*. This will be null while you are stuck in the loop, but as soon as you press any other key, it will store that. It then passes to LOOP WHILE A$="" and because *A$* isn't null any more it comes out of the loop. The next line prints out the key that you did press.

Run the program in the usual way. Notice that you don't have to press Return. As soon as you press the key the program moves on.

INKEY$ is very useful when you want to use keys for making movements in games. Sometimes, you use letter keys to move around the screen particularly if you don't have a mouse or a joystick. INKEY$ is ideal for this. You can also use it to make the computer make a move when you press the cursor up, down, left or right keys.

Another situation where you just press a key and something happens, is when you use menus, like the ones on your word processor. Often you have a choice, you can press a number or a letter, and whatever option they stand for, will start to run. Many menus have a highlight bar as well and you can usually choose to move the highlight with the cursor keys until it is over the option you want, then you press Return to choose it. The other option is to press the number or letter without the Return key. It is this last one that you do with INKEY$.

If you have GW-BASIC

Type NEW to start a new program, and then enter:

```
10 PRINT "SAMPLE MENU PROGRAM"
20 PRINT "1. Word process"
30 PRINT "2. Spreadsheet"
40 PRINT "3. Database"
50 PRINT "4. Exit"
60 A$=INKEY$:IF A$="" GOTO 60
```

```
70 IF A$="1" THEN PRINT "WORD"
80 IF A$="W" THEN PRINT "WORD"
90 IF A$="2" THEN PRINT "SPREAD"
100 IF A$="S" THEN PRINT "SPREAD"
110 IF A$="3" THEN PRINT "DATA"
120 IF A$="D" THEN PRINT "DATA"
130 IF A$="4" THEN END
140 IF A$="E" THEN END
```

Lines 70 to 140 look very similar. You do not need to type each of them out in full. Once you have typed in 70, type:

```
EDIT 70
```

The cursor will be over the 7 in line 70. Type 8 to change this to make line 80. Move the cursor along to the 1. Change this to W and then type <Rn> to register the new line. Because you changed the 7 to 8, you have a new line 80, in addition to the old line 70. Create all the next lines in the same way. This time you will need to change the WORD to SPREAD and so on.

Put <caps lock> on and press <F2> to run the program.

If you have QBASIC

Use the GW-BASIC program listed in the above section leaving out the line numbers but replace line 60 with the lines:

```
DO
AS = INKEY$
LOOP WHILE A$ = ""
```

Some of the lines are very similar like lines 70 and 80. Type in line 70 and instead of typing it all out again, copy it down on to the next line. Move the cursor key so that it is at the beginning of the line you are going to copy.

Hold down the shift key and, at the same time, move the <rightarrow> key until you reach the end of the line. You will see that the whole line is highlighted as you move along. Release the keys. What you have done is to mark the line out as a block.

Move the cursor down to the start of the line below, the position you want to copy the line to. Press <Alt-E> to select the Edit menu. <Arrowdown> until the Copy is highlighted and press <Rn> to select. You could use the mouse keys instead. Alternatively, you could leave out using the menu and just press the hotkey <Shift-Insert>.

You get what looks like a menu written on the screen. Press 1, 2 or 3 or W, S or D and you get a statement shown up on the screen, WORD, SPREAD or DATA. You did not need to press <Rn> after the words or numbers to get this. Normally, of course, instead of, for example, PRINT "WORD", you would have something like GOSUB 2000 if you are using GW-BASIC or a label if you are using QBASIC, to load the word processor.

Try running the program again and putting in a 4 or an E. This time the computer does do something other than outputting to the screen. It brings the program to an end.

This is a rather unsophisticated menu. It only lets you put in upper case letters and it also gets lost if you put in the wrong letter or number. In a full program, you would need to do what is called *error trapping*, putting tests in your program that deal with the user pressing the wrong keys. There are also shorter ways of writing lines 70 and 140, but written out in this way, it is easier to see what is happening.

Exercises

❏ What program lines can you add to the menu program, so that it will also respond to a lower case w, s, d or e?

❏ Difficult but interesting to think about: how would you *error trap* or deal with the user keying the wrong letter, by sending him back to the menu again.

8.7 Making Noises

The PC is not a brilliant soundmaker and is quite disappointing compared with some computers like the Amiga or even the good old BBC. These have more than one voice channel and you can make the sound of a 3-voice or 3-instrument orchestra, for example. With the PC it is one voice or instrument only. However, this one voice can make quite a variety of noises.

There are three different noise commands:

❏ BEEP

❏ PLAY

❏ SOUND

8.7.1 BEEP

This is the simplest command as it makes just one sound – a warning one. It is the warning bell, the sound you get when you do something wrong.

If you have GW-BASIC

Try typing

```
BEEP
```

Press <Rn> and you get the familiar warning sound. The computer responds to this immediately. In this situation, you are using BEEP as a direct command but you could build it into your programs.

If you have QBASIC

Type:

```
BEEP
```

and run the program.

You can make programs, with your own warnings. For example, suppose you want someone to type in only the numbers 1 to 6, perhaps in answer to a menu. Any other numbers would be wrong and you want to warn them of this by making the computer BEEP. Try this little patch of program.

If you have GW-BASIC

```
10 PRINT "SELECT A NUMBER FROM 1 TO 6"
20 PRINT "NORMALLY THIS WOULD HAVE BEEN A PROPER MENU"
30 X$=INKEY$:IF X$="" THEN 30
40 IF X$<"1" OR X$>"6" THEN BEEP:GOTO 10
50 IF X$>"0" AND X$<"7" THEN PRINT "YOU GET YOUR CHOICE"
```

Line 30 keeps the computer waiting until you press some key.

Line 40 looks to see if the key is less than 1 or greater than 6 and if it is, it sounds the warning bell and goes back to the beginning of the program and waits until you put something more desirable in.

Line 50 tests to see if you are putting in the correct number, from 1 to 6. If you do, it tells you that you get your choice. Normally the program would go on further at this point and carry out whatever options are given on the menu.

If you have QBASIC

You need to use a different loop for line 30, where you go on testing the value of INKEY$, until it is something other than null. You also have a problem making the program go back to the beginning of the menu if you put the wrong thing in. For this you need to label the first bit of the program – in this case START seems as good a name as any. To show that it is a label, you must follow it with a colon, :.

The whole program should look like this:

```
START:
CLS
PRINT "Select a number from 1 to 6"
PRINT "normally this would have been a proper menu"
DO
X$ = INKEY$
LOOP WHILE X$ = ""
IF X$ < "1" OR X$ > "6" THEN BEEP: GOTO START
IF X$ > "0" OR X$ < "7" THEN PRINT "You get your choice"
```

Run the program by using the hotkey combination, <Shift-F5>. The explanation given in the section on GW-BASIC also applies to QBASIC.

You need to put the numbers in quotations marks, because *X$* is a string, so the numbers have to be treated as strings as well.

8.7.2 The PLAY Command

You can put music on to your PC using letters for notes. Look through your early piano or recorder books at home and see if you can find some very easy music with just a few notes between middle C and B just below upper C. The music should be all crotchets, the usually early practice exercises. The way to produce notes is to use the PLAY command followed by the letters of the notes in quotes. Here is the beginning of Good King Wenceslas.

```
10 PLAY "GGGA GG"
```

When you want a note which is longer or shorter than a crotchet, you have to set a different note length. When you first start using the PLAY command, the default value is a crotchet. To set another length of note, use the letter L followed by a number. The table below shows what the different numbers mean. Every time the length of note changes in your music, you will need to reset the L value.

L1	Semi breve
L2	Minim
L4	Crotchet (Default)
L8	Quaver
L16	Semi quaver
L64	Demi semi quaver

For example, here is the next line of Good King Wenceslas.

```
20 PLAY "L2 D L4 EDEF+ L2 GG"
```

If you have a sharp or a flat, use a + or a − respectively. Notice the F sharp in line 20.

If the notes go below middle C or above B, you will need to tell the computer to go into another octave. Middle C up to B is called Octave 4 and this is the default value which you get when you start to use the PLAY command. The octave starting at higher C is Octave 5 and the one below middle C is Octave 3. To move into these type O5 or O3 and then go on to give the note letters in the usual way. If you change an octave, like going back into Octave 4, you will need to register the change with another O4. Notice that you use the letter O, not the zero symbol.

Go on to add:

```
30 PLAY "L4 O5 DC O4 BABA L2 G"
```

To continue with the music. This time you will see the new symbols, > and <. These increase or decrease the octave by 1. This is quicker than messing around with O followed by a number.

```
40 PLAY "L4 EDEF+ L2 GG L4 DDEF+"
50 PLAY "GG L2 A L4 > DC < BA L2 G > C < L1 G"
```

8.7.3 The SOUND Command

The command has the syntax: SOUND *frequency, duration*

The first number is the highness or lowness of the note. It can vary between 37 and 32,767 and can produce sounds well away from the particular ones you might recognise as music. Middle C has a frequency of 523, Upper C is 1046.

The second number is the length of the note and can vary from 0 to 65535. 9 would represent half a second – how long would 65535 last? I don't recommend using a very long number for the duration unless you are first happy with the frequency number you put in. Experiment with some different numbers and see what sounds you make.

For example, SOUND 900, 40 would be a possibility. Try some different number combinations. If you are using GW-BASIC, you can do this by trying one after another as direct commands. If you are using QBASIC, you'll have to put a string of them in a program and run it.

You can also write programs to put one sound after another in regular steps. Here is an example:

```
10 FOR N=40 TO 2000 STEP 40
20 SOUND N,25
30 NEXT N
```

8.7.4 Building up a Library of Sound

As you try things out or look at programs in magazines you will collect a little library of sound. It is a good idea to store these together in a big sound program.

If you have GW-BASIC

Start high up at about line 5000 and set out each sound or piece of music separately. Start each bit with a REM so that you can see clearly what it is and end it with a RETURN. This will send the computer back to the program you called it from. For example:

```
5000 REM BARBARA'S MUSIC LIBRARY
5010 REM 'GOOD KING WENCESLAS
5020 PLAY etc
5030 PLAY etc
5040 PLAY etc
. . . . . . .
5090 RETURN
5100 REM 'OLD KING COLE
5110 PLAY etc
5120 PLAY etc
5130 PLAY etc
. . . . .
5190 RETURN
```

You can use a command called MERGE to add this library on to your other programs. You could then call up Good King Wenceslas with GOSUB 5010 and Old King Cole with GOSUB 5100, earlier on in your main program.

If you have QBASIC

Because you don't use line numbers, you will need to use labels instead. You can call up the sound with a label name. It must always end with the colon symbol, :. This is how QBASIC knows that you are using a label. Your main music program would look something like this:

```
COLE:
PLAY etc
PLAY etc
PLAY etc
WENCESLAS:
PLAY etc
PLAY etc
PLAY etc
```

More BASIC Programming

As in the previous chapter I shall be using GW-BASIC and QBASIC for these sample programs. You can assume that if QBASIC is not specifically mentioned, the listings will work by simply leaving out the line numbers and running the resulting program.

9.1 Time

When you boot up make sure that you put in the correct date and time. If your computer has an inbuilt clock and battery it will automatically do this.

Try typing:

```
10 PRINT TIME$
```

Run the program and you get the time, with hours followed by minutes followed by seconds.

Try typing:

```
20 PRINT DATE$
```

This time you get the date as well, in this case in the form of the month, then the day and then the year, the American way of writing it. It is possible that your BASIC will give you the English way, with the day first then the month.

Try:

```
30 PRINT RIGHT$(DATE$,2) <Rn>
```

RIGHT$ is called a string function. You feed in the string given immediately after the first bracket, in this case *DATE$*, and it picks out some characters on the right or at the end of that string. The number of characters it is going to pick out are given in the number that comes after the comma, second in the bracket. In this case, you get the last two numbers only – the year.

```
40 PRINT LEFT$(DATE$,2)
```

The LEFT$ function works in the same way as RIGHT$, except that it picks out the character to the left or the beginning of the string you feed into it, in this case the number of the month.

```
50 PRINT MID$(DATE$,4,2)
```

The function MID$ does much the same thing as RIGHT$ and LEFT$, except that it picks out characters in the middle of a string. It needs two numbers to show what these are. The first shows where it will start. In this case, the 4 means that it starts with the 4th character along. The second number says how many characters it will go on to pick out, in this case 2. In this situation, it picks out two characters starting four along, which is the day part of the date.

Note that TIME$ and DATE$ are string functions even though they contain numbers. This is because the numbers in a date are separated by hyphens (-) or colons (:) so that you can write the time and date in the usual way. A pure number would not accept the hyphens or colons.

You can set the time yourself with, for example:

```
TIME$="0:0:0"
```

If you do this, you will reset the system clock and the time you put in will appear in anything else you do, until you set the clock back again, so it is probably better not to try this out if you have an inbuilt clock. If you do set it, remember to put the actual time between quotes to register that it is a string.

If you want to use the various bits of DATE$ and TIME$, you get strings, not numbers, out of LEFT$, RIGHT$ and MID$. For example, MID$(DATE$,4,2) returns the day as 10 say, and not as the number 10. To get the number so that you can do arithmetic on it, you need to turn the string into a number which you can do by taking its VAL, for example, VAL(MID$(DATE$,4,2)). VAL turns a string into a number.

You can use the TIME$ function to make a simple digital clock. All it does is to keep on printing the time in the middle of the screen. You put a little delay loop between each print, so it reprints about every second. I use a fast 386 computer, so you may need a much lower number if you have an 8086. It's not a wonderful clock, because it flickers too much.

```
10 FOR N=1 TO 50
20 LOCATE 12,40
```

```
30 PRINT TIME$
40 IF INKEY$=CHR$(27) THEN END
50 FOR J=1 TO 5000:NEXT
60 NEXT N
```

The program prints the time just 50 times. This is because it is a trial program and once you have seen it working, that is enough. Obviously you could leave out the *do it 50 times* instruction if you were making a real clock.

LOCATE 12,40 is a new command. If you didn't have it in, the PRINT would put the time in the cursor start position at the top left hand corner. LOCATE positions the cursor somewhere else on the screen. It starts with the row, then gives the column. The top left hand corner is 1,1. There are 25 rows down and either 40 or 80 columns across. This means that 12,40 should be roughly in the middle.

9.1.1 Timing Things

It can be quite interesting to time how long things take. For example, how quickly you can do some arithmetic or press a key on the computer. You can compare your speeds with those of your friends.

You can also time how long it takes for the computer to do something, like draw 100 circles or do a calculation or run more or less any program. This kind of method is used in what are called Benchmark tests – you get different computers to do the same thing and time them to see which is the quickest.

A useful BASIC statement here is TIMER. You cannot set this yourself – it is what is called *read-only* and returns the number of seconds since midnight. Try it now by typing:

```
PRINT TIMER
```

and a few seconds later with another:

```
PRINT TIMER
```

You can use this as the basis for timing things. Try this little program:

```
10 START = TIMER
20 PRINT "To test your reaction press a 4"
30 A$=INKEY$ :IFA$ <>"4" THEN GOTO 25
40 FINISH = TIMER
50 PRINT FINISH - START
```

If you have QBASIC replace line 30 with:

```
DO
LOOP WHILE INKEY$<>"4"
```

To use TIMER as a timer you have to read it on two occasions. You do this at the beginning of the program and call its value at that point, *START*. You then write the lines of program that set out your test, in this case to press the number key 4. You then read it again, and this time, call its value *FINISH*. Both *START* and *FINISH* refer to the number of seconds since midnight – to get the time between them (between the beginning of the test and the time when you pressed the key) you need to subtract the START time from the FINISH time and print out the result.

What would happen if you started this program just before midnight and finished it just after?

You can also put a FOR N= 1 TO 5 . . . . . NEXT N loop right round the whole program. This makes it run five times and you can see if your reactions get any faster.

9.1.2 Making an Egg Timer

You can also use this kind of program to time things you want to do like boiling an egg or spending half an hour doing some work. This program puts a timer on for 15 seconds because you don't want to spend any longer than that seeing whether it will work.

```
10 START = TIMER
20 FINISH = TIMER
30 X = FINISH - START
40 IF X>=15 THEN BEEP:GOTO 60
50 GOTO 20
60 END
```

Lines 40 and 50 continually test to see if the difference between *FINISH* and *START* has reached 15 seconds. If it hasn't, it goes on and does another test. If it has, it gives you the warning BEEP. You could put GOSUB followed by the line number of one of your favourite tunes instead.

If you have QBASIC you need labels instead of line numbers for the GOTOs.

```
START = TIMER
TIMING:
FINISH = TIMER
X = FINISH - START
IF X>=15 THEN GOTO FINAL
GOTO TIMING
FINAL:
BEEP
END
```

START reads the time at the moment you start to run the program. You then move into the part of the program called *TIMING:*. The fact that it is a label is indicated by the colon. What this does is to read the time again. If this is more than 15 seconds, it goes on to the bit of the program labelled *FINAL:*. If not, it goes back to the beginning of *TIMING:* and repeats the whole procedure again. The label *FINAL:* produces the BEEP sound and ends the program.

9.2 Tables and Columns

This section is about arrays, which is a fancy word for lists and tables of information stored in your computer. I am afraid it doesn't sound very exciting but it is useful and when you look at ready made programs you will be able to spot arrays all over the place.

There are one dimensional and many (multi) dimensional arrays. A one dimensional array is just a list of figures like:

32
16
91
45
80
69

or the names of the months in a list like:

January
February
March
April
May
June

A two dimensional array is a table of values, with more than one column like:

Jan	Feb	March	April	
Bread	6.32	9.41	2.04	5.09
Books	4.9	90.00	2.99	9.99
Papers	0.40	0.40	0.80	1.25

Can you think of some examples for yourself, first a one dimensional array and then a two dimensional array or table?

Now go back to the first list. There were six figures in it. To put them into the computer, you could use an array called *Mark*. The first element is called *mark(1)*, the second *mark(2)*, right up to *mark(6)*. In this situation:

mark(1) = 32

mark(2) = 16

mark(3) = 91

For a two dimensional array you put two figures in the brackets, separated by a comma. Bread in February was 9.41. This is row 1, column 2 of the table. Call the array Spend, for spending.

spend(1,1) = 6.32

spend(1,2) = 9.41

spend(1,3) = 2.04

spend(2,2) = 0.00

The first number in the brackets stands for row, the second number for column. It could be the other way round, the only important thing is that you know how your array works.

What is spend(2,4) and spend(3,1)?

This is all a bit complicated, you might say, so why do it? Well, M(1) = 2 can be written more quickly than *the first entry on the list is 2* and S(1,3) is quicker than *the spending on bread in March* or worse still, *the entry in row 1, column 3*. Arrays are a good short way of describing your data.

They become even more useful when you can use FOR N = 1 TO somenumber to load your computer up with data. When you have huge tables and very long lists they are even more useful.

They are also useful when combined with READ..DATA statements. To illustrate what this means, here is a program which will read in the numbers in the first list and then print them on the screen to show that it has, in fact, read them in properly.

Start off with:

```
20 READ F
30 PRINT F
50 DATA 32,16,91,45,80,69
```

The READ in line 20 reads the first figure in the list after the DATA in line 50. As the program stands at the moment, that is all that happens.

Add lines:

```
32 READ F
34 PRINT F
```

and run the program again.

With QBASIC add the two new lines before the DATA statement.

What happens now? READ F now reads the next figure in the data list.

Instead of going on adding READ..DATA program lines you could use a FOR...NEXT loop to read all the figures after the data statement. Change your program by omitting lines 32 and 34 and adding:

```
5 FOR N = 1 TO 6
35 NEXT N
```

What happens if you try to make the program read more data than you have put in? Change the 6 in line 5 to 7 and run the program again to see what happens.

With QBASIC change your program so it reads as follows:

```
CLS
FOR N= 1 TO 6
READ F
PRINT F
NEXT N
DATA 32,16,91,45,80,69
```

Run the program again to see what happens.

So where do arrays come into this? So far, you have just read in the data and printed it out straightaway and you only needed one memory box to do this, which was called *F*. So when *N* was 1, *F* was 32, when *N* was 2, *F* became 16 and so on. There was only one value in *F* at one time and all the old ones were forgotten. Now computers are supposed to have good memories so that doesn't seem very sensible does it?. If you want it to remember all six numbers you have got to think up the names of six memory boxes and what could be more convenient than labelling them *M(1)*, *M(2)* and so on.

Start a new program. This puts the six numbers into the six memory boxes of the array, *M*. When they are all saved into memory, it will then print them out and add them up. Right at the end of the program it prints out the final total.

```
10 DIM M(6)
20 FOR N = 1 TO 6
30 READ M(N)
40 NEXT N
50 FOR N = 1 TO 6
60 PRINT M(N)
```

```
70 NEXT N
80 LET SUM = M(1) + M(2) + M(3) + M(4) + M(5) + M(6)
90 PRINT SUM
100 DATA 32,16,91,45,80,69
```

The first line declares an array. It is not necessary for arrays with less than 10 data elements, but it is a good idea to get in the habit or a more complicated program may fail to run and you will spend hours wondering why. It just tells the computer you are going to use an array called *M* and it will not have more than six elements (the number in the bracket). You might use less.

You can use several arrays in the same program. The next program puts six nouns in an array called *noun$* and six verbs in *verb$*.

```
10 DIM noun$(6),verb$(6)
20 FOR N = 1 TO 6
30 READ noun$(N)
40 NEXT N
50 FOR N = 1 TO 6
60 READ verb$(N)
70 NEXT N
100 DATA "HORSE","COW","DOG","SHEEP","HUMAN","CAT"
110 DATA "JUMPS","SINGS","WALKS","SMILES","HOWLS","SMELLS"
```

You need to use the dollar sign in the array name to show the computer that you are going to store strings and you must use quotation marks around the data. Commas are used to separate the information.

You can use this program to make random sentences.

Add the line:

```
80 PRINT noun$(INT(RND*6));" ";verb$(INT(RND*6))
```

To produce 10 of these sentences, add lines:

```
75 FOR J = 1 TO 10
85 NEXT J
```

With QBASIC insert the following lines after READ verb$ (N) ; NEXT N:

```
FOR J = 1 TO 10
PRINT noun$(INT(RND*6)+1);" ";verb$(INT(RND*6)+1)
NEXT J
```

You can mix arrays in your DATA statements, so that you read in the first entry in one array, the first in another, the two second entries together and so on. For example, suppose you want to use the names of the months with their number of days. You want two columns, side by side.

January	31
February	28
March	31

and so on. Use *month$* and *days*. They tie together very naturally because, of course, *month$(1)* goes with *days(1)*, *month$(2)* with *day(2)* and so on.

Here is a program that does this.

```
10 DIM month$(12), days(12)
20 FOR N = 1 TO 12
30 READ month$(N),days(N)
40 PRINT month$(N);" HAS ";days(N);" DAYS"
50 NEXT N
60 DATA "JANUARY",31,"FEBRUARY",28,"MARCH",31,
70 DATA "APRIL",30,"MAY",31,"JUNE",30,"JULY",31
80 DATA "AUGUST",30,"SEPTEMBER",30,"OCTOBER",31
90 DATA "NOVEMBER",30,"DECEMBER",31
```

Notice how the data can be spread out over several programming lines – you don't have to have the same amount on each line but you do need to start a new line with a fresh DATA.

Look through ready made programs in books and magazines and look at the DATA statements they contain.

Happy arrays!

9.3 Writing All Over The Screen

When you write with a word processor, your text runs all the way along the line and then goes down the page, line after line. This time though, you are going to leave gaps between words and write things in different places all over the screen. You might find this useful for making a fun party invitation or for making a screen display, perhaps as an introduction to one of your own programs. You can even use letters to make simple pictures.

Try the following program:

```
10 PRINT "123456789012345678901234567890123456789 0"
20 PRINT "A","WAS","AN","OLD","COMPUTER"
30 PRINT 1,12,123,12345,123456
```

Make sure you put all the commas in. Run the program and see what happens.

What do the commas do? What happens when you replace the WAS in line 20 with a really long word or collection of characters, say about 20 or so. Line 10 in the program acts as a kind of grid so you can see how the spacing works.

Replace the commas with semi-colons. When you do this don't type the whole line again, edit it by moving the cursor up to the line you want to change or by typing, say, EDIT 20. Run the program again. What happens now?

You can make patterns or pictures with letters, like a diamond.

```
   x
  x x
 x   x
x     x
 x   x
  x x
   x
```

To do this, you will want to put spaces between letters. It is probably easiest just to use the spacebar, but you can also use the SPC() command. Try this program:

Type NEW and then:

```
10 CLS
20 PRINT SPC(6) "X" SPC(0) "X"
30 PRINT SPC(5) "X" SPC(2) "X"
40 PRINT SPC(4) "X" SPC(4) "X"
50 PRINT SPC(3) "X" SPC(6) "X"
60 PRINT SPC(2) "X" SPC(8) "X"
70 PRINT SPC(1) "X" SPC(10) "X"
```

Don't forget the trick I showed you earlier in Chapter 8 that does away with typing in each line. Use EDIT 20 and modify that line. Using QBASIC, copy it and change it.

Run the program. You should get half a diamond. To finish it add row 80 the same as row 60, row 90 the same as row 50 and so on.

You could do the above program in a very few lines, like this:

```
20 FOR N=0 TO 5
30 PRINT SPC(6-N) "X" SPC(2*N) "X"
40 NEXT N.
```

If you do want to plan out some more character pictures, use grid paper. There are 80 characters across the screen, 25 rows down. You can use ordinary square paper or special computer grid forms if you can get hold of them.

What do you use to type down the screen, line after line, in the usual way but you don't want to always start on the left hand side? The answer is TAB, just like using the TAB key to move a few spaces at one time when using a word processor. Type NEW and then:

```
10 PRINT TAB(12) "SILLY"
20 PRINT TAB(16) "OLD"
```

```
30 PRINT TAB(17) "THING"
40 PRINT TAB(61) "YOU ARE"
```

Run the program and see what happens. Notice that you still go down the lines, you just start in from the side.

What would you do if you wanted to dance around the screen, printing something at the bottom, then at the top, then in the middle, not just going straight down? You would use the command LOCATE.

LOCATE 3,5 places the cursor at row 3 i.e. 3 characters down and 5 characters or columns over to the right, measuring rows from the top of the screen. The first number runs from 1 to 25, the second from 1 to 80. Type NEW and then try:

```
10 CLS
20 LOCATE 12,1
30 PRINT "THE SILLY"
40 LOCATE 6,6
50 PRINT "PROGRAM"
60 LOCATE 3,50
70 PRINT "COMPANY"
```

Run it and see what happens. You can turn it into a *moving screen* by putting in delay loops. Try adding:

```
15 FOR N = 1 TO 10000:NEXT N
```

and then copy this to a new line 35 and 55. You may find this number too fast or too slow, depending on what kind of chip you have. Change it until you get something that works on your machine.

For all but the last program, you can replace the PRINT with LPRINT and the output will appear on your printer rather than on the screen.

9.4 String Functions

These examples deal with strings – collections of letters or words or numbers that are not used for arithmetic.

Try this program:

```
10 LET A$ = "REFRIGERATOR"
20 LET B$ = "OVEN"
30 PRINT LEN(A$)
40 PRINT LEN(B$)
```

Run it and see what happens. What do you think LEN does?

Add two more lines:

```
50 PRINT LEFT$(A$,3)
60 PRINT LEFT$(B$,2)
```

Keep lines 10 and 20 and replace lines 30 to 60 with:

```
30 FOR N = 1 TO LEN(A$)
40 PRINT LEFT$(A$,N)
50 NEXT N
60 END
```

What do you think RIGHT$ would do? Replace the LEFT$ in line 40 with RIGHT$.

There is another one as well. This looks a bit different because it has two numbers in the brackets. Try a new program.

```
10 LET A$ = "COMPUTER"
20 PRINT MID$(A$,2,3)
30 PRINT MID$(A$,2,4)
```

What do the two numbers mean?

The first says what character you are going to start with, in this case the second which is O. The second tells you how many characters to take, in this case, three in line 20 and then four in line 30.

You could use LEFT$, RIGHT$ and MID$ in adventure games. Suppose people have got the opportunity to go north, south, east or west. These all begin with different letters. If you test for the whole word you would need it to be typed and spelt correctly. This might be rather hopeful. Instead, use LEFT$ to pick off just the first letter and test for that.

Try this program:
```
10 PRINT "WHAT DIRECTION WILL YOU GO IN?"
20 PRINT "USE CAPITAL LETTERS"
30 INPUT D$
40 IF LEFT$(D$,1) = "N" THEN PRINT "YOU GO NORTH INTO THE CAVE"
50 IF LEFT$(D$,1) = "S" THEN PRINT "YOU GO SOUTH INTO THE SEA"
60 IF LEFT$(D$,1) = "E" THEN PRINT "YOU GO INTO THE SALT MARSHES"
70 IF LEFT$(D$,1) = "W" THEN PRINT "YOU GO WEST TO THE CASTLE"
```

Here again remember the shortcuts in GW-BASIC (EDIT) and QBASIC (Copy) that will allow you to modify an existing line to avoid having to type in new similar ones.

Another use of string functions is to create your own database. You can put all the information for one person or thing into one long string all tied up together. You must allow the same number of characters for each field and fill them up with spaces if an individual one is not long enough. For example, here are my two son's records.

```
10 RECORD1$ = "WILLIAM    290584PEWLEY DOWN FIRST"
20 RECORD2$ = "MATTHEW    190178R.G.S              "
```

I have left 11 spaces for the first name, 6 for their date of birth and 17 for the name of their school. I can pick these bits of information out using the string functions.

`LEFT$(RECORD1$,11)` will give me the name

`MID$(RECORD1$,12,6)` will give me the birth date

`RIGHT$(RECORD1$,17)` will give me the school. Try some more records for yourself.

9.5 Starting to write a Word Processor

This section will show you how to store some text on to a floppy or hard disk. One of the main purposes of word processing is to store writing on to a disk so that you can call it up another day and look at it, change it and maybe print it out.

The first part of the program invites the user to input a tiny bit of text and to save it into a file called DATA1. Try:

```
10 PRINT "Type what you want"
20 PRINT "Do not use carriage return"
30 LINE INPUT A$
40 OPEN "DATA1" FOR OUTPUT AS #1
50 WRITE #1,A$
60 CLOSE
```

Lines 10 and 20 are instructions using PRINT statements. It is important that you do not press carriage return as this effects the way the text will be treated by the file commands.

When you use a commercial word processor you do not press carriage return at the end of the line but usually just type on – the program does the word wrapping for you. LINE INPUT in line 30 works much like the ordinary INPUT command – but it allows you to put in commas and quotation marks.

Line 40 opens up the communications channel for data to go from your program to the disk. If you are using a double disk drive and want to save to the disk in drive B use "B:DATA1" instead of "DATA1". The communication channel you use is number 1, hence the #1 – you can use 1, 2 or 3. Line 50 actually writes the text into the file. Line 60 is very important. When you have finished dealing with a file you must close it – otherwise some funny things may happen.

Now try running the program. When it asks you to type in some text use the following:

TAURUS YOU WILL HAVE A BAD DAY TODAY GEMINI YOU HAVE GOT AN EASTER
SURPRISE COMING

Keep it all in capitals – it is part of a horoscope. You will hear the disk drive
whirring as it saves your text. Then type:

```
FILES
```

or

```
FILES B:
```

if you have saved your data on the B: drive and see that the file is saved.

The next thing is to see if you can recover this file. Start a new program with the
following lines:

```
10 OPEN "DATA1" FOR INPUT AS #2
20 INPUT #2,B$
30 PRINT B
90 CLOSE
```

Try running this. You should get back what you put in. Remember to type
`"B:DATA1"` instead of `"DATA1"` if you have stored the data in the
B: drive.

The next thing to try is to take out just a part of the text – for example the TAURUS
part only.

Add:

```
100 L=LEN(B$)
110 G=INSTR(B$,"GEMINI")
120 TAURUS$=LEFT$(B$,G-1)
130 PRINT TAURUS$
```

Try running it.

In line 100 `LEN(B$)` gives the number of characters in the whole piece of text – this
will be needed later. You can add PRINT L if you want to see what this is. In line
110, `INSTR(B$,"GEMINI")` tells you where in the string you can find GEMINI.
The computer searches through *B$* until it finds GEMINI and it returns the number of
characters along. In this case the answer happens to be 38. The TAURUS message
ends at one character less than this and is on the left position of the string, so in line
120 use LEFT$ with 1 less than G.

Can you think how you would get GEMINI's horoscope out?

If you can't, try adding on to the program:

```
140 GEMINI$=RIGHT$(B$,L-G+1)
150 PRINT GEMINI$
```

Exercises

❏ This is a crude beginning and there is an awful lot that you could add. You could develop the word processing side of it a bit more by, for example, providing a menu at the beginning of the program and making options of writing some text, of choosing the filename yourself and of saving or recovering it.

❏ Try to develop the horoscope side a bit more. Provide all the months of the year and write some user friendly instructions so that people can pick out their own sign.

Good luck!

9.6 Starting Graphics with Pixel Painting

Graphics is the process of making computer pictures on the screen. Don't get too excited or get your mouse straight out of the cupboard – GW-BASIC makes you do it the hard way, point by point or line by line. Some newer BASICs like Amiga BASIC allow you to draw simple pictures with the mouse and build these into your programs.

The first thing that you have to do is tell the computer to set up a special screen for graphics purposes. The usual screen you use for text and for writing your programs is SCREEN 0. This is called a default screen, and is what the computer gives you automatically unless you ask for something else.

A graphics program will need to begin by setting up another screen, with the SCREEN 1 or SCREEN 2 command if you have a CGA monitor or with a SCREEN 7, 8 or 9 if you have a CGA or EGA monitor and the right version of BASICA. If you have an old monochrome monitor you can only use a text screen and you cannot write programs that use graphics or run any ready made application programs like games or business packages that use graphics.

Computer graphics work by lighting up or colouring in little squares or pixels. The more pixels you have on the screen, the more detail you get, or in computer language, the higher the resolution. More pixels require more memory though. Colour requires even more memory – it gobbles it up like nothing on earth. If your screen is black or white, each pixel can only be either black or white. If your screen has 16 colours, the computer has 16 choices for each pixel. That really overloads the memory. For this reason, a higher resolution (more pixels to light up) usually means that less colours are available.

The table below shows the resolution and colour options available in the different monitors.

CGA

Screen	Resolution	Colours	Text across x Down
0	Text Only		80 (or 40) x 25
1	320 x 200	Yes	40 x 25
2	640 x 200	No	40 X 25

VGA or EGA

0	Text Only		80 (or 40) x 25
1	320 X 200	Yes (3)	40 x 25
2	640 x 200	No	40 x 25
7	640 x 200	Yes (16)	40 x 25
8	640 x 200	Yes (16)	80 x 25
9	640 x 350	Yes (64,16)	80 x 25

The higher the resolution, the less chunky and the more detailed the graphics will be. When you get 40 x 25 text this will look a bit chunky and may be disappointing.

So when you start a graphics program, it will begin with a line like:

```
10 SCREEN 2
```

This also has the effect of clearing the screen.

9.7.1 Lighting up Individual Pixels

It is possible to light up each pixel one by one. PSET lights it up, PRESET turns it back to the background colour. The syntax is PSET(*numberx, numbery*) where the first number stands for the number of pixels along the screen and the second stands for the number down the screen, starting from the top. This is a bit like the graph co-ordinates in maths, except that in maths, the y value is measured up from the bottom of the page rather than down.

Try some yourself:

```
10 SCREEN 2
20 PSET(10,10)
30 PSET(50,50)
40 PSET (100,100)
```

Add some more lines and run it again:

```
50 PSET(600,10)
60 PSET(500,200)
70 PSET(200,200)
```

Try some more of your own. You can make some quite interesting programs out of lighting up pixels. Start a new program and type in:

```
10 SCREEN 2
20 FOR J=0 TO 319 STEP 4
30 FOR K=0 TO 199 STEP 4
40 PSET(J,K)
50 NEXT K
60 NEXT J
70 END
```

What this program does is to start with *J=0*. *J* is the x co-ordinate so the program starts at the left hand side. It then runs through all the values of *K* which is the y co-ordinate before it goes to *J=1*. It then runs through all the values of *K* before it goes to *J=2*. This means that the program runs down the screen going from left to right. Step 4 means that it only lights up every fourth pixel which produces a dotted grid all over the screen. Change the 4 after STEP in lines 20 and 30 to get some different patterns.

You can use random numbers to make a chance pattern. To do this use a variation of PSET. PSET on its own just lights up a pixel but you can use PSET(X,Y),1 to light up a pixel and PSET(X,Y),0 to turn one off (this makes PSET work like PRESET). Change line 40 so that it looks like this:

```
40 PSET(J,K),INT(RND*2)
```

The bit after the second comma produces either a 0 or a 1 in random sequence so pixels are either lit up or turned off. To make it really random add:

```
5 RANDOMIZE TIMER
```

You can see the result of this program in Figure 9.1.

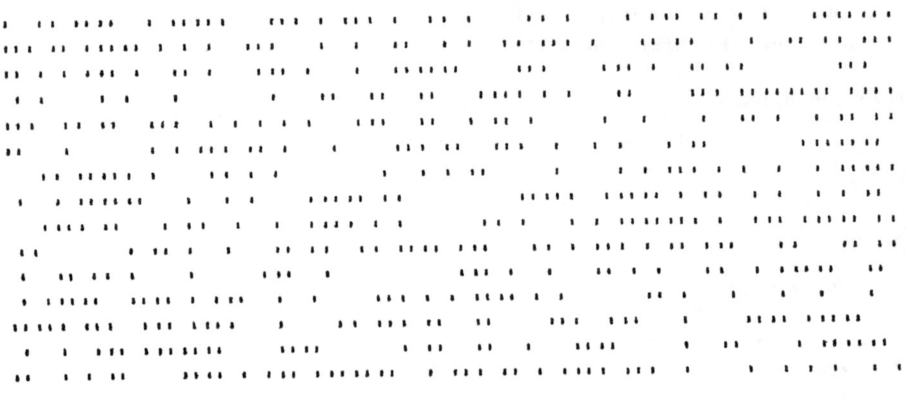

Figure 9.1: Using PSET at random

9.7 Making Pictures and Curves with Lines

Like all graphics programs, start by setting up a graphics screen. Type:

```
10 SCREEN 2
```

The pixel painting section used the PC's default screen co-ordinates run down the screen instead of up, and use strange numbers like 320 and 640. You can make life much easier for yourself by setting your own co-ordinates with the WINDOW command. You start with the co-ordinates of the left hand bottom corner and end with the top right hand corner:

```
20 WINDOW (0,0) - (10,10)
```

sets a co-ordinate screen from (0,0) at the bottom left hand corner to (10,10) in the top right.

Now add:

```
30 LINE (1,1) - (9,9)
```

Run the program and see what happens. Add:

```
40 LINE (1,9) - (9,1)
```

Run it again. What happens now? Re-do lines 30 and 40 and add line 50:

```
30 LINE (1,1) - (5,9)
40 LINE -(9,1)
50 LINE (3,5) - (7,5)
```

Line 40 draws a line from the last point given in the previous line, in this case (5,9).

Make up some other letters or simple shapes and pictures that interest you. Plot them out on square paper before you do the programming.

A good technique is to use READ.....DATA statements. You start with a single figure for the number of points and then just put in the two x and y co-ordinates. Here is an example program to draw the seagull in Figure 9.2.

```
10 SCREEN 2 : CLS
20 WINDOW (-640,-450) - (639,349)
30 RESTORE
40 READ POINTS
50 READ X,Y:PSET (X,Y)
60 FOR J = 2 TO POINTS
70 READ X,Y : LINE -(X,Y)
80 NEXT J
90 DATA 17,-110,70
```

```
100 DATA -120,90,-110,100,-90,100,-30,70
110 DATA 100,240,300,160,130,180,40,0
120 DATA 140,-60,60,-130,0,-40,-140,-130
130 DATA -220,-390,-200,-70,-70,30,-110,70
```

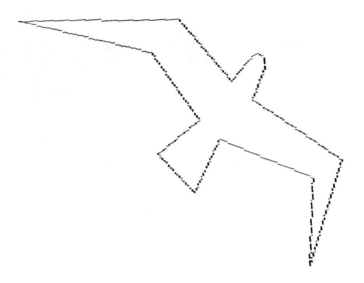

Figure 9.2: Drawing a seagull

This is one situation where you need to adapt the program to QBASIC. Replace line 30 with GOTO SEAGULL, line 70 with SEAGULL: and remove line 140.

You can use the line command to draw the mathematical curves in Figure 9.3. Try:

```
10 SCREEN 2 : CLS
20 WINDOW (-10,-1.1)) - (10,1.1)
30 PSET(-10, SIN (-10))
40 FOR X = -10 TO 10 STEP .2
50 Y = SIN(X) :LINE - (X,Y)
60 NEXT X
```

9.8 Going Round in Circles

GW-BASIC has a CIRCLE command. There are two things you need to know to draw a circle – its centre, expressed here in x and y co-ordinates, and its radius – the distance of the edge of the circle from the centre.

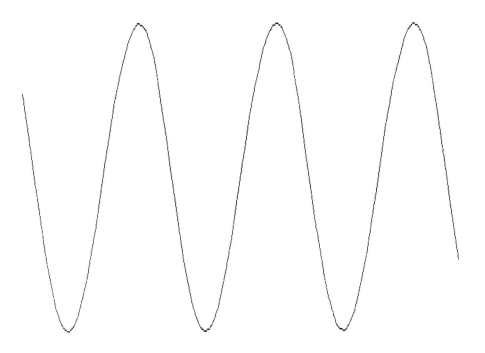

Figure 9.3: Mathematical curves

Put the computer into graphics mode by typing:

```
10 SCREEN 2
```

It is useful to set the co-ordinates so that they start from the bottom left corner and run 1000 along and 1000 up. To do this type:

```
20 WINDOW (0,0) - (1000,1000)
```

Then try:

```
30 CIRCLE (500,500),200
```

and run the program. It will draw a circle with its centre in the middle of the screen.

Exercises

❏ Add some extra lines to draw some more circles – experiment with different centre co-ordinates and different radii. Add one line at a time and then run the program to see what the effect of each extra line is.

❏ Make a whole collection of circles within circles. To do this you keep the same centre and just use different radii. These are called concentric circles. An example to produce Figure 9.4 would be:

```
10 SCREEN 2
20 WINDOW (0,0) - (1000,1000)
30 CIRCLE (500,500),50
40 CIRCLE (500,500),100
50 CIRCLE (500,500),150
60 CIRCLE (500,500),200
```

and so on, making the radius go up by 50 each time.

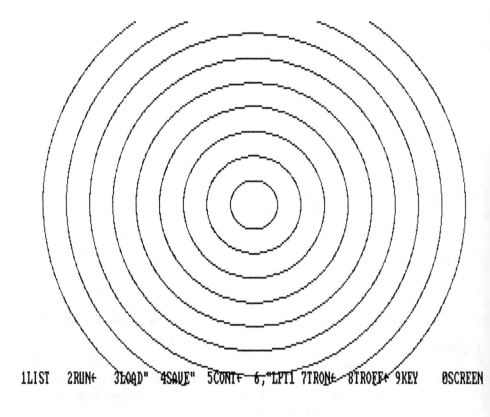

1LIST   2RUN‹   3LOAD"   4SAUE"   5CONT‹ 6,"LPT1 7TRON‹ 8TROFF‹ 9KEY   0SCREEN

Figure 9.4: Concentric circles

You could use a FOR...NEXT loop to save all the lines of CIRCLE commands. Replace line 30 onwards with:

```
30 FOR R=50 to 450 STEP 50
40 CIRCLE (500,500),R
50 NEXT R
```

It looks neater but only do it if you are happy – you can get just the same effect with all the CIRCLE statements.

❏ Add another set of concentric circles with a different centre – you can fill your screen with some quite interesting patterns this way.

9.8.1 Random Circles

It is also possible to make the computer draw random circles and that can make some quite interesting patterns.

Start a new program and type the same lines 10 and 20 to set up the screen and co-ordinate system.

Then add:

```
25 RANDOMIZE TIMER
30 FOR N=1 to 10
40 LET Y=INT(RND*1000)
50 LET X=INT(RND*1000)
60 LET R=INT(RND*200)
70 CIRCLE (X,Y),R
80 NEXT N
```

This draws 10 circles (line 30, for N=1 to 10 sets this up) with the centre co-ordinates *X* and *Y* chosen randomly (lines 40 and 50) up to 1000, their greatest possible value and, *R*, the radius chosen randomly up to 200 (line 60). Change the end value of *N* in line 30 to draw a different number of circles as Figure 9.5.

If you have a colour monitor you can add an extra number after the radius to make the circle a different colour e.g. CIRCLE (500,500),200,3 – put a comma after the radius before you put in the colour number. You must change the Screen 2 to Screen 1, though, because Screen 2 does not produce colours. If you have an EGA or VGA monitor, change it to Screen 7 and then you can have Colours 0 to 16. Try the same circle with different numbers and you could add a random colour element to get an even more interesting display.

9.9 Ellipses and Parts of Circles

An ellipse is like a circle that has been squashed, either from on top which makes it wider than it is high or from both sides, which makes it an egg shape.

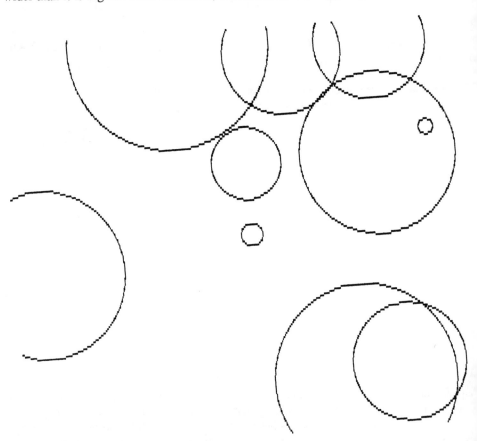

Figure 9.5: Random circles

In fact you can draw an ellipse using the circle command – you just need to add something extra on to the end. An ellipse has a centre much like a circle and the radius is the horizontal or along distance from this centre to the edge. The distance up from the centre would be just the same for a circle but for an ellipse it will be different, shorter for an ellipse squashed down from the top, and larger for an egg shape.

What you need to do is to type four commas after the radius and then put in a decimal number like .2 or .6. You have to try out different ones to see what sort of ellipse you get.

Try typing:

```
10 SCREEN 2
20 WINDOW (0,0) - (1000,1000)
```

This is just to set up a graphics screen and the co-ordinate system. Then try:

```
30 CIRCLE (500,500),200,,,,.2
```

and run the program.

Then add another ellipse:

```
40 CIRCLE (500,500),200,,,,.6
```

Try a few more. What number would you use to make a circle?

Try making some concentric ellipses like the concentric circles in the last example.

9.9.1 Parts of Circles and Ellipses

You can make parts of circles and ellipses. You need to put in a rather strange value for the points on the circle where it is to start and stop drawing.

Try the usual line 10 and line 20 then:

```
30 CIRCLE (500,500),200,,5,6,.2
```

and run it. Replace the 5 and 6 with some different numbers – they can be decimals but should always be less that 6. Work out roughly where the different numbers take you.

If you want to do a part circle rather than an ellipse take off the last comma and the decimal number at the end. So, for example:

```
30 CIRCLE (500,500),200,,5,6
```

would produce part of a circle and not an ellipse.

Now you might realise that 6 doesn't quite take you around to the horizontal. How would you deal with that?

Using compass directions: North is straight up and South straight down. West is horizontally along to the left and East horizontally along to the right.

Now East is zero or 2*PI, West is PI, and North being half a turn between the two will be PI/2. South is another half turn from West so it will be PI + PI/2 which is 3*PI/2.

Now try:

```
5 PI = 4*ATN(1)
30 CIRCLE (500,500),200,,0,PI
```

You should get a semi-circle from East to West. Try some more.

PI is roughly 3.142 and that is why the numbers 5 and 6 worked and produced a shape in the South East type of direction, because 6 is a bit less than twice 3.142 which would have been pure East.

Exercises

❑ Play around and try some more values.

❑ Make some drawings with parts of circles and ellipses like a face with a big circle for the head, two little circles for the eyes and a part circle for the mouth. Make it smile and make it look sad.

❑ (Very difficult) Try and draw some clouds or the petals of a flower. Good luck!

9.10 Using Colour in BASIC

Obviously you need a colour monitor to use this section, although a black and white one would produce some variations on grey. Exactly what you can do with colour depends on the type of monitor you have, whether it is CGA, EGA or VGA and also on the version of MS-DOS you use. This makes colour quite complicated. All I can do in an introductory book like this, is to give you the most general versions, and leave you to dip into your manual to get the full glories of whatever colours you do have. These programs also vary from version to version, this section uses GWBASIC version 3.3. Make sure you are in screen 0.

9.10.1 Coloured Writing

The command COLOR *number1, number 2*, e.g. COLOR 5,7 lets you do coloured writing on a newly coloured background. Start a little program:

```
10 REM: COLOURED WRITING
20 CLS
30 COLOR 1,7
40 PRINT "This should be blue on white"
50 COLOR 2,7
60 PRINT "This should be green on white"
```

Run it and see what happens. You get a background bar, wherever there is writing, which produces the effect of a written strip part of the way across the screen.

COLOR *number1, number2* makes number 2 the background colour and number 1 the writing colour. Here is a table showing what colour goes with what number.

0	Black	8	Grey
1	Blue	9	Bright blue
2	Green	10	Bright green
3	Cyan	11	Bright cyan
4	Red	12	Bright red
5	Magenta	13	Bright magenta
6	Brown	14	Bright yellow
7	Dim white	15	Bright white

If you add 16 to the foreground or writing colour you will get a blinking effect. Here are some more lines in my demonstration program, but do experiment with your own.

```
70 COLOR 3,7
80 PRINT "This should be red on white"
90 COLOR 10,7
100 PRINT "This should be light green on white"
110 COLOR 11,0
120 PRINT "This should be light cyan on black"
130 COLOR 3,0
140 PRINT "This should be cyan on black"
150 COLOR 14,6
160 PRINT "This should be yellow on brown"
170 COLOR 5,15
180 PRINT "This should be magenta on bright white"
190 COLOR 12,0
200 PRINT "This should be light red on black"
210 REM: TO DEMONSTRATE REVERSE VIDEO
220 COLOR 1,7
230 PRINT "Blue on white again"
240 COLOR 7,1
250 PRINT "Reverse video. White on blue"
260 COLOR 7,0
270 PRINT "Back to normal again"
280 END
```

9.10.2 Writing in Coloured Boxes

You can use the colour command and PRINT statements with spaces in them to make coloured boxes on the screen, in which you can put writing. There are easier ways of drawing boxes, using the LINE command, but you need to do this in screen 1 upwards and if you only have a lower version of GW-BASIC and/or a CGA Monitor, you will find that you can only do the larger, chunkier, 40 characters to the line writing which doesn't look so good.

Here is a program which puts two coloured boxes on the screen.

```
10 REM: BOXES OF WRITING
20 CLS
30 COLOR 12,7
40 LOCATE 5,50
50 PRINT "in this box        "
60 LOCATE 6,50
70 PRINT "print is in        "
80 LOCATE 7,50
90 PRINT "light red on       "
100 LOCATE 8,50
110 PRINT "white            "
120 LOCATE 9,50
130 PRINT "                "
140 COLOR 14,6
150 LOCATE 15,10
160 PRINT "in this box              "
170 LOCATE 16,10
180 PRINT "print is in yellow on brown"
190 LOCATE 17,10
200 PRINT "                         "
210 LOCATE 18,10
220 END
```

The quotes marks in the PRINT statements line up and this is how you make a box. You need to use LOCATE before every PRINT line so that you get the coloured written bar in the right place. If you didn't do this, the cursor will go over to the left again.

9.10.3 Using Colours in Graphics, the CGA Paint Box

In graphics mode, you get a different choice of colours, depending on your type of monitor and version of GW-BASIC.

With a CGA monitor, you can only choose two graphics screens: Screen 1 and Screen 2. In CGA, only Screen 1 provides any choice of colour. In fact, what it does is to provide you with a choice of four colours at one time. There are two separate sets of the four colours but you can only have one of these in operation. If you change to another set during the course of your program, anything you drew previously will be redrawn in the new colour choice, so you can only use one of these sets at one time.

One of the colours in each set, the colour numbered 0, is the same as the background colour, so you only have three real choices of new colours at one time, six in all.

Here is a program which draws four boxes on the screen, to demonstrate the colours you get in each set. It shows the first set, with the command COLOR 0,0, puts in a delay loop to make a pause, then changes to the second colour set with COLOR 0,1 and automatically draws the boxes again in the new colour set.

```
10 REM: coloured in boxes to demonstrate palettes
```

```
20 CLS
30 SCREEN 1
40 WINDOW (0,0) - (100,100)
50 COLOR 0,0
60 GOSUB 590
70 COLOR 0,1
80 GOSUB 590
90 END
590 REM: procedure to draw boxes
600 LINE (20,60)-(50,90),0,BF
610 LINE (60,60)-(90,90),1,BF
620 LINE (20,20)-(50,50),2,BF
630 LINE (60,20)-(90,50),3,BF
640 FOR N=1 TO 50000:NEXT N
650 RETURN
```

If you are using QBASIC, you will need to make an adjustment for the GOSUBs, replacing them with suitable labels.

Lines 600 to 630 draw the boxes. The BF makes a filled in box and the number before that, the 0, 1, 2 or 3, decides what colour you will use.

The COLOR command in lines 50 and 110 sets the background colour with the first number. In this case it leaves it as black, but you have 15 other choices, numbered 0, 1, 2 through to 15. These correspond to the list of text colours in Section 9.10.1. The second number lets you choose between the two sets of colours, a set being called a palette. One is 0, the other 1. Below is a table, showing what colours each of these palettes contains. For example, COLOR 0,1 produces a background of colour 0 which is black and chooses the second palette, palette 1.

Colour number	Palette 0	Palette 1
0	Black	Black
1	Green	Cyan
2	Red	Magenta
3	Brown	White

9.10.4 The EGA Paintbox

GW-BASIC doesn't give any special support to VGA screens, over and above the EGA. However the EGA option allows you to have 16 colours on the screen at one time, which is a great improvement over CGA. It provides 64 colours altogether, and instead of giving you a choice of a fixed particular set, it lets you choose exactly which 16 you want, using the PALETTE command.

The program given below colours in 16 boxes, giving the standard set of colours you get if you don't make any changes with the PALETTE command. It stays like that, until you press any key and then it changes both background and coloured squares, so that you get all 64 colours flashing in front of you. It appears to wipe out each box in turn. If you get fed up with the display, you just press <Esc> to come out of it.

```
10 REM : ega palette
20 CLS : KEY OFF
30 SCREEN 9
40 WINDOW (-1,-1) - (5,5)
50 COLR = 0
60 FOR X = 0 TO 3
70 FOR Y = 0 TO 3
80 LINE (X,Y)-(X+1,Y+1),COLR,BF
90 COLR = COLR + 1
100 NEXT Y
110 NEXT X
120 X$=INKEY$:IF X$="" THEN 120
125 FOR PAL = 0 TO 15
130 FOR COLB = 0 TO 64
140 PALETTE PAL, COLB
150 FOR N=1 TO 10000:NEXT
155 X$=INKEY$:IF X$=CHR$(27) THEN END
160 NEXT COLB
165 NEXT PAL
170 SCREEN 0
180 END
```

Replace line 120 with a DO..WHILE LOOP in Q BASIC.

To get a screen that uses all these colours, you need to go into SCREEN 9. Line 120 leaves the 16 initial squares sitting there, until you press any key. Then you get the fancy display. This is done in line 140, with the PALETTE PAL, COLB. *PAL* only goes through 16 numbers because that is all that you can have at one time. *COLB* runs through 64, because you have the choice of assigning any of the 64 colours available to just 16 *PAL* places at one time. If you like, you have the numbers 0 to 15 for your colours, and you can choose exactly what colours, out of 64, these numbers will represent.

9.11 Worms, Fireworks and Raindrops

9.11.1 Making a moving Worm

It is amazing what you can do by drawing circles in different places and then rubbing bits of them out. To draw a circle, you use the first part of the CIRCLE command. For example:

```
CIRCLE (30,60),20,2
```

draws a circle which has an x co-ordinate of 30 and a y co-ordinate of 60 for its centre. It has a radius of 20 and is drawn in colour 2. You can go on and add other bits to the CIRCLE command to produce pie slices and ellipses, but we are not interested in those at the moment.

You make a worm by drawing 12 little circles, one after the other. Try:

```
10 REM: MAKING WORMS
20 SCREEN 1
30 WINDOW (0,0)-(100,100)
40 DIM XCENT(12), YCENT(12)
50 FOR N=0 TO 11
60 XCENT(1+N)=50+N
70 YCENT(1+N)=50+N
80 CIRCLE(XCENT(1+N),YCENT(1+N)),1,1
90 NEXT N
```

The screen co-ordinates are set with line 30 so that they run from the bottom left hand corner, 100 along and 100 up. This makes it easier to know what you are doing. Each circle is given a radius of 1. The x co-ordinates of the 12 circles are *XCENT(1)*, *XCENT(2)* up to *XCENT(12)* and the corresponding y co-ordinates are *YCENT(1)*, *YCENT(2)* up to *YCENT(12)*. *XCENT* and *YCENT* are both arrays which are declared in line 40. The rest of the listing puts starting values into these arrays, so that *XCENT(1)* and *YCENT(1)* both start at 50, right in the middle of the screen. *XCENT(2)* is 51, *XCENT(3)* is 52 and so on. Line 80 actually draws the circles, and if you run the program you will find that you do have what looks like a worm sitting in the middle of the screen.

The next thing you can do is make the worm start moving. The idea is that if you press one of four chosen keys, it will move in a different direction. I chose Q and Z to move vertically, and B and M to go left and right. Any other keys would do provided you make the necessary changes to lines 120 to 150. When you press one of the keys, the program draws a new circle with just one co-ordinate value changed. Try lines:

```
100 LET A$=INKEY$:IF A$="" THEN 100
110 CIRCLE(XCENT(1),YCENT(1)),1,0
120 IF A$="Q" THEN LET YCENT(12)=YCENT(12)+1
130 IF A$="Z" THEN LET YCENT(12)=YCENT(12)-1
140 IF A$="B" THEN LET XCENT(12)=XCENT(12)-1
150 IF A$="M" THEN LET XCENT(12)=XCENT(12)+1
160 IF A$=CHR$(27) THEN SCREEN 0 :END
170 CIRCLE(XCENT(12),YCENT(12)),1,1
```

Line 110 draws the first of the 12 circles in the same colour as the background, which effectively wipes it out. This is a very important line. If you leave it out, you just get a continuous snake trail all over the screen. The only trouble with the program as it stands is that we have a new circle number 12, and we have taken away the first circle, but we are left with all the others in the same place as before. What we want to do is to make the old number 2 circle the new number 1 circle, the old number 3 the new number 2, the old number 12 the new number 11 and so on. Then you can go through the whole procedure all over again and you really will get a moving worm. Make sure you have *caps lock* on when you run the program.

You can do this with the following lines of code:

```
180 FOR N=1 TO 11
190 XCENT(N)=XCENT(N+1)
195 YCENT(N)=YCENT(N+1)
200 NEXT N
```

Line 110 is a standard line. It tests whether you have pressed the Escape key, which has the ASCII value 27 and if you have, it takes you out of the program.

At the moment, the program only lets you make one worm move. Put in:

```
210 GOTO 100
```

and the program will loop round and round until you press the Escape key.

9.11.2 A Falling Raindrop

You can vary the worm program so that you have just one circle, which steadily moves from the centre top of the screen down to the bottom. As it does this, its radius gets steadily larger, and this gives the appearance of a falling raindrop. Here is the listing:

```
10 REM: SINGLE RAINDROP
20 KEY OFF:CLS
30 SCREEN 1
40 WINDOW (0,0)-(100,100)
50 R = 1
60 XCENT(1)=50:YCENT(1)=99
70 XCENT(2)=50:YCENT(2)=99
80 FOR N=1 TO 50
90 FOR J=1 TO 1000:NEXT J
100 CIRCLE(XCENT(1),YCENT(1)),R,0
110 R=R*1.1
120 CIRCLE(XCENT(2),YCENT(2)),R,1
130 XCENT(1)=XCENT(2):YCENT(1)=YCENT(2)
140 A$=INKEY$:IF A$=CHR$(27) THEN SCREEN 0:END
150 NEXT N
160 SCREEN 0:KEY ON
```

This time, there are just two circles. *XCENT(2)* and *YCENT(2)* are the co-ordinates of the centre of the second circle, *XCENT(1)* and *YCENT(1)* are the co-ordinates of the first, which is drawn in the background colour to wipe it out and to give the effect of movement. R=R*1.1 makes the radius of the circle get slowly larger. Experiment with some different values and see what effects you get. Just like worms, line 130 swaps the values over, so that the new circle becomes the old circle in the next round through the loop. A delay loop is necessary to stop the whole thing going so quickly that you can't see it.

9.11.3 A Single Firework

Another variation on the theme is to make a single circle move slowly up the screen diagonally. This time the radius stays constant, but both the x and y co-ordinates change at the same time, to get the diagonal movement. Again you only need two circles, a new and an old one.

```
10 REM: ONE FIREWORK
20 KEY OFF:CLS
30 SCREEN 1
40 WINDOW (0,0)-(100,100)
50 R = 1
60 XCENT(1)=50:YCENT(1)=50
70 XCENT(2)=50:YCENT(2)=50
80 FOR N=1 TO 40
90 FOR J=1 TO 1000:NEXT J
100 CIRCLE(XCENT(1),YCENT(1)),R,0
110 XCENT(2)=XCENT(1)+1:YCENT(2)=YCENT(1)+1
120 CIRCLE(XCENT(2),YCENT(2)),R,2
130 XCENT(1)=XCENT(2):YCENT(1)=YCENT(2)
140 A$=INKEY$:IF A$=CHR$(27) THEN SCREEN 0:END
150 NEXT N
160 SCREEN 0:KEY ON
```

9.12 Writing Longer Programs

All the books tell you that you must plan at your desk before you get anywhere near a computer. If you hope to write a professional program, they are, of course, quite right.

However when you first start writing longer programs, they will probably be quite small, perhaps just a matter of sticking one or two of the bits of this and the previous chapter together. It may be quite easy to see how the various bits tie up and, if so, you can go straight ahead and program. For example, I wrote a program called Happy Birthday. I decided that it would play the familiar tune and produce a picture of a birthday cake with candles. So my program consisted of two bits:

Play tune

Draw picture

All I really had to do was to decide which had to come first. Now it takes some time to play a tune whereas the computer draws a picture almost straightaway. This meant that it was sensible to:

Draw a picture (which stays there)

Play a tune

And that was as much overall planning as I needed to do.

The picture needed rather more planning. I drew it on graph paper and I had to fiddle with the different numbers for the ellipse parameter before it looked right. In fact this was really where most of the planning went.

An adventure game like King's Quest might have 30 or 40 screens with different graphics layouts. Different things happen on each screen and as you move in different directions you end up in different places. You would need to plan complicated graphics for each screen, and list out the various happenings and tie them all together.

In practice you will tend to write longer programs that never quite get finished. If you are computing for fun there is absolutely nothing wrong with this. You will probably get involved in one or two small bits of a project and want to see if you can make these work. Once you have found whether they will or will not, you will lose interest. Fair enough. This kind of approach is called prototyping.

For example, I decided to write a program to keep an eye on my bank balance. What really began to interest me was how to write data to the disk, recover it and update it. I got involved with the technical question of file handling. In fact even if I had finished the program, I would never have remembered to put all cheque transactions on to the computer – I hadn't been much good at doing this on my cheque book stubs.

To practise planning, start by looking at a ready made program and doing a screen analysis. Choose one that is similar to the kind of thing that you will write.

First establish in general terms what the program is trying to do. An example might be, to test French Vocabulary or a number guessing game for children aged 5 to 7.

The next step is to do a screen analysis, rather like storyboarding in the film industry. Take several sheets of paper and make three columns. The one on the immediate left is narrow and is headed Screen Number. As a program runs from one screen to another, you will number the screens. For example, a program might start by displaying a title screen. Call this Number 1. Then it might provide another screen with some instructions on how to play a game, call this screen Number 2. It might then give you a level one games playing screen with lots of action going on. This would be Number 3. If you get to a higher level, you go on to a new screen, which is

Number 4. There could be a fresh screen to give you the final overall score. This would be Number 5. Finally, you might get a menu asking if you want to play another game. Call this Number 6.

Make the next two columns about the same size. Head the first one, Appearance of Screen and the last one, Action.

Now go through some of your ready made programs, filling the form in as you go. If they run very quickly, you may have to start at the beginning again, to be able to do this. For Screen Appearance, you could draw a little picture showing where everything is. In the Action column, write what actually goes on.

For example, Screen Number 1, might have a drawing of a large letter title page. Action would be: *Writing scrolls slowly up the screen giving the title.*

Screen 2 could be, text only: *Explains the game.*

Screen 3 could be a drawing of a sky, stars, meteorites all over the place, and a small space ship. The action could be something like: *Steer space ship from bottom left to top right hand corner, trying not to hit the missiles. If a hit occurs, strength score is reduced by 1000 and if it reaches zero, the space ship disappears into a dot.*

Do screen analysis for some of the commercial programs you run. It makes you look at them more carefully and gives you a better understanding of how they are put together.

Then plan some out for the programs you are going to write yourself.

10

What goes on inside the Computer?

10.1 Versatility

How would you answer the question, what is a computer? Well, you might say it's a machine. How would you tell someone what that is, for example, a car or a washing machine? You might say that you use a car for travelling, taking you to work or shopping and that someone drives it. You use a washing machine to wash clothes.

What do you use a computer for? Playing games might be the first answer. But you can play games with a games console. So what is special about a computer? Is there anything else you can do with it? The answer is a very definite yes, although if you are a true beginner, you may find it hard to think of anything else.

❑ You can word process – write letters or even books, change them, add and take bits away and print the end result.

❑ You can get a paint package and make pictures.

❑ You can make 3D designs for architecture, for designing tools and cars and aeroplanes, or designing a new kitchen.

❑ You can do accounts and sort out your finances.

❑ You can store information, rearrange it and call it up another way.

❑ You can spend hours learning about how a computer works and using programs to examine what is happening inside.

You can do all kinds of things with a computer and that is what makes it very different from other machines. It is very versatile and it has many different functions.

Another thing about machines is that, unlike plants or animals, they are not living things. They won't do anything on their own: breathe, sleep, move or eat. They need power or energy to run. For a computer or washing machine, it is electricity; for a car it is petrol or diesel. A computer is quite modest in its use of electricity, although the monitor is more power hungry, like a television set. The car, in contrast, is a real energy guzzler, using up the world's scarce resources and spewing waste gases into the atmosphere, that, in time, lead to global warming.

Although machines need energy to run, they also need more than that. They all need instructions. For a washing machine these are easy. You turn a selection dial, depending on the type of clothes you are going to wash, and press or pull out a button – a one-off instruction and the machine gets on with it. This is only possible because the machine does more or less the same thing every time you use it.

The car, on the other hand, needs instructions all the time you are travelling. You have to start it, select its speed, change its gear and steer it. It needs your attention all the time, because there is so much uncertainty in driving – different roads and plenty of other cars to steer round and past. Research is going on to develop cars that drive themselves, that can sense other cars and obstacles and keep them at a certain distance, that can respond to electronic bumps in the road and weather hazards and adjust their speed and direction. Providing everyone is moving along a straight motorway this might work, but there is not much hope of a car driving itself along a winding country road with the odd stray tractor, sheep or cow.

The computer can do so many different things that it needs to be told what it is going to do right at the beginning, whether it is going to play a game, make a spreadsheet or write a letter. Sometimes, like a car, it will need your ongoing activity. We are a long way from providing computers that can read our minds and do all our work for us. On other occasions, we can start by feeding some instructions into the computer and then go away and leave it to get on with the job. This is called batch processing and while you sleep at night millions of computers are busy printing out pay checks and other routine documents.

Some of the most intelligent computer programs can respond to different situations, just like the car driver, and alter their behaviour accordingly. These are called real time systems. Air traffic control systems are being developed to read radar screens, to assess the positions of aircraft and to give pilots the necessary instructions. You can book a plane ticket in South America and the computer can realise that someone has already booked the last seat on the plane a few seconds before in South Africa and warn you accordingly. Though it still needs someone to feed in the request for a ticket.

When the computer appears to work on its own it is only following a program that can cover all the things that might happen and give the computer some rules to carry out in different situations. The more complicated the situation, the more complicated the program. It must be loaded in before the computer can carry out its tasks.

So machines need energy and they need instructions. Is there anything else?

Well, an empty washing machine isn't a lot of use. You usually put some dirty clothes into the drum and when it has done its jobs, you take out clean and usually slightly wet clothes. A car is less obvious, but the end result is arriving in another place.

Because the computer does so many different things, what you put in and what you get out varies. When you write, you type in letters using the keyboard and eventually print out the finished document. With accounts you feed in your expenses and daily takings and get out who owes what and the kind of balance sheet that your accountant likes. When you make a picture, you feed in the movements of the mouse and the computer turns this into a picture on the screen. When you play games, you press buttons on the keyboard or move a joystick and the computer responds by zapping a few aliens. This is what we call input and output. You put something into the computer, the input. The computer does something to it, or processes it and something different comes out, the output.

Machine	Input	Process	Output
Washing	Dirty clothes	Washes	Clean, wet clothes
Tumble dryer	Clean, wet clothes	Dries	Dry clothes
Cooker	Raw foods	Cooks	Cooked food
Computer games	Joystick moves	Notices moves Reacts to them	Zapped or missed aliens
Word processor	Press letters on keyboard	Echo on screen Puts document together	Prints out document

10.2 Input and Output

There are two kinds of things you can put into your computer: instructions – the program, and things you want it to work on or process – the data. Now pushing a dial and dirty clothes look rather different, whereas a set of instructions or program and the material your computer is going to work on, may look rather the same. They will both be written as a file on a disk and will be in the same computer language. In fact, the only language the computer itself can understand is very simple – just a mixture of 0s and 1s, and everything that goes in must be translated into this language.

So if a computer is a machine that takes things in, does something to them and sends out the finished result, it will need a method of doing this. The extra items used for this purpose are called peripherals or input/output devices.

One common input device is the keyboard. You use this to type in letters and numbers, and out of these you build instructions, like MS-DOS commands, or put in data like a written letter, work essays or books.

The mouse is another popular input device. Businessmen have always had the attitude that female typists are the ones to use keyboards and the mouse developed as an executive's alternative. It often goes with what we call a graphical user interface, a series of little pictures or icons on the screen. You use the mouse by moving it around on the computer desk. As you do this, the cursor moves around on the screen. Place the cursor on top of the picture of what you want to select, perhaps a program you want to run, click a little button on the top of the mouse and the computer responds by running whatever it is you select.

If you play games, one input device you may well come across, is the joystick. It makes a little picture on the screen (an aeroplane or little person) move very quickly. You can press a firebutton to shoot. It can be used to make the picture move very quickly which is what you want when you play an action game.

Where does the output appear? The printer is an obvious answer. You can print out your writing or picture. We call this hard copy.

The monitor is also an output device. Sometimes it just echoes what you have typed in at the keyboard, like when you type in an MS-DOS command. The input was actually the key presses you made on the keyboard as you typed the command in, but it is useful to see this echoed on the screen as you type, so that you can see that you have done it correctly. When it obeys the command and puts its own message on the screen, like:

```
Failure reading drive A
```

this is output.

The disk drive is what you might call an input/output device. Sometimes the computer will read from it, calling up instructions or pieces of work that it is going to use. On other occasions, it will save finished bits of work or programs that you have written for future use. In the first situation, it is an input device, in the second, it is an output device.

There are lots of other input/output devices like electronic sensors, electronic keyboards, speech synthesisers, and digitisers to capture photographic quality pictures and put them on your screen. You may well be tempted to buy the odd one or two of these and you will get plenty of fun out of them, but they are beyond the scope of this book. A keyboard, perhaps a mouse, disk drive and printer will normally be your starting devices.

10.3 The Computer's Language

The computer itself can only understand two things, on or off. For example, when it reads from a disk, it either notices that a small area is magnetised or that it is demagnetised. This is translated into an electric current where there are two voltage levels, the higher representing on or off, the lower representing the opposite. Some computers like the higher voltage to be on, the lower voltage off. Others do things the opposite way round.

Now you could ask: if the only thing the computer can understand is on or off, how do I get it to understand my instructions and the data or material it is going to act on? There are 26 letters in the alphabet, 10 number digits (0,1,2,3...9) and some other quite funny characters on the keyboard.

The answer lies in codes. In the Second World War, the British and the Germans needed to pass on secret war messages. They had to try and develop codes that the other side wouldn't be able to crack and they also had to try and break down the other side's messages. At the end of six years, a lot had been learned about codes in general and this made a major contribution to the rapid growth in computing in the next 50 years.

So how do you make a code out of on/off switches? Suppose we label on as 1, off as 0. Now put two switches together and you get four possibilities. You can have:

```
00
01
10
11
```

If you have three switches, there are eight possibilities:

```
000
001
010
011
100
101
110
111
```

So one switch gives you two possibilities. Two switches give you 2 x 2 = 4 possibilities, three give you 2 x 2 x 2 = 8, while eight give you 2 x 2 x 2 x 2 x 2 x 2 x 2 x 2 = 256.

Now 256 combinations can cover 26 upper case letters, A, B, C, D etc, 26 lower case letters, a, b, c, d etc. and the 10 digits, 0, 1, 2,....9. This occupies only 62 of the various choices, and leaves nearly 200 others, like + or -, <, >, and some of the other things on the keyboard.

How do you decide what collection of 0s and 1s will go with what? Well it doesn't really matter as long as you remember what the various collections of 0s and 1s mean. But once you have decided, it is a good idea to stick to it and it is also a good idea for everyone to use the same set of codes. Now, so far in this book, I have had to point out that there isn't one kind of PC or printer, there are several. This though, is one area, where people have come together and made an agreement, in what we call ASCII codes. ASCII is short for American Standard Code for Information Interchange.

The computer understands all that and at least it is standard, but it doesn't look at all meaningful. And how are you going to remember whole collections of eight 0s and 1s? It may suit the computer's mind but it doesn't suit mine. Well these collections of 0s and 1s are what we call binary numbers and we can turn them into the kinds of numbers we do understand.

When we use our numbering system, we have 10 digits, 0, 1, 2,...9 but we can use them to make millions and millions of different numbers. We do this by using places.

The numbers 12 and 21 use the same digits 1 and 2 but putting them in a different order gives two different numbers. In 12 the 1 is in the second place from the left, this represents one 10. The 2 is in the unit place, so it represents two 1s: 10 plus 2 equals 12.

For the second number, the 2 is in the 10s place, which means two 10s or 20. The 1 is in the unit place, one unit is 1. So 20 plus 1 equals 21.

```
10,000    1000    100    10    Units
    6         2      3     4        5
```

This number contains six 10,000s, that is, 60,000, two 1000s which is 2000, three 100s which is 300, four 10s which is 40 and five units which is 5. As you move to the left, the value of each place is 10 times the last one.

❏ The first place on the right is units

❏ The second is 10 x 1 which is 10

❏ The third is 10 x 10 which is 100

❏ The fourth is 10 x 100 which is 1000 and so on.

We have 10 digits, 0, 1, 2,...9 and 10 fingers to go with them.

Our computer uses just two digits, 0 and 1. We call this binary arithmetic. The values from the right are: units, 2 x 1 = 2, 2 x 2 = 4, 2 x 4 = 8.

The binary number 001000001 which is the ASCII code for capital A, consists of:

```
256   128  64  32  16  8  4  2  units
  0     0   1   0   0  0  0  0   1
```

This has one 64 and one unit which makes 65 altogether, in our decimal numbering system. And since we are happier with what we are used to, this is a bit easier to remember.

The upper case letters of the alphabet are given by decimal 65 to 90, the lower case letters by decimal 97 to 122.

After the letters and digits, there are nearly 200 codes available to stand for other things. Decimal 0 to 32 are what we call control codes. For example, 27 stands for the Escape key, 10 for line feed, 13 for carriage return. Code 7 stands for the beep sound that the computer makes when you do something wrong. High numbers beyond 128 give what are called graphics characters, like partly filled in squares or hearts, clubs, diamonds and spades, the playing card symbols. These can be built up to make quite complicated pictures in what are known as text graphics.

What about proper graphics? How does the computer turn a string of 0s and 1s into pictures. To do this it divides the screen up into a whole series of small squares or pixels. For a black and white system it is easy, 1 means light up the square, 0 means don't. So a small picture on an 8 x 8 square grid could have:

```
row 1        00111100
row 2        11111111
row 3        01111110
row 4        01011010
row 5        01111110
row 6        01000010
row 7        01111110
row 8        00111100
```

and this could have many other pictures joined on to it, right down and across the screen.

What happens with colours? Well you can use binary numbers to represent different colours. Using a 2 digit binary number, you have four choices:

```
00
01
10
11
```

which means you could have four colours: 00 could stand for black, 11 for white, 01 for red and 10 for blue.

You would now use two digits for each square rather than the one you used for a simple black and white system. The stream 010011010101 would mean first square red, second square black, third square white, fourth, fifth and sixth squares red.

3 digit binary numbers give you the choice of:

```
000
001
010
011
100
101
110
111
```

which allows you to have eight colours altogether.

4 digit binary numbers allow you to choose from 16 colours.

This is why the computer screen lets you choose mono (2 colours, black and white), 4, 8, or 16 colours rather than 3, 5 or 13.

10.4 The Computer's Brain

When you load up programs from the disk drive, they will already be written in machine code. When you write commands and work data with your keyboard, mouse or other input device, they will be translated into machine code. Program instructions and data are stored in the computer's memory.

The brain part of the computer, where all the processing goes on, is called the Central Processing Unit or CPU. This is also split up into different parts.

The part of the CPU where the real *thinking* or processing goes on, is called the Arithmetic and Logic Unit or ALU. In fact computer thinking is really quite simple. It can add two things together or subtract them, it can compare them and return a 0 or a 1 depending on whether they are the same or not. It can also do what are called logical operations on two things, like AND, OR, NAND and NOR. What these do is to take two inputs, 0s and 1s, and give a different single output, depending on which operation you are using. So two 1s might result in a 1, or a 0. What makes the computer a good thinker is the speed and accuracy at which it works and the fact that all kinds of complex logical operations can be built up out of these simple commands.

Because the computer handles two inputs at one time, it needs somewhere else to store one of them. It can keep one in the ALU, but it needs another place for the second one. This is called the accumulator.

It also has temporary memory addresses inside its CPU or central brain, where it stores more things to work on. This makes its operations even quicker. These temporary memory cells are called registers.

One of these is called an instruction register. This stores the memory address of the next instruction the CPU is going to carry out. The actual instruction will have to be fetched from the memory address where it is stored. Once this is done, it will be executed or carried out.

Finally, there is the control unit. Fetching and executing instructions, receiving and sending data and instructions from memory and from input and output devices, so that they are all in the right place at the right time, is a real operation in itself. The control unit manages and co-ordinates all this, by sending electrical signals in turn to all the various memory addresses, processing units and input and output devices.

Appendix

Magazines

Computer Shopper (has some excellent articles for a little more than a beginner)
Microdecision
Personal Computer Directory (First edition, Winter 1991)
PC Answers
PC Plus
PC Shareware Magazine
PC Today
PC Format (about games but some good hardware articles as well)
Shareware Shopper
What Micro?

Educational Software Suppliers

Davidson ABLAC
ABLAC Computec Ltd
South Devon House
Newton Abbot
Devon
TQ12 2BP

Tel: (0626) 331464

*They are quite a new company, supplying American based educational software that
has been adapted to the British National Curriculum.*

Rickitt Educational Media
Ilton
Ilminster
Somerset TA19 9HS

Tel: (0460) 57152

Rickitts are a major supplier of all kinds of educational software from all the major companies. They produce a useful catalogue divided by age range and subject.

Shareware Suppliers

Advantage (PCT)
56 Bath Road
Cheltenham GL53 7HJ

Tel: (0242)224340

College Shareware UK
Dept PCD
The College Business Centre
Uttoxeter New Road
Derby
DE22 3WZ

Tel: (0332) 294447

Gemini Shareware Limited
The Court House
110 High Street
Nailsea
Bristol BS19 1AH

Tel: (0275) 810477 (orders)
     (0800) 373000 (orders)
     (0275) 858965 (queries)

Shareware Marketing
3A Queen Street
Seaton
Devon
EX12 2NY

Tel: (0297) 24088

INDEX

V
VGA 12

W

X
XGA 12